CLASS OF '59

CLASS OF '59

From Bailey to Wooller: The Golden Age of County Cricket

CHRIS WESTCOTT

MAINSTREAM
PUBLISHING

EDINBURGH AND LONDON

First published in Great Britain in 2000 by
MAINSTREAM PUBLISHING COMPANY (EDINBURGH) LTD
7 Albany Street
Edinburgh EH1 3UG

ISBN 1 84018 239 3

A catalogue record for this book is available from the British Library

Typeset in Sabon
Printed in Great Britain by Butler & Tanner Ltd, Frome and London

Contents

Foreword   7
Introduction   9
1   Trevor Bailey   11
2   Wilf Wooller   15
3   Roy Tattersall   21
4   Colin McCool   26
5   Donald Carr   31
6   Les Jackson   36
7   Alan Moss   40
8   Robin Marlar   44
9   John Pretlove   47
10   Martin Horton   52
11   Frank Tyson   59
12   Reg Simpson   65
13   Godfrey Evans   69
14   Don Shepherd   75
15   Maurice Tremlett   80
16   Eric Bedser   84
17   Brian Boshier   87
18   Fred Titmus   92
19   Ray Illingworth   100
20   Brian Taylor   112
21   Derek Shackleton   119
22   Derek (Dick) Richardson   123
23   Gamini Goonesena   129
24   Mike (M.J.K.) Smith   134
25   Keith Andrew   140
26   Willie Watson   145
27   Maurice Hallam   152
28   Cyril Washbrook   158
29   Alan Oakman   163
30   Alan Wharton   168
31   Leo Harrison   174
32   Jim Parks   178
33   George Tribe   185
34   William (Gilbert) Parkhouse   190

35	Don Kenyon	193
36	Norman Horner	197
37	Fred Trueman	202
38	Doug Insole	209
39	Malcolm Hilton	216
40	Allan Watkins	220
41	Vic Wilson	225
42	Jack Robertson	228
43	Alec Bedser	232
44	Don Smith	235
45	Colin Ingleby-Mackenzie	238
46	Roy Marshall	243
47	Brian Close	247
48	Raman Subba Row	259
Acknowledgements		263
Appendix		265

Foreword

Embellishing history with more history, Chris Westcott has come up with a minor classic. We collectors of unconsidered trifles indulge ourselves for love and passion, for obsession, for cussedness, and because, well, we haven't the heart to throw anything away. A 'collectible' first inspires and then beguiles, and our passing crazes speckle the course of our lives, leaving behind markers which, if rediscovered, can warm history into life.

Which is what happened in 1996 when Westcott was crawling around the attic of his home and came across a carefully hoarded bundle of cards depicting county cricketers of the 1950s playing in England. In themselves they were a rewarding find. Collectors of such collectible (and 'swappable') ephemera – or those of a certain age, anyway, will remember the handsome A&BC chewing-gum cards. Chris's father had 'laid down' the full set in mint condition when his son was but a lad of five. Obviously he hoped his son – or grandson – would discover them in a far distant future. Discover and enjoy.

His son went one better than that. He traced every one of the 48 subjects featured in the cards – or in the case of death their surviving relatives. If ever

7

there was a case of a picture postcard coming to life, then this, dear reader, is it. These are their true stories, all 48 of them. And like real life, some are sad and poignant, others happy and glorious.

Lithographs of the nineteenth century players were the first true great cricketing collectibles. After 1868, when the first edition of the magazine *Vanity Fair* was published, a craze began for collecting cricketers' cartoons (which it occasionally published, full page and printed in chrome-lithography along with politicians, lawyers, landowners etc.). In all, between the issue of 9 June 1877 (W.G. Grace, of course) and 13 August 1913 (E.W. Dillon, captain of Kent) 31 cricketers were featured. All but nine of them were drawn by 'Spy', who was Sir Leslie Ward RA. The originals are now worth a fortune, although copies once torn from the magazine remain pleasantly collectible.

In the first quarter of the century, there was a popular swell to collect copies of *The Empire's Cricketers* (folio-size and drawn by A. Chevallier Tayler). These were sold and swapped by men and schoolboys with obsessive joy and, by nice coincidence, there were only 48 of them – there were to be only 48 A&BC cards as well.

I was common-as-muck, I'm afraid. I was a cigarette card collector. No rarity there, they flooded all markets. A generation before Chris Westcott, I nevertheless proudly had what I reckoned to be a full collection of every Gloucestershire man who had ever been cigarette carded – Sinfield, Parker, Hammond, Wilson, right up to Lambert, Wells, Emmett, Crapp and Graveney T.W. The day before we moved house from Stonehouse to Cheltenham in 1960, my dear old dad wantonly, unthinkingly scattered them all on the back-garden bonfire. I was left bereft. My dad was no romantic like Westcott *père*. And, to be sure, I am no romantic like Westcott *fils*. For now he has brought this common or garden commercially-inspired collectors' craze triumphantly and almost, to animate flesh and blood. Oddly, no Gloucestershire men among the prized and select 48. Where are they now? All inside these highly original and beautifully crafted pages. Read on.

Frank Keating

Introduction

Have you ever found in the house somewhere, perhaps the attic or spare room, an old set of cards slavishly collected as a youngster, dusted them down and wondered whatever happened to the players? Well, that's exactly what I did in 1996 when I came across this set of 48 county cricketers from a card series produced in 1959 by A&BC. Only I went one step further and resolved to track down and interview the cricketers so as to produce this tribute to coincide with the 40th anniversary of the cards being produced. Little did I realise at the time what a monumental task that would be! Over the last three years the search has taken me across the length and breadth of the UK, to South Africa and Australia and has become something of a driving obsession.

Cricketer cards have been collected since the turn of the century and during the '20s and '30s were issued in quite significant numbers. The full name of A&BC is the American & British Chewing Gum Co., which was the British subsidiary of Topps Chewing Gum. The company first produced cards in 1953 and in total issued over 150 sets, with football being the dominant subject. In 1959 the company branched into cricket for the first time with this particular set. That was followed by a series of 48 Test series cricketers, issued in 1961. In the mid-'70s the A&BC name disappeared to be replaced by the parent company of Topps UK Ltd, which still produces cards today.

Whoever selected these 48 county cricketers chose well, with all the counties represented except Gloucestershire, much to the chagrin of Frank Keating. With the exception of one or two giants in cricket at that time, the leading players in county cricket are highlighted during a period where, whilst attendances had declined since the halcyon post-war days, championship matches were still well supported.

The front of the card shows each player unusually superimposed on scenes reflecting a proliferation of blue sky, wholly appropriate for the summer in question, by an artist seemingly with a penchant for conifers! The reverse provides information on each cricketer and statistics for the 1958 season. You will find each reverse reproduced in the appendix to this book (page 265 onwards).

Along with each cricketer's recollections of the period you will also find the most memorable match they played in and their proudest moment in the game. Interestingly, Australia features as opponents in a third of the matches recalled, which is not entirely surprising in view of the significance always placed on competing with our traditional foes. At the other end of the spectrum the annual Varsity match at the outset of a first-class career is the game etched in the cerebral minds of three of our players.

The book is not designed to unearth any great controversial issues, although the honesty of some of the contributors is both illuminating and enlightening. It is more a nostalgic stroll across the landscape of a bygone age and I sincerely hope this tribute gives as much pleasure to the reader as it did for me when compiling.

It has been a great privilege to meet the players concerned, who have been wholly supportive of my endeavours and I thank them sincerely for their assistance. Where the cricketers are sadly no longer with us their relatives have kindly supported me.

I am very grateful to Charles Frewin for giving an unknown the opportunity for an opening in the field of writing and also to Frank Keating for penning such a splendid foreword.

The book itself is dedicated to my wife Linda, who has been my constant source of companionship and encouragement during the time it has taken to complete this work. It would not have been possible but for her immense tolerance and patience.

Chris Westcott

–1–

Trevor Bailey (b. 1923)

Essex, Cambridge University and England

At the beginning of 1959 I was with MCC in Australia. The final Test I played was in Melbourne when I got a pair against Ray Lindwall. On that last tour, I had back trouble for the first time but didn't miss a Test match. I had to have an operation when I got back to England which was successful and probably accounted for why I had a very good summer in 1959 [scoring 2,000 runs and taking 100 wickets, Bailey was the first player to achieve that feat since 1933]. I didn't get into the England side though which is rather ironic. However, I loved county cricket and obviously enjoyed that season as I was probably batting better at that time than I had ever done.

During the '60s I toured with the International Cavaliers on a couple of occasions, including a trip to the West Indies in 1964–5. We took three young players, Alan Knott, Keith Fletcher and Ron Headley, which was not a bad choice. Knott was understudying Godfrey Evans and I told him the next time he came out there he would be playing for England, which turned out to be correct. His outlook on cricket was excellent – I sent him in as night watchman on one occasion when Wes Hall was bowling, simply because this was the sort of thing he would have to do. Being an intelligent young player, he realised what a marvellous experience it was for him, which also applied to Fletcher.

I was captain of Essex from 1961 to 1966. We were struggling at the time as we had little money and were short of players. I had a bad leg for some time and in 1967 decided to call it a day. We were a very poor side and I was beginning to struggle to get runs and take wickets.

I was also the county secretary from 1954 to 1967. I was originally toying with the idea of full-time teaching in the late '40s when Essex asked me to be assistant secretary. I carried on teaching for a time then went to Australia in 1950, so after that and playing football as well, teaching was not feasible. Looking back I found combining the secretarial role with playing cricket fairly easy. We weren't chief executives in those days and it was very good fun.

I have spent 20 years with *The Financial Times* as their cricket and football correspondent. I studied English and History at Cambridge which helped. I also wrote at least a dozen books, the first one with Denys Wilcox on coaching.

I also ran a public relations business in London for over 25 years and had wholesale and retailing interests in the toy industry, so it was quite a varied life. In addition I have hosted a great number of overseas touring parties, the first one when Ray Illingworth was captain and we won the Ashes in 1971, the last one to Australia in 1998.

Memorable Game

This has to be at The Oval in 1953 where we won back the Ashes which Australia had held for 19 years, so it was about time they came back. It was a great moment and the most satisfactory team performance. It was a good series for me as I scored some runs and took wickets.

15, 17, 18, 19 August 1953. England won by 8 wickets

Bailey played his part to the full, particularly in the first innings when scoring a valuable 64 runs including seven fours, without offering a chance. His last-wicket partnership of 44 with Alec Bedser ensured that England gained a psychological advantage as they established a first-innings lead.

Australia

A.L. Hassett c Evans b Bedser	53	lbw b Laker	10
A.R. Morris lbw b Bedser	16	lbw b Lock	26
K.R. Miller lbw b Bedser	1	c Trueman b Laker	0
R.N. Harvey c Hutton b Trueman	36	b Lock	1
G.B. Hole c Evans b Trueman	37	lbw b Laker	17
J.H. de Courcey c Evans b Trueman	5	run out	4
R.G. Archer c and b Bedser	10	c Edrich b Lock	49
A.K. Davidson c Edrich b Laker	22	b Lock	21
R.R. Lindwall c Evans b Trueman	62	c Compton b Laker	12
G.R. Langley c Edrich b Lock	18	c Trueman b Lock	2

W.A. Johnston not out	9	not out	6
B 4, n-b 2	6	B 11, l-b 3	14
	275		162

1/38 2/41 3/107 4/107 5/118 6/160
7/160 8/207 9/245

1/23 2/59 3/60 4/61 5/61
6/85 7/135 8/140 9/144

England

L. Hutton b Johnston	82	run out	17
W.J. Edrich lbw b Lindwall	21	not out	55
P.B.H. May c Archer b Johnston	39	c Davidson b Miller	37
D.C.S. Compton c Langley b Lindwall	16	not out	22
T.W. Graveney c Miller b Lindwall	4		
T.E. Bailey b Archer	64		
T.G. Evans run out	28		
J.C. Laker c Langley b Miller	1		
G.A.R. Lock c Davidson b Lindwall	4		
F.S. Trueman b Johnston	10		
A.V. Bedser not out	22		
B 9, l-b 5, w 1	15	l-b 1	1
	306	(2 wkts)	132

1/37 2/137 3/154 4/167 5/170
6/210 7/225 8/237 9/262

1/24 2/88

England Bowling

	O	M	R	W	O	M	R	W
Bedser	29	3	88	3	11	2	24	0
Trueman	24.3	3	86	4	2	1	4	0
Bailey	14	3	42	1				
Lock	9	2	19	1	21	9	45	5
Laker	5	0	34	1	16.5	2	75	4

Australia Bowling

	O	M	R	W	O	M	R	W
Lindwall	32	7	70	4	21	5	46	0
Miller	34	12	65	1	11	3	24	1
Johnston	45	16	94	3	29	14	52	0
Davidson	10	1	26	0				
Archer	10.3	2	25	1	1	1	0	0
Hole	11	6	11	0				
Hassett					1	0	4	0
Morris					.5	0	5	0

Umpires: F.S. Lee and D. Davies

The final Test against the West Indies at Jamaica in 1954, which we had to win, must come very high on the list as well. I was opening the batting and bowling and it was my best bowling performance on a very good batting wicket. [England won by nine wickets and Bailey's 7–34 in 16 overs at the time was the best bowling analysis for England against West Indies.]

Proudest Moment

I am not sure what my proudest moment in cricket was but I can recall my most exciting. In 1938 I was 14 and playing happily in the Dulwich College Colts getting some runs and wickets. I remember when MCC came down to play the school they had a young professional called Jack Robertson who scored a century. Then for the game against Bedford School they were short of one bowler and brought me in to play. The Dulwich College first XI team used to be pinned up on a notice board and all those boys with Colours had their initials in front. The last name on the list was Bailey T.E., as I hadn't got my Colours at that stage.

I remember it being there and putting my hand up and asking to be excused so I could just gaze at it. I remained in the team for the rest of that summer. We won all our remaining school matches, which hadn't occurred for 50-odd years. Alan Shirreff, who was the captain, received a classic letter saying, 'Dear Shirreff, congratulations on a superb performance' enclosing a small crock of gold. Being a sensible individual Alan decided that the whole team would go to the London Palladium to see a show and have dinner beforehand. At 14 I had never been to a show in my life. My parents then picked me up and I went home. The small crock of gold was five guineas, the writer P.G. Wodehouse! A historic moment.

A tough competitor and outstanding all-rounder, 'Barnacle' Bailey scored 28,642 runs (33.42) including 28 centuries and took 2,082 wickets (23.13) and 425 catches. In 61 Test matches he scored 2,290 runs (29.74) including one century, took 132 wickets (29.21) and 32 catches.

–2–

Wilf Wooller (1912–1997)

Cambridge University and Glamorgan

As told by Mrs Enid Wooller

Wilf played for Glamorgan as captain until 1960 when he retired at the age of 48. He had a bit of a bad spell with his depression around that time, which was a throwback to his war days, and saw a psychiatrist. He got over it although he never planned for the future – he always thought the future would take care of itself. We were also in a bungalow with the five young children, Jackie, Brian, Penny, Nick and Jon, which I think got on top of him, though he would have had 22 children given the chance! Wilf then shared the captaincy of Glamorgan's second XI with Phil Clift for a while and played cricket for St. Fagan's in 1961, his last year of regular club cricket. He actually played once more for Glamorgan in 1962 against Middlesex at Newport when Ossie Wheatley, his successor, was unavailable.

He was a very modest man even though he was also abrasive and always wanted to win. He knew his facts and had very definite ideas which were invariably right. He would put a lot of people's backs up, although off the field he was a completely different person. When Glamorgan used to play the early bank holiday game in Cardiff the players from both counties would play golf, then come back to our house for tea. The opposition

15

couldn't believe it was the same chap they played against the day before, as he was so completely different, especially with his children. The lads in the team, who were so much younger than Wilf, did appreciate what he said, even though he was a hard captain. Matthew Maynard said he always tried to follow Wilfred's rules of playing the game.

He was an amateur with Glamorgan and also had an insurance business which he continued on retirement from cricket – he enjoyed going to the office. He was originally more of a figurehead in a partnership with Hugh Ferguson Jones, a lovely man who was godfather to our first baby.

Wilf was a Test selector from 1955 to 1961 and was good at it. England had an excellent record when Wilf was involved and he had a wonderful time. He admired Peter May, the England captain at the time, very much. He thought he was the best English cricketer of his era. Another chap he greatly admired was Gubby Allen. Wilf used to stay with him when he was a Test selector – he would come up to London on the overnight train and have breakfast with him.

Wilf remained secretary at Glamorgan until retiring on his 65th birthday in 1977, although he felt he could have continued in an administrative capacity for a few more years. I was always disappointed he didn't get involved in that way after he finished as secretary, as I felt he had more to offer. It left quite a void in his life, although he did become a J.P. in later years.

He wrote about rugby and cricket for *The Sunday Telegraph* from 1961 and would receive a little card every Thursday asking him to cover a particular rugby match. Then in 1988 for about four weeks nothing came and suddenly Wilfred received a letter from David Gryce, *The Sunday Telegraph* sports editor, saying they had been taken over by *The Daily Telegraph* and he was no longer the editor. They were getting new blood in and that was all it said. I was furious and Wilf was very upset about it, as he had written for them for over 25 years. They didn't even say what a good job he had done, let alone apologise for the loss of income. People used to phone and say what a good article he'd written, he was an excellent writer – always controversial! Wilf always wrote exactly what he thought and everybody who read his articles agreed with him. As soon as Rugby Union went professional Wilf lost interest in the game – he said it would never work. Wilf became depressed again when he stopped writing, but it soon passed.

From the early '60s he also became involved in cricket TV broadcasting for quite a while and was commentating for BBC Wales when Gary Sobers hit the record six sixes in an over for Nottinghamshire at Swansea in 1968. He was never involved in rugby TV but did quite a few radio interviews over the phone with Vincent Kane about forthcoming rugby matches.

Wilf was a good golfer who enjoyed the game but didn't play a lot. He adored fishing and was very successful. We used to fish in·west Wales at Caernarfon where salmon fishing was expensive, but he was told by a chap he could fish any time along this particular stretch of river. His greatest achievement was catching five salmon in one day and the heaviest was something like 20 lbs – we even took a photo of it. It was a delicacy but with such a big family it soon went! Prior to that he would fish for trout in a place called Cwrt-yr-ala near Cardiff. We also used to go on holiday to our caravan in west Wales where Wilf would go sea fishing and catch whitebait as well. I would haul the net in and Wilf would say he'd make a fisherman of me, but he didn't.

He was a very good gardener if not a tidy one. He didn't believe in set gardens as he said nothing in nature was straight. I looked after the inside of the house and he would look after the outside – he never did anything inside the house! Everything he touched grew until about 1994, when he decided he didn't want to do much more. So I took over and became quite excited as I had never gardened before. He was so pleased for me – we had a lean-to which was extended for Wilf and he loved sitting there in the evenings where all my successes were.

He was also a very good chess player going back to his university and POW days and an excellent card player, particularly bridge. When we played another couple every week, he would never play by the rules. The other wife would say, 'Wilfred you can't say that, don't let your partner see what you have got.' He would reply, 'Look at the score, who's winning?' She would respond, 'You are,' to which he would reply, 'There you are, it doesn't matter about the calling, I win!' He also loved bowls and when he retired and was asked in an interview if there was anything he wanted to do that he had not, he said he would really like to play bowls for Wales!

He was a very good teacher especially with his children. I would take over the children's science and maths homework and he would do their history and geography. He was a great family man – we have eight grandchildren, two boys and six girls. He didn't enjoy them so much when they were babies as when they started talking. He was a great party man and when we had our ruby wedding anniversary in 1988 it was a scream as the boys all put their dinner jackets on for a party. Wilf typically said, 'I'm not putting mine on.' Jackie the oldest child said, 'Dad you have got to, you have been married 40 years.' He agreed in the end to put his dinner jacket on but would not change his beige trousers! He was very fit and active even though he ate and drank too much. He had four brothers but sadly there is only Roy left now. Roy would say, 'Wilfred you eat all the wrong things,' to which Wilf would reply, 'Roy, I am perfectly healthy,' and he was.

He was never at a loss to tell a story and when in his eighties helped Andrew Hignell write a biography of him. It took a tremendous amount out of him though, and was at the wrong time in his life. He spent hours reading the notes for his biography and it was really too much for him.

We went to a big 80th birthday party in November 1996 and he really looked well, as he liked the sun and had a good tan. Even in February 1997 Vincent Kane interviewed him about the rugby and he was as clear as a bell, although Wilfred's problem was his circulation. He was wonderful to nurse as he found it progressively more difficult to get upstairs and so appreciated my help. He also found it very difficult to move from one room to another. Then in March 1997 he went into Llandough hospital and even in the hospital bed looked well. He was only in hospital for about four days in the end, and died peacefully at the age of 85 – he went the way he would have wanted.

An extraordinary thing happened when he died. All the family were gathered there and one of the boys suggested we got James, the eldest grandchild to join us. As James and his father Nick were walking back to us at 5.10 p.m. a TV programme of memorable sporting moments with Roy Castle was being shown. At the very moment they walked towards where Wilfred was, it showed Gary Sobers hitting those sixes against Glamorgan and I could hear Wilf's voice commentating. It really was eerie, difficult to believe and shortly after Wilf passed away. I remember at the funeral the one thing Matthew Maynard said he would miss was Wilf coming into the dressing-room and saying, 'Now look here Matthew, set your field properly.'

Memorable Game

I think Wilf's most memorable game could well be when Glamorgan beat South Africa at Swansea in 1951 – he worked hard for that victory.

4, 6 August 1951 Glamorgan won by 64 runs

As Wooller was carried shoulder-high from the field, the crowd of 25,000 sang the Welsh national anthem in recognition of being the only county to defeat the South Africans that summer. The players celebrated with champagne and glasses were raised in recognition of the fine performances of Muncer and McConnon, who took 17 wickets between them.

Glamorgan

E. Davies c van Ryneveld b Mansell	19	c Endean b Melle	9
P.B. Clift c Fullerton b Melle	0	c Melle b Mansell	0
B.L. Muncer lbw b Rowan	30	b Rowan	8
W.E. Jones c Tayfield b Mansell	13	c Rowan b Mansell	10
A.J. Watkins c Mansell b Rowan	26	run out	11
W. Wooller c Nourse b Mansell	1	c Mansell b Rowan	46
B. Hedges c van Ryneveld b Rowan	6	c Endean b Mansell	10
J. Pleass c van Ryneveld b Mansell	1	c Fullerton b Mansell	29

18

J. McConnon c McLean b Mansell	4	c Nourse b Rowan 0
H.G. Davies b Rowan	1	not out 8
D. Shepherd not out	0	c van Ryneveld b Rowan 0
B 6, l-b 4	10	B 9, l-b 6, w 1 16
	111	147

1/13 2/39 3/63 4/77 5/89 6/105
7/106 8/108 9/110

1/3 2/42 3/48 4/63 5/85
6/107 7/130 8/134 9/147

South Africa

J.H.B. Waite c Clift b Wooller	1	c H. Davies b McConnon 17
W.R. Endean c Watkins b Muncer	13	c Watkins b Muncer 35
C.B. van Ryneveld c Shepherd b Wooller	4	c Wooller b McConnon 1
A.D. Nourse c Watkins b Muncer	6	c Watkins b Muncer 2
J.E. Cheetham lbw b Muncer	2	c Watkins b McConnon 1
R.A. McLean c Clift b Muncer	0	lbw b Muncer 10
G.M. Fullerton b Muncer	2	b McConnon 0
P.N.F. Mansell b Wooller	21	c sub b McConnon 0
A.M.B. Rowan not out	49	c sub b Muncer 7
H. Tayfield c Wooller b Muncer	0	not out 0
M.G. Melle b Muncer	4	c Clift b McConnon 0
B 9	9	B 4 l-b 6 10
	111	83

1/1 2/12 3/27 4/27 5/29 6/33 7/34
8/88 9/95

1/54 2/54 3/61 4/61 5/68
6/68 7/68 8/72 9/72

South Africa Bowling

	O	M	R	W	O	M	R	W
Melle	5	0	19	1	9	0	16	1
Mansell	26	11	37	5	36	9	73	4
Rowan	21.4	7	45	4	28	14	42	4

Glamorgan Bowling

	O	M	R	W	O	M	R	W
Wooller	15	3	41	3				
Muncer	23.4	12	45	7	8.5	3	16	4
McConnon	9	3	16	0	10	2	27	6
Watkins					6	1	12	0
Shepherd					4	0	18	0

Umpires: H.L. Parkin and L.J. Todd

Proudest Moment

I think this was when he led Glamorgan to their first County Championship title in 1948. We have always lived in Cardiff and had a flat overlooking the cricket ground when we were first married. Every morning when we were playing at home that season he would have the boys on the ground at nine o'clock practising! It was such a shame he didn't live to see them win it again in 1997 as he would have loved that. His other proudest moment in cricket was when he was made President of Glamorgan CCC in 1991. When Rowe Harding, who he had known for a long time, died Tony Lewis rang him up and said the county would like him to become president. He was so delighted he shed a tear and loved being still connected with the club. He wasn't well at the time and was absolutely overcome. It gave him that little bit of a boost – Glamorgan was so very important to him.

A tough competitor, all-rounder and excellent close fielder, Wooller scored 13,593 runs (22.57), took 958 wickets (26.96) and 412 catches.

–3–

Roy Tattersall (b. 1922)

Lancashire and England

I was very disillusioned in 1959 and especially in 1960, as I was not playing much for Lancashire First XI and it was a mystery to me why I was not in the side. I didn't feel I had lost any form as every full season I played in I had taken more than a hundred wickets. In those days you couldn't go to the committee and ask them why – you were just not invited into the committee room. I was being stopped in the street and asked why I was not playing for Lancashire – was I injured or had I done anything wrong? We always had six batsmen, four bowlers and a wicket-keeper. The bowlers were expected to get the wickets and any runs we scored were looked on as a bonus, the batters vice-versa, and we were a better team for that. Then they had a change in the committee and decided to blood all-rounders instead of specialists and we were powerless to do anything about it. I do think it was because of this policy that some good players were left out of that side as well as myself – Alan Wharton and Malcolm Hilton spring to mind. The ironic thing was that the all-rounders didn't live up to expectations. The chairman of the committee at that time, has since apologised to me as I felt I had at least another three years of first-class cricket in me.

In 1960, my last season, Malcolm Hilton and I had a joint benefit game;

we had both taken 1,000 wickets for Lancashire. I was the first to be capped and it was in seniority that a benefit was awarded. In fact Brian Statham was also due a benefit that year but had one in 1961. Our benefit game was the Roses match on August bank holiday at Old Trafford on a glorious day, the ground was packed with about 30,000 spectators and they were turning people away. I was 12th man and Malcolm was playing in a second team game at Scarborough! It was a great game, with Lancashire winning off the last ball with four byes.

We had a good second XI team in 1960 and won the Minor Counties Championship. My last game for Lancashire was against Norfolk at the Colmans Mustard ground. In those days there was a northern and southern section of the Minor Counties and whoever finished top would play against each other. Norfolk finished top of the southern section. We had a good contest, especially between Bill Edrich, who was playing for them, and myself, and beat them. I bowled about 30 overs for 26 runs and took 5 wickets, thoroughly enjoyed it and finished on a high.

I came to Kidderminster in 1961 as professional and coach for the cricket club. I also started work with Brintons, the biggest carpet firm in Kidderminster, where I worked for 26 years. I was working five days a week and playing cricket on a Sunday, plus coaching three nights per week and it was too much. We didn't know anyone down here and my wife Phyllis was unhappy with all the family being up north. So after a season I stopped as pro but still played for them and did some voluntary coaching. I actually played for Kidderminster for about five seasons and still watch them play occasionally. When we came down to Kidderminster we started a family and now have three daughters living in Guildford, Leicester and Stroud.

I played one game in 1964 for MCC against Lancashire at Old Trafford and took six wickets for 60-odd! It was the Lancashire centenary game and they asked me to play with Len Hutton and Denis Compton – it proved I could still play a bit!

I was a NatWest adjudicator for 15 years until 1997, am president of the Old Players' association, vice-president and life member of Lancashire CCC and I am also a member of Warwickshire CCC. When Ian Botham and Graham Dilley came to Worcester it was a job getting into the ground in the car as I had just had hip replacement operations on both legs for the fifth time and was on crutches, whereas Edgbaston had a big car park.

I was always keen on football. I played for about 12 months when I joined Lancashire but packed it in when I became concerned I might get injured, bearing in mind cricket was my livelihood. I was always a big fan of Bolton Wanderers in the Nat Lofthouse era and saw the 1958 and the Matthews 1953 Cup finals – the players became friends of mine.

I used to enjoy watching Stirling Moss at Oulton Park and was thrilled when I bought my first car instead of having to catch three buses to Old

Trafford with all my kit. It was a pleasure in those days – we used to drive out to the Lake District and the Ribble Valley at weekends.

Memorable Game

This was the second Test match at Lord's against South Africa in 1951 when I took 7–52 in the first innings and 12–101 in the match.

It was classed as 'my match' so I have particularly happy memories. I had three excellent leg-fielders for Lancashire – Ken Grieves, John Ikin and Geoff Edrich. Geoff was like the Rock of Gibraltar and Ken, being a goalkeeper, had glue on his fingers! One of the greatest fielders you could have in the leg-trap was Johnny Ikin. My abiding memory of the South African match is that Johnny took a catch to dismiss Eric Rowan in the leg-trap when he was horizontal. He was a terrific fielder with excellent anticipation and always said it was the best catch he ever took. It was only two or three yards from the bat but Eric hit it hard and John dived to catch it.

He watched me bowl, not the batsman to see where it was pitching. If the batsman went forward he would go forward and likewise if the batsman went on the back foot he would go back. The Test actually finished on the Saturday after two and a half days, and in the evening, I received the inaugural Cricketer of the Year award chosen by the Cricket Writers' Association for the 1950 season. We had a dinner at Fleet Street, held by the association, which the England and South African teams were invited to, and Sir Stanley Rous presented the trophy to me, which I was very proud of.

21, 22, 23 June 1951. England won by 10 wickets

In his first appearance for England at Lord's, Tattersall predominantly bowled over the wicket at medium pace. On a rain-affected pitch he varied his pace splendidly to take 9 of the 14 wickets to fall on the second day.

England

L. Hutton lbw b McCarthy	12	not out	12
J.T. Ikin b Mann	51	not out	4
R.T. Simpson lbw b McCarthy	26		
D.C.S. Compton lbw b McCarthy	79		
W. Watson c McCarthy b Chubb	79		
F.R. Brown b Chubb	1		
T.G. Evans c Fullerton b McCarthy	0		
J.H. Wardle lbw b Chubb	18		
A.V. Bedser not out	26		
J.B. Statham b Chubb	1		
R. Tattersall b Chubb	1		
B 8, l-b 9	17		
	311	No wkt	16

1/20 2/89 3/103 4/225 5/226 6/231 7/265 8/299 9/301

South Africa

E.A.B. Rowan c Ikin b Tattersall	24		c Ikin b Statham	10
J.H.B. Waite c Hutton b Wardle	15		c Compton b Tattersall	17
D.J. McGlew c Evans b Tattersall	3		b Tattersall	2
A.D. Nourse c Watson b Tattersall	20		lbw b Wardle	3
J.E. Cheetham c Hutton b Tattersall	15		b Statham	54
G.M. Fullerton b Tattersall	12		lbw b Bedser	60
C.B. van Ryneveld lbw b Wardle	0		c Ikin b Tattersall	18
A.M.B. Rowan c Ikin b Tattersall	3		c Brown b Bedser	10
N.B.F. Mann c Brown b Tattersall	14		c Brown b Tattersall	13
G.W.A. Chubb c Tattersall b Wardle	5		b Tattersall	3
C.N. McCarthy not out	1		not out	2
L-b 3	3		B 11, l-b 8	19
	115			211

1/25 2/38 3/47 4/72 5/88 6/91
7/91 8/103 9/112

1/21 2/29 3/32 4/58 5/152
6/160 7/178 8/196 9/200

South Africa Bowling

	O	M	R	W	O	M	R	W
McCarthy	23	2	76	4				
Chubb	34.4	9	77	5				
A. Rowan	13	1	63	0				
Mann	32	12	51	1				
van Ryneveld	5	0	27	0				
Nourse					2	0	9	0
E. Rowan					1.5	0	7	0

England Bowling

	O	M	R	W	O	M	R	W
Bedser	8	5	7	0	24	8	53	2
Statham	6	3	7	0	18	6	33	2
Tattersall	28	10	52	7	32.2	14	49	5
Wardle	22.5	10	46	3	20	5	44	1
Compton					2	0	13	0

Umpires: F.S. Lee and H. Elliott

I also remember a game in 1953 against Yorkshire at Headingley when I took 14 wickets in the match which, against the old enemy, was very satisfying. I also took 13 wickets the same season at Bath when we beat Somerset, the game was over by 5.30 p.m. on the Saturday – the first day! We won the toss and put them in. Brian Statham opened up one end and myself the other. I used to vary my pace depending on the wicket and on that day I bowled fairly quick off-spinners and felt I could do anything with the ball. The very first one I bowled moved quite a bit and we got them out for 55 and I took 7 wickets for 25 runs. We went in and scored a quick 158 using the 'long handle' and attacking them. They went back in later in the day, the wicket was still taking spin and they were out for 79 and I took another 6 wickets! We had been scheduled to stay at our hotel for four days, but booked out and motored home in an Austin 10 the same day.

Proudest Moment

For me this was when I was chosen for my first Test match in Adelaide, the fourth Test, in 1950. It was always my ambition to play for England. I was actually disappointed not to make the MCC tour party to Australia at the end of the season. I played in the Gents v. Players match at Lord's and bearing in mind the team was chosen from that game, I had a good game and felt I had a chance. I also took most wickets in the country and finished top of the bowling averages so I couldn't have done any more. At about Christmas time, I was at St. Dunstan's in Swindon attending a sports forum. There was a lot of speculation in the press about me going to Australia but I dismissed it as paper talk. Then someone told me I had been called up and that I was to return home as soon as I could. So I telephoned Geoffrey Howard to confirm it, which he did, and returned on the milk train via London. I listened to the third Test match on the radio and played in the fourth! Brian Statham and I flew out there on a Constellation aircraft with propellers – it was our first flight and took four days! Then we beat them in the fifth Test at Melbourne when I put on 74 with Reg Simpson for the last wicket. When I batted I was surrounded by fielders and remember surviving an lbw appeal from Jack Iverson, a freak spin bowler, to a ball which pitched outside the leg stump. Reg was 92 not out when I came in and I was there to help him reach his century on his birthday. He finished on 156 not out and it was Australia's first defeat in 26 Tests. Lindsay Hassett the Australian captain sent champagne into our dressing-room, so it was a memorable start for me.

A first-rate right-arm off-break bowler, 'Tatt' scored 2,040 runs (9.35) and took 1,369 wickets (18.04) and 143 catches. In 16 Test matches he scored 50 runs (5), took 58 wickets (26.08) and 8 catches.

–4–

Colin McCool (1915–1986)

New South Wales, Queensland, Somerset and Australia

In 1959 McCool embarked on the fourth season of a successful campaign with Somerset and was granted a testimonial which raised three thousand pounds. He scored 1,769 runs and took 64 wickets in a year he felt was his best ever. There were two simple reasons for a surge of form in the autumn of his career at the age of 43. Firstly the summer was long and hot, the wickets were covered and conditions were exactly the same as he had known in Australia, with pitches fast and true. Secondly McCool also had continuity of cricket and, playing every day, was able to retain his form in Australian-style conditions which played to his strengths. He found that he had a sight of the ball and the pace of the pitch from the very first delivery that he received. So he reverted to his old Australian batting habits using his natural strength, particularly square of the wicket, where he excelled in cutting and hooking.

Somerset skipper Maurice Tremlett had decided early on that he needed McCool's batting more than his bowling. He put him in at number four and told him not to take any silly risks. McCool bore the brunt of a frail batting side and from 1956 to 1960 scored about 1,500 runs a year for them. Consequently he felt that he was not always put on to bowl enough, though he always got on well with Tremlett, who he felt did a great job as captain. McCool thrived on cricket and was one of the principal reasons for a revival in Somerset's fortunes. Hence when he retired from first-class cricket at the end of the 1960 season at the age of 44, McCool felt that he had become a far better player than when playing Test cricket in Australia. He was a more complete player technically through having to play in conditions that were constantly changing, and playing on English wickets with their tremendous variations.

With his wife Dorothy and young family, McCool returned to his native Australia after the end of the 1960 season. He had not quite come to terms with the West Country, though was flattered that in his last season a number of Somerset supporters tried to start a fund to pay his passage to and from Australia, so that he could have another season as a Somerset player, however impractical. It had been his original intention to come to England in 1953 and play just two seasons in the Lancashire League – as it turned out he stayed eight years! He missed the sunshine though: 'There's no winter,' he said, 'and the beer's better; and the bloody off-spinners don't turn!'

The McCools returned to Brisbane, where they had retained their home and Colin was able to resume working for the Government in the city transport department. He found time to write an interesting, thoughtful book, *Cricket Is a Game*, in 1961 and the '60s saw him help bring up their daughter and three sons, Russell, Ross and Raymond.

The family moved to Umina in New South Wales in the early '60s and on retirement McCool was able to pursue his hobby of gardening, encouraged by Dorothy, to the extent that it became his main interest. The garden at Umina was to become his pride and joy.

McCool never had a day's illness in his life and was always in good health – the only time he suffered was from a worn spinning finger, a legacy of his triumphs way back in 1946–7, when he was Australia's leading wicket-taker in the Test matches against the touring MCC side. It was therefore a tremendous shock to the family when he was diagnosed with cancer in 1985 and within six months passed away, in April 1986 at the age of 70.

McCool's favourite sportsman, county colleague and fellow Australian Bill Alley said at the time of his death: 'As a batsman Colin gave the county tremendous service and he was at his most brilliant on turning wickets of the kind we used to have at Weston and Bath. He used to get inside the ball and drive it even when it was turning square. He was an independent sort of character, always very relaxed in the dressing-room. He would sit in the corner puffing his pipe or even going to sleep with his pads on until it was time to bat. He would talk to the young players and quietly encourage them – but he could also put the fear of God into anyone he thought was a bit cocky.'

Memorable Game

The most memorable game McCool played in may well have been the third Test at Durban in 1950, where he made a significant contribution. The pitch took spin from the second day and, having dismissed Australia for 75, South Africa did not enforce the follow-on in an intriguing tactical match. McCool, who added a crucial 106 for the sixth wicket with Neil Harvey to see Australia home, rated it as one of his best innings, for until then he had had little experience of wet wickets. He was also fascinated by the tactical battle between two great cricketing brains, skippers Lindsay Hassett and Dudley Nourse.

20, 21, 23, 24 January 1950. Australia won by 5 wickets

With the forecast of further rain, it was Nourse's view that he should bat again and build a commanding lead in order to reduce his side's chances of losing. What he didn't bargain for was the ability of the Australians to keep the South Africans at the wicket without them realising that the pitch was turning. So Hassett avoided using the spinners and with splendid fielding to match prevented an early declaration, which would have made life difficult for the Australians, particularly after the damage inflicted by Tayfield in the first innings. The plan worked a treat. South Africa were contained to a score of 99, batting most of the day and were given no indication of a turning wicket. Thus Australia only had to bat during the last session – even then they lost Moroney, Hassett and Miller. On the final day, though, Australia fought back to gain a remarkable victory with ten minutes to spare.

South Africa

E.A.B. Rowan c Johnston b Miller	143	c Saggers b Lindwall	4
O.E. Wynne b Johnston	18	b Johnson	29
J.D. Nel c and b Johnson	14	lbw b Johnston	20
A.D. Nourse c Saggers b Johnston	66	c McCool b Johnson	27
W.W. Wade b Lindwall	24	b Johnston	0
N.B.F. Mann b Johnston	9	lbw b Johnson	0
J.E. Cheetham c Hassett b Johnston	4	c Hassett b Johnson	1
J.C. Watkins b Lindwall	5	st Saggers b Johnson	2
H.J. Tayfield run out	15	b Johnston	3
V.I. Smith b Lindwall	1	b Johnston	4
C.N. McCarthy not out	0	not out	2
B 3, l-b 7, n-b 2	12	B 5, l-b 1, n-b 1	7
	311		99

1/32 2/75 3/242 4/264 5/283 6/289 7/293 8/304 9/308

1/9 2/51 3/85 4/85 5/88 6/90 7/93 8/93 9/93

Australia

A.R. Morris c Smith b Tayfield	25	hit wkt b Tayfield	44
J. Moroney b Tayfield	10	lbw b Tayfield	10
I.W. Johnson lbw b Tayfield	2		
K.R. Miller b Tayfield	2	lbw b Mann	10
A.L. Hassett lbw b Tayfield	2	lbw b Mann	11
R.A. Saggers c Cheetham b Mann	2		
C.L. McCool lbw b Mann	1	not out	39
R.R. Lindwall b Mann	7		
R.N. Harvey c and b Tayfield	2	not out	151
S.J.E. Loxton c Cheetham b Tayfield	16	b Mann	54
W.A. Johnston not out	2		
B 3, l-b 1	4	B 7, l-b 9, n-b 1	17
	75	(5 wkts)	336

1/31 2/35 3/37 4/39 5/42 6/45 7/46
8/53 9/63

1/14 2/33 3/59 4/95 5/230

Australia Bowling

	O	M	R	W	O	M	R	W
Lindwall	19	3	47	3	4	1	7	1
Miller	24	5	73	1	7	0	12	0
McCool	13	3	35	0				
Johnston	31.2	5	75	4	18.2	6	39	4
Loxton	6	1	31	0				
Johnson	16	5	38	1	17	2	34	5

South Africa Bowling

	O	M	R	W	O	M	R	W
McCarthy	6	2	8	0	12	3	32	0
Watkins	4	1	9	0	6	2	10	0
Mann	10	1	31	3	51.6	13	101	3
Tayfield	8.4	1	23	7	49	5	144	2
Smith					5	0	32	0

Umpires: J.V. Hart-Davis and B.V. Malan

His 'double' for Somerset of 90 and 116 (in 95 minutes) against the touring Australians in 1956 was equally as sweetly satisfying a performance as any in McCool's illustrious career.

Proudest Moment

Apart from representing his country, McCool's proudest moment may well have been catching his boyhood idol on his debut for New South Wales in 1939. Test cricketer Arthur Chipperfield had just retired as the champions of the Sheffield Shield played the Rest of Australia. McCool took his place on the back of scoring runs and showing great promise in the field for Paddington. In the event he took five catches including a caught-and-bowled.

All was eclipsed though, in the second innings by a catch at first slip to dismiss Don Bradman off the bowling of Albert Cheetham's medium-paced out-swinger for two. It was a memory to remain with McCool for the rest of his life, and on the first occasion he had ever played in the same match as Bradman. It also revived memories when, as a boy, McCool had slipped through a hole in the fence at Sydney to watch Bradman practice with McCabe and Archie Jackson and get his autograph on a dirty scrap of paper.

McCool also took pride in being able to adapt to English conditions and derived great satisfaction over the years from his performances on wet wickets. It was felt by English players that overseas batsmen couldn't play on soft, wet wickets, where the ball turns and stops and refuses to come on to the bat. McCool was able to disprove that theory and successfully balanced a more cautious approach to his batting with his natural flair and inventiveness.

A short but powerful right-handed stroke-playing batsman and leg-break bowler, McCool scored 12,420 runs (32.94) including 18 centuries, took 602 wickets (27.48), 261 catches and 1 stumping. In 14 Test matches, he scored 459 runs (35.30) including 1 century, took 36 wickets (26.61) and 14 catches.

–5–

Donald Carr (b. 1926)

Oxford University, Derbyshire and England

The number of runs I scored for Derbyshire in 1959 [over 2,000] was, and still is, a record for the club. It was a very good summer and pitches by and large around the country were better to bat on than the norm. I was a better and more successful player on straight up and down pitches rather than slow turners. I had a good final month of the season in the main and managed to get a century in each innings at Canterbury. That was the first year during my time with Derbyshire that the batting had as much bearing on the results as the bowling. With Les Jackson, Cliff Gladwin, Derek Morgan and latterly Harold Rhodes we didn't very often have to field a full day. We were surprised if any team scored 300 against us. The batting improved with confidence.

I skippered the team until 1962 when I became assistant secretary at MCC on Billy Griffith's promotion to secretary. I thought that if I were to remain in cricket this would be as good a job as I could have. I had previously been secretary at Derbyshire for three years and before that assistant secretary to a wonderful old boy called Will Taylor, who had been secretary for 51 years.

I played a handful of games in 1963, my first innings that year being against Sussex when I scored a hundred much to everyone's amazement, and horror for Billy Griffith, who had given me the time off to play. When

31

the Gillette Cup started that year Derbyshire played Hampshire in the first round and they asked me to play without any practice. I have never been so exhausted in my life! I did absolutely nothing on the field but we won off the last ball of the game and I thought, 'thank goodness I have retired!' I subsequently played a bit of cricket for Free Foresters and MCC and in 1967 captained Repton in the inaugural year of the Cricketer Cup, when we beat Radley in the final. I played in the Cricketer Cup for four or five years and we probably should have won it more times. We had a very good side, including Richard Hutton, who had a year off from Yorkshire.

I worked with the TCCB from its inauguration in 1968. In the late '60s MCC provided a secretariat, but when Billy Griffith retired in 1974 it was decided to have a separate secretary of the TCCB which I was appointed to, and Jack Bailey became secretary of MCC. It was a combined role with secretary of the Cricket Council which I held until 1986. Since then I have been involved in various committees but am now retired to all intents and purposes.

I was England cricket manager on the MCC tours to South Africa in 1964–5, India/Pakistan in 1972–3 and the West Indies in 1973–4 and have many memories of these times. India in 1972–3 was Tony Greig's first tour. I said to him when we left England, 'You've got that awful South African accent and as South Africa is not the most popular place in the Indian sub-continent, I suggest you keep your mouth shut, within reason!' He said, 'Don't worry about it man, I'll be all right.' He arrived in India, all 6' 7" of him, fair hair, big smile and within a week all the boys and girls in India wanted to see him more than anyone else. They called him 'MrTonyGreig' in one word and he was marvellous – he played well too. He had this infectious ability to attract people. Much as I hated him over the Packer business I couldn't help enjoying his company.

The West Indies tour was certainly very eventful. The Kallicharran incident happened during the first Test in Port-of-Spain, Trinidad. Tony Greig was fielding in his usual position about two yards from the bat on the off-side for last ball of the day with Bernard Julien batting and Kallicharran up the bowlers end. Julien successfully blocked the ball and Alan Knott took the bails off and turned round towards the pavilion. Greigy picked up the ball, turned the other way, threw it and knocked the middle stump as Alvin was walking out of his ground back to the pavilion. The umpire Sang Hue hadn't called time and there was a hush round the ground. Kally was about 50 not out and almost knocked my foot out as I was standing on the steps when he smashed his bat on the ground. That was one of the nastiest moments I have ever been involved in. Mike Denness, the captain and I had about an hour with the umpires and the West Indies' authorities after the close of play. The umpires accepted that they didn't want him out but Sang Hue said he had given him out because he was out and there was no way he could not be out, but we asked to withdraw our appeal. Jeff Stollmeyer, who was the senior man in Trinidad cricket said that if he wasn't allowed to bat the following day, he feared for the trouble there would be with the crowd. We eventually obtained agreement to withdraw our appeal and in fact after that the law of cricket was changed to allow an appeal to be withdrawn. Greigy just acted on instinct when he threw the wicket down – he was certainly very competitive.

The final Test, also in Trinidad was most exciting. The West Indies needed 220-odd to win in the final innings and we were flying home at the end of the game. So I was not there at the ground at the start of the day's play, but finishing off accounts, packing and listening on the radio. Tony Greig started bowling them out and whilst I thought we would lose quite comfortably at the start of the day, suddenly it was becoming a close run thing. By this time I left what I was doing and rushed down the stairs of the hotel. Out from the swimming pool area, her hair in rollers, came Mrs Stuart Surridge, who became the first lady president of Surrey. She had been listening to the radio as well, so took her curlers out and we dashed to the ground. We finished up winning by 26 runs and whilst we had been so outplayed in the series, that win levelled the scores.

I still play golf, back permitting, and follow football. I enjoy photography although my family wouldn't say that I am a very good photographer! At that time (1959) I had been on tour a few times and liked to take my camera with me.

I didn't quite succeed in my ambition to lead Derbyshire to the Championship. In 1957 we were top of the table with Lancashire in July. Then losing the toss in 10 of the last 11 matches we dropped to fourth place and Les Jackson was injured as well. Our batting was never consistent enough to quite mount a serious challenge for the Championship. Our spinning department was also not strong enough.

Memorable Game

I suppose that was the third Victory Test match at Lord's in 1945 – I was only 18 at the time. The game itself wasn't very memorable, but to play with W.R. Hammond captaining the side was a great thrill.

14, 16, 17 July 1945. Australia won by 4 wickets

About 84,000 people attended the Victory match and England played three of the best schoolboy cricketers of that year, Carr, Dewes and White. However Australia always had the edge and spinner Cristofani varied his pace and flight to good effect in his first game of the series.

England

L Hutton b Miller	104	c Sismey b Cristofani	69
C. Washbrook c Sismey b Williams	8	not out	13
J.G. Dewes b Miller	27	b Miller	0
W.R. Hammond st Sismey b Pepper	13	absent ill	
Hon. L.R. White st Sismey b Cristofani	11	lbw b Cristofani	4
W.J. Edrich lbw b Cristofani	38	b Miller	58
D.B. Carr b Miller	4	c Pepper b Cristofani	1
S.C. Griffith c Pepper b Cristofani	36	c Pepper b Cristofani	0
R. Pollard not out	1	b Miller	9
W. Roberts b Cristofani	1	b Ellis	0
D.V.P. Wright lbw b Ellis	5	c Hassett b Cristofani	6
B 2, l-b 1, n-b 3	6	L-b 3, n-b 1	4
	254		**164**

Australia

R.S. Whitington b Pollard	19	c Griffith b Pollard	0
J.A. Workman c Edrich b Wright	7	b Wright	30
A.G. Cheetham b Roberts	5	not out	9
A.L. Hassett lbw b Pollard	68	c Edrich b Wright	24
K.R. Miller b Pollard	7	not out	71
C.G. Pepper lbw b Pollard	0	lbw b Edrich	18
D.K. Carmody c White b Pollard	32	c Edrich b Roberts	1
D.R. Cristofani b Roberts	32		
S.G. Sismey c Griffith b Pollard	9	lbw b Pollard	51
R.G. Williams b Wright	4		
R.S. Ellis not out	0		
L-b 4, n-b 7	11	B 1, l-b 15, n-b 5	21
	194	(six wkts)	**225**

Australia Bowling

	O	M	R	W	O	M	R	W
Williams	19	6	45	1	3	0	10	0
Cheetham	19	4	47	0	4	0	7	0
Pepper	19	2	44	1	10	3	22	0
Ellis	19.1	6	25	1	14	1	29	1
Miller	18	3	44	3	16	2	42	3
Cristofani	13	1	43	4	29.3	8	49	5
Whitington					1	0	1	0

England Bowling

	O	M	R	W	O	M	R	W
Edrich	7	0	25	0	12	1	37	1
Pollard	23	4	75	6	21	4	71	2
Wright	24.1	3	49	2	25	4	59	2

Roberts	14	5	24	2	13	4	24	1
Carr	3	1	10	0	6	2	13	0

Also, winning the university match in 1951 against a very strong Cambridge side when we were the underdogs was most enjoyable. Beating Yorkshire in Les Jackson's benefit match at Burton-on-Trent in 1957 was my favourite for Derbyshire. We eventually won in the last over of the match and I was rather pleased with myself for judging the declaration well! When Laurie Johnson caught the last man at second slip next to me I was so pleased for Les.

Proudest Moment

The proudest moment in cricket for me was being selected to play for England against India in 1951 [Carr made his England debut at Delhi in a drawn game, scoring 76 in the second innings].

A class right-handed batsman, slow left-arm bowler and brilliant close fielder, Carr scored 19,250 runs (28.68), including 24 centuries, took 328 wickets (34.71) and 500 catches. In 2 Test matches, he scored 135 runs (33.75) and took 2 wickets (70.00).

35

–6–

Les Jackson (b. 1921)

Derbyshire and England

In 1959 I had trouble with a trapped nerve in my hip bone. Stan Weaver, the old Newcastle United player, who was our masseur at the time, would strap me up. I used to breathe in and he pulled the muscle away from the hip bone – I was like that for half a season! My feet also used to bleed – Derbyshire skipper Donald Carr used to say, 'Why didn't you tell me?' I told him things were going fine, I wasn't worried and was happy to carry on. I was thought of as a hard nut being a miner and if I was playing cricket, it didn't matter. In addition to breaking a finger, I remember dislocating another which was put back into place on the field and I carried on! I was being paid and felt it was my job to get on with. I was quite happy as I loved the game, that was the main thing. Cricket today is a game of money with no loyalty. My wages were equivalent to fifty pounds a month.

There was no secret to my bowling possibly other than holding the ball in one position with the seam between the two main fingers and the thumb underneath. The only other thing I can think of is the difference in action, as my arm would be a little higher or lower at certain times. Before the start of the 1949 season Derbyshire sent me down to Alf Gover's school in London for a fortnight with Derek Morgan and Arnold Hamer to try and change my action. After a couple of days Alf said, 'What did they send you for?' I said, 'As far I know, something to do with my action.' He told me to carry on, because trying to change it might throw it out altogether.

I know Ted Dexter was very complimentary about my bowling, particularly at Derby where Walter Goodyear, one of the finest groundsmen in the country, used to prepare the wickets to suit me and Cliff Gladwin. When Ted came in once, one ball pitched on leg and missed off, then another pitched on off and missed leg. He looked at me and said, 'Which bloody way is it going?' I said, 'You'll find out in a bit.' Then one pitched on, he missed and it bowled him. His favourite saying was, 'You don't know which bloody road they are going do you?' to which I said, 'I don't!'

I have met various players, at dinners over the years, that I used to play against. As soon as they come through the door they put their hand up and tell me to start rubbing the inside of their leg, as I never hit them on the pad, always on the inside of the leg! It was gratifying to know that opposing teams didn't like coming to Derby to face Cliff and me. I remember saying to Walter Goodyear the match before we faced Northamptonshire (and Frank Tyson) one year at Derby that he couldn't prepare a fast wicket. We beat them but I never said that to Walter again as Frank was the quickest thing I have ever seen!

I started to play cricket for the local side, working down the colliery at the time. Whilst I made my debut for the county in 1947 at the late age of 26, it was in 1948 that I walked into the side and stayed there. Bill Copson was injured at Burton-on-Trent and Derbyshire sent for me.

I finally retired in 1963 holding all the main records for a Derbyshire bowler. The colliery gave me a job over the winter months on the surface and I went to work at Mansfield on retirement for the National Coal Board as a driver, then went back to Bolsover, the area headquarters. I chauffeured Mr Siddall, the director of the NCB, to London and he agreed that I could retire in 1983 when I reached 62. I have lived in Whitwell all my life apart from about three years. I used to do a lot of gardening when I first finished cricket and that kept me busy.

Memorable Game

This was probably my benefit match in 1957 against Yorkshire at Burton-on-Trent. We beat them for the first time and I did fairly well as regards wickets, five in the first innings and six in the second.

25, 27, 28 May 1957. Derbyshire won by 84 runs

Jackson fittingly took the final Yorkshire wicket of Platt to secure an excellent victory for Derbyshire with just seven minutes to spare.

Derbyshire

A. Hamer b Platt	8	lbw b Trueman	13
C. Lee c Trueman b Illingworth	39	c Watson b Platt	2
J. Kelly c Watson b Wardle	106	c Binks b Trueman	0
A.C. Revill c Close b Illingworth	9	b Platt	15
D.B. Carr c Binks b Illingworth	40	not out	92
G.O. Dawkes c Watson b Trueman	28	b Trueman	75
H.L. Johnson c Taylor b Trueman	2	not out	31
D.C. Morgan c Wilson b Taylor	21		
E. Smith c Sutcliffe b Wardle	16		
C. Gladwin not out	8		
L. Jackson b Trueman	1		
B 9, l-b 5	14	B 2, l-b 1	3
	292	(5 wkts decl.)	231

1/12 2/57 3/67 4/152 5/198 6/204
7/242 8/277 9/291

1/4 2/11 3/30
4/36 5/146

Yorkshire

D.B. Close st Dawkes b Smith	120	b Jackson	11
K. Taylor b Jackson	20	c Morgan b Jackson	5
J.V. Wilson b Gladwin	7	c Hamer b Carr	40
R. Illingworth b Jackson	16	c Dawkes b Jackson	44
W. Watson c Jackson b Gladwin	0	b Revill	50
D.E.V. Padgett run out	2	c Morgan b Carr	15
W.H.H. Sutcliffe c and b Gladwin	6	not out	40
J.G. Binks c Lee b Jackson	2	c Gladwin b Jackson	9
J.H. Wardle b Jackson	22	c Morgan b Carr	0
F.S. Trueman b Jackson	2	lbw b Jackson	0
R.K. Platt not out	1	c Johnson b Jackson	17
B 1	1	B 4, l-b 5	9
	199		220

1/65 2/107 3/145 4/149 5/161 6/165
7/173 8/175 9/188

1/13 2/20 3/97 4/107 5/108
6/148 7/202 8/215 9/215

Yorkshire Bowling

	O	M	R	W	O	M	R	W
Trueman	23.1	3	68	3	22	0	103	3
Platt	25	4	87	1	21	8	55	2
Taylor	19	7	31	1				
Illingworth	19	5	51	3	3	0	18	0
Wardle	17	7	30	2	9	3	27	0
Close	3	0	11	0	6	2	25	0

Derbyshire Bowling

Jackson	28.4	7	51	5	29	11	63	6
Gladwin	29	7	57	3	13	2	42	0
Morgan	17	3	51	0	4	0	16	0
Smith	14	7	35	1	14	7	33	0
Carr	1	0	4	0	22	3	63	3
Revill					8	4	14	1

Umpires: T.W. Spencer and J.S. Buller

My most memorable bowling performances were 9–60 against Lancashire at Manchester in 1952 and 9 wickets (conceding just 17 runs) against Cambridge in 1959. I got the first nine out at Fenners, then Donald Carr put Derek Morgan on and with his second ball he bowled the number 10 or 11 out. I looked at Derek but didn't say anything – the look was good enough to kill!

Proudest Moment

My proudest moment in cricket was when I walked onto the pitch at Manchester for my first Test match against New Zealand in July 1949. It was early in my career and I didn't know too many players. When I walked into the dressing-room and saw Denis Compton, Bill Edrich and Godfrey Evans I was very nervous. However, as soon as I put my foot on the cricket pitch everything went blank, irrespective of the crowd, and the nerves went. It was exactly the same the other time I played for England in 1961 against Australia at Leeds.

Playing for England was always in the back of my mind. After that first Test in 1949 there was a glut of very good bowlers like Fred Trueman, Brian Statham, Peter Loader and Frank Tyson. I don't think I missed out playing for England because I was with an unfashionable county and it never worried me. In 1961 I was playing at Derby when I was recalled to the England side for the third Test. When I went up to Leeds on the Friday night Brian Statham was there and the only chance I had of getting in the team was if he wasn't fit. Brian failed a fitness test in the nets and I was in. When I look back I only played once against Australia in a Test match and we won in three days. Freddie Trueman bowled them out as fast as they came in, but I did my share and got a couple of wickets [England won by 8 wickets, Jackson taking 2 wickets in each innings].

A strong, hostile, right-arm, fast-medium bowler, Jackson scored 2,083 runs (av. 6.19), took 1,733 wickets (17.36) and 136 catches. In two Test matches, he scored 15 runs (15.00), took 7 wickets (22.14) and 1 catch.

–7–

Alan Moss (b. 1930)

Middlesex and England

My best season was probably 1960, when I took 136 wickets at the age of 29. I also had a good year in 1961 with 106 wickets at just over 12 runs apiece, which was quite astonishing but then it was when I was at my fittest. I had a couple of bad injuries earlier in my career – one was against Australia in 1956 at Trent Bridge and I didn't play again that season. Then I paralysed myself at Headingley from the waist down against India in 1959.

I finished cricket early, at the age of 32, as I had a job to go to and didn't like the way we were playing. When I wasn't abroad, I had been in printing and publishing during the winter. My guv'nor asked me if I was going to tour again which I couldn't answer, so he offered me a job for life. I became a Free Forester just, as in one of my qualifying matches I turned up late – I thought it was an afternoon start but it was 11.30 a.m. My proposer or seconder, Dennis Silk spoke up for me and I played one game for them in 1968. I found that people expected me to knock over wickets though, and I really wasn't in the frame of mind to get worked up about it. I had worn my back out anyway, so I didn't play cricket after that.

I went on the committee for Middlesex in the late '60s, was treasurer for 11 years and appointed chairman in April 1996. Giving back to the game for me is quite exciting and good fun even though it's a lot of hard work. I am still in printing – I have my own business now but it is a consultancy. I was on Robert Maxwell's Board for two years and was with BPC for 17 years, so it's been my life. Cricket does take a lot of my time and affects my business, there's no doubt about that.

Whilst photography was my hobby in 1959, I've still got the cameras but no longer the incentive. I love travel – I didn't tour Australia but I have been over as my son lives there. I saw quite a bit of the world with cricket – Pakistan, South Africa, West Indies three times, America and Canada, so it's been a very good life. The prettiest country I went to was Kenya.

Memorable Game

One of the most memorable games I played in was the first Test against Australia at Trent Bridge in 1956. I had been picked ahead of the others, Statham, Trueman and Tyson. Brian broke down at the nets and we went in with Bailey, Moss, Laker, Lock and Appleyard. It was a great boost to be picked against the Australians, although I had only bowled four overs when I slipped in the field and tore my inside. Alan Davidson was also injured badly in the ankle, and walking on sticks, and I was bent like an old man! It's strange to remember it just for the four overs.

7, 8, 9, 11, 12 June 1956. Match drawn

After a rain-affected opening two days, Moss was injured fielding brilliantly a firm drive from Harvey at cover early into the third day. Adverse weather conditions dominated the Test as the game ended in a draw.

England

P.E. Richardson c Langley b Miller	81	c Langley b Archer	73
M.C. Cowdrey c Miller b Davidson	25	c Langley b Miller	81
T.W. Graveney c Archer b Johnson	8	not out	10
P.B.H. May c Langley b Miller	73		
W. Watson lbw b Archer	0	c Langley b Miller	8
T.E. Bailey c Miller b Archer	14		
T.G. Evans c Langley b Miller	0	not out	8
J.C. Laker not out	9		
G.A.R. Lock lbw b Miller	0		
R. Appleyard not out	1		
A.E. Moss did not bat			
B 5, l-b 1	6	B 4, l-b 1, w 2, n-b 1	8
	(8 wkts dec) 217		(3 wkts dec) 188
1/53 2/72 3/180 4/181		1/151 2/163	
5/201 6/203 7/213 8/214		3/178	

Australia

C.C. McDonald lbw b Lock	1	c Lock b Laker	6
J.W. Burke c Lock b Laker	11	not out	58
R.N. Harvey lbw b Lock	64	b Lock	3
P. Burge c sub. b Lock	7	not out	35
K.R. Miller lbw b Laker	0	lbw b Laker	4
R.G. Archer c Lock b Appleyard	33		
R. Benaud b Appleyard	17		
I.W. Johnson c Bailey b Laker	12		
R.R. Lindwall c Bailey b Laker	0		
G.R. Langley not out	0		
A.K. Davidson absent hurt	0		
L-b 3	3	B 10, l-b 3, n-b 1	14
	148	(3 wkts)	120

1/10 2/12 3/33 4/36 5/90 6/110
7/148 8/148 9/148

1/13 2/18 3/41

Australia Bowling

	O	M	R	W	O	M	R	W
Lindwall	15	4	43	0				
Miller	33	5	69	4	19	2	58	2
Davidson	10	1	22	1				
Archer	31	10	51	2	9	0	46	1
Johnson	14	7	26	1	12	2	29	0
Burke	1	1	0	0	3	1	6	0
Benaud					18	4	41	0

England Bowling

	O	M	R	W	O	M	R	W
Moss	4	3	1	0				
Bailey	3	1	8	0	9	3	16	0
Laker	29.1	11	58	4	30	19	29	2
Lock	36	16	61	3	22	11	23	1
Appleyard	11	4	17	2	19	6	32	0
Graveney					6	3	6	0

Umpires: T.J. Bartley and J.S. Buller

I also remember my first Test match which was against the West Indies in January 1954 in Jamaica. We went in with four seamers which in those days was unusual – Trueman, Statham, Bailey and Moss. The spinner was Lock and we left out Laker and Wardle, who was not happy and felt I shouldn't have been playing. As it turned out he was probably right! It was a thrilling match, we went out with all the drums banging and fiery Fred was going to pin them to the sightscreen, but the only thing that got pinned to the sightscreen was the ball [West Indies won by 140 runs]! It was a very good [drawn] series and exciting for me to be picked for the tour as I was only 23 when I arrived in the Caribbean.

Whilst I didn't get many opportunities for England because of the number of top class bowlers at the time, I have far more sympathy for Les Jackson, who I think was hard done by. He was a terrific bowler and it was said he couldn't bowl away from Derbyshire which I think was grossly unfair. He would easily walk into the side today on his record alone. He was a hard man and a great competitor.

Proudest Moment

My proudest moment in cricket was being asked to become treasurer of Middlesex CCC, as I was the first professional of my era ever to hold office here at Lord's, MCC or Middlesex. The other great moment in my life was in 1953 when I was at home and Don Bennett, who was staying with us, went out to get the paper while I was still in bed. He came back and said to me, 'You're going to the West Indies.' I learnt about it in the paper and that moment sticks in my mind – he stood there with *The Telegraph* and I said to him, 'You lying so and so!'

A tall and strong right-arm fast bowler, Moss scored 1,671 runs (6.99), took 1,301 wickets (20.78) and 143 catches. In 9 Test matches he scored 61 runs (10.16), took 21 wickets (29.80) and 1 catch.

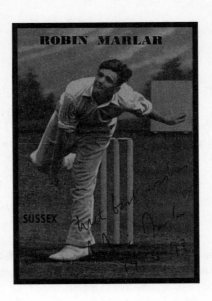

–8–

Robin Marlar (b. 1931)

Cambridge University and Sussex

I played for Sussex regularly until 1960, captaining the county from 1955 to 1959. There was a bit of a problem in 1968 when I came back and played in three matches as a member of the committee, just to see what was going on. It was the time when Jim Parks was handing over to Mike Griffith.

I briefly went full-time into journalism until going into industry. I was rugby writer for *The Telegraph* and also worked for *The Sunday Times*. I was also secretary of the Cricket Writers' club for a few years – only because I had an office! I worked in a world-wide head-hunting business from 1968 and on my own from 1971, which I combined with writing. My most satisfying piece of journalism is always the last one.

I've had the very best job in cricket journalism for 26 years and been very happy. The last year as chairman (1997) of Sussex CCC has been difficult. If the vote had gone for two divisions I don't think I would have stayed on for a second year. I was very critical when those six ex-committee guys walked out. One of my present colleagues, Jim May said, 'What are you going to do about it?' I went to New Zealand during the winter and thought no more about it. When I came back and the campaign started I realised what a great honour it was to be the chairman of the county, especially to be only the third captain of the club to take the chair after Arthur Gilligan and A.J. Holmes.

I have a house in France so that has partially fulfilled my ambition to live abroad during the winter. It's to avoid something called snow which I am desperately allergic to!

Memorable Game

The most memorable game I played in was the Varsity game at Lord's as captain of Cambridge in 1953. We were losing but worked very hard to get back into the game with Dennis Silk's runs and won by two wickets in the end.

4, 6, 7 July 1953. Cambridge won by two wickets

Marlar bowled tirelessly in the match from both ends, skilfully flighting his off-breaks to take 12 wickets. In one lethal spell of 5 overs in the Oxford second innings, he took 4 wickets for 5 runs.

Oxford

H.B. Birrell c Alexander b Hayward	6	b Hayward	0
J.C. Marshall c Alexander b Marlar	21	c Alexander b Dickinson	26
C.C.P. Williams lbw b Marlar	40	c Hayward b Marlar	5
M.C. Cowdrey c Silk b Marlar	116	c Alexander b Marlar	0
A.L. Dowding lbw b Marlar	7	c Subba Row b Marlar	9
J.P. Fellows-Smith b Dickinson	33	c Alexander b Marlar	49
J.M. Allan run out	2	c Lumsden b Marlar	7
A.P. Walshe c Marlar b Dickinson	29	b Marlar	2
G.H. McKinna c Crookes b Hayward	0	c Bushby b Marlar	3
D.K. Fasken b Marlar	20	c Lumsden b Hayward	3
D.C.P. R. Jowett not out	6	not out	0
B 18, l-b 12, n-b 2	32	B 8, l-b 2, n-b 2	12
	312		116

1/18 2/57 3/121 4/150 5/223
6/241 7/254 8/259 9/300

1/5 2/18 3/18 4/29 5/74
6/101 7/110 8/115 9/116

Cambridge

M.H. Bushby c Dowding b Allan	10	b Jowett	21
D.R.W. Silk c Fellows-Smith b Allan	22	not out	116
V.R. Lumsden c Fellows-Smith b Fasken	16	c Williams b Fasken	14
R. Subba Row c Marshall b Jowett	6	lbw b Jowett	28
F.C.M. Alexander b McKinna	31	c Marshall b Allen	7
W. Knightley-Smith c C'drey b McKinna	20	c Williams b Fasken	10
L.K. Lewis b Jowett	22	c Williams b McKinna	2
D.V. Crookes c Fasken b Cowdrey	25	st Walshe b Allan	5

W.I.D. Hayward not out		6	run out		6
D.C. Dickinson b Jowett		0			
R.G. Marlar b Allan		11	not out		9
B 16, l-b 3, w 2, n-b 1		22	B 19, l-b 1		20
		191		(8 wkts)	238

1/19 2/46 3/66 4/66 5/115
6/125 7/167 8/174 9/174

1/40 2/57 3/114 4/125
5/155 6/164 7/167 8/186

Cambridge Bowling

	O	M	R	W	O	M	R	W
Hayward	34	11	88	2	22.4	10	27	2
Dickinson	21.5	4	58	2	5	1	10	1
Marlar	37	14	94	5	25	8	49	7
Lumsden	3	1	6	0				
Subba Row	6	0	26	0	6	3	18	0
Crookes	1	0	8	0				

Oxford Bowling

	O	M	R	W	O	M	R	W
McKinna	17	9	14	2	20	4	45	1
Fasken	17	7	28	1	22	5	48	2
Jowett	31	11	57	3	32	15	50	2
Allan	30.3	13	65	3	33.5	12	61	2
Cowdrey	2	1	3	1				
Fellows-Smith	2	1	2	0	1	0	3	0
Birrell					5	2	11	0

Umpires: F. Chester and H.G. Baldwin

Proudest Moment

It's difficult to say – my top score of 64 against the Australians at Hove in 1956 was probably the proudest. The most satisfying was getting Ted Dexter to play for the county and then becoming captain. Everyone was after him at the time and I persuaded him that Brighton was the nearest place in England to Milan where he was born! One was also always proud when one helped the team to win.

An amateur and right-arm off-break bowler, Marlar scored 3,033 runs (9.72), took 970 wickets (25.22) and 136 catches.

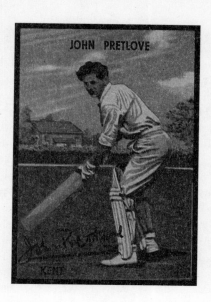

–9–

John Pretlove (b. 1932)

Cambridge University and Kent

1959 was my last season playing first-class cricket. I stopped in fact halfway through. The day I was due at Canterbury for pre-season nets, I received a letter from Lord's inviting me on a minor MCC tour to Canada, ending up with a week in America. I remember reading the letter and saying to Ann, my wife of five months, 'Look at this.' She read it through, burst into tears and said, 'Of course you must go!' Les Ames, who never thought much of me as a player, advised me to go as that sort of opportunity didn't often crop up. The invitation was right out of the blue and I don't know why I was asked, but assume it was because of the Varsity connection. With the tour being between July and September, there were a lot of schoolmasters and Varsity Blues and the Varsity match was over early in July.

The 1959 season started well and I had changed my style a bit. For a little chap, I was using a long handle bat, trying to strike it in the arc between mid-off and mid-on if it was pitched up to me, irrespective of whether it was quick or slow bowling. Les asked me after a month if the trip to Canada was still on but didn't say any more. A month on and, after I had scored 60 runs very quickly against the clock playing Glamorgan at Dartford, Les asked, 'You are still going on this trip aren't you?' The last match I played for Kent was at Westcliff against Essex. We won a really good game of cricket, which swung back and forward, by 28 runs. I literally sailed off into the sunset two days later as we went to Canada by boat on the SS *Corinthia* – it took five days to sail across!

The group of 13 included Ian Bedford, famous for bowling out Bradman and who sadly died later in the '60s, Roger Prideaux, Alan Smith, Dennis Silk, Mike Bushby, Chris Howland, who now lives in Petts Wood, J.R. Thompson, one of the all-time great racquets players and Bob Barber. We were seen off by Billy Griffith, the secretary of MCC and set sail on the Friday night along the Scottish coast to pick up the main body of passengers. The next day we noticed on the board 'Saturday night is get-together night', so Dennis Silk called the players together and there was a bit of a party. I remember missing breakfast but finding a bar at about 10.30 a.m. that was open for a 'hair of the dog'. There was a crowd of passengers who had clearly been there all night. It was obvious they knew each other very well, so I asked them who they were. One of them held his glass up, shaking, and said, 'We are the Canadian Rifle team – we have been to Bisley.' I don't think at that stage they could have hit a sightscreen from 20 yards!

I used to sit and talk to four charming Canadian ladies who played bridge every night. On the third night out, three of them were sitting there looking very miserable and I asked them why. One of them said, 'Mary has *mal de mer* and there's no bridge.' I offered to make up the four and they quickly chained me to the table! One of the ladies, with steel-rimmed specs and dripping with diamonds said, 'We like to play for a little stake of ten cents to keep the interest,' to which I agreed. I was on the winning side for a very enjoyable three rubbers until dinner time, when I was showered with Canadian dollars. I couldn't work it out, as there hadn't been huge points difference until I tumbled the fact that we had been playing ten cents a point! If I had lost, all my cash for the trip would have gone.

The boat docked at Montreal where we were greeted by the Canadian Cricket Association. There were a lot of mean looking armed police and customs people waiting and I remember Jack Bailey, who had certainly enjoyed himself on the trip over, appearing at the top of the slope leading to the huge customs room. At the far end of the hall there was this huge sign saying 'Drink Canada dry'. Jack said as he removed his sunglasses, 'Skipper, we've done the boat, now let's try the country!' We played 28 matches, two three-day games against Canada at Toronto, a two-day game against the States and 25 one-dayers all over Canada. I reckon we all saw more of Canada than most Canadians do in a lifetime – Montreal, Ottawa, Toronto, then on a plane to Vancouver. We played on this wonderful ground called Brockton Point, which Don Bradman describes as the most spectacular ground he has ever seen. On one end there is the sightscreen and you don't get the play stopped for people, but when a great liner goes sailing past over the top of the screen! We had a week's cricket broken by a weekend in Vancouver Island. Then we took a Greyhound bus and came back via Winnipeg and Calgary, then by train to Toronto. On to Philadelphia, where we played a game, then finally a game in New York before catching the *Queen Mary* back to Southampton, where I was met by my dear wife.

Kent had done quite well in 1959 when I finished and I wouldn't swap those few years I played for the county. The '50s was a tremendous time to play – there were so many characters who are still around, I am glad to see. There followed many years of club cricket – for Brentwood and then Bromley, with quite a lot of midweek games for the Stoics.

I left cricket to go into the construction industry, where I have been ever since. I started with Blue Circle, where I was for five years, before moving on to Ready Mixed Concrete for 20 years. I was a director of Hall & Co. and ran two of their four operating companies. I took early retirement from RMC in December 1985 at the age of 53 and started a business of my own, before a friend of mine talked me into going back into a big company. I joined Costain in July 1986 and worked full-time until the end of 1992 and have been a consultant since.

I won a Blue at cricket, and also soccer and captained the Cambridge University side. I also played rugby fives and was open singles champion for four years. I played with four different partners and won the open doubles eight times, mostly with Dennis Silk, a friend for over 40 years, who was our best man and is our daughter's godfather. I still play rugby fives but as a coach now rather than competitively. I also took golf up after cricket but play off a poor 18 handicap.

My nickname of 'Pretters' came from Brian Johnston, like 'Aggers' or 'Blowers'. My name lent itself to that and a lot of people still use it.

Memorable Game

The most memorable game I played in was the Kent v. Surrey game in 1958 at Blackheath when I scored 78 and 29 against the likes of Loader, Bedser, Laker and Lock. Lock took 15 wickets in the match and scored 57 and it looked at one time as if he was going to take them to a win.

12, 14, 15 July 1958. Kent won by 29 runs
Kent were indebted to Pretlove, who top-scored in the first innings, as an entertaining match concluded in Kent's favour by a slender margin with less than 20 minutes to spare.

Kent

R.C. Wilson b Fletcher b Laker	44	c A. Bedser b Lock	10
J. Prodger c Stewart b Lock	4	b Lock	21
S.E. Leary c and b Lock	26	c and b Lock	39
M.C. Cowdrey c Stewart b Lock	6	c May b Lock	5
J.F. Pretlove c Clark b Lock	78	b E. Bedser	29
T.G. Evans c Lock b Laker	1	c and b Lock	10
J. Pettiford c Fletcher b Lock	63	c Stewart b Lock	12
D.J. Halfyard c Clark b Lock	10	c May b Lock	30
G. Smith c Fletcher b Lock	26	b E. Bedser	0
A. Brown lbw b Lock	0	b E. Bedser	8
J.C.T. Page not out	0	not out	1
B 16, l-b 16, n-b 1	33	L-b 6	6
	291		171

1/26 2/78 3/88 4/99 5/106 6/233
7/244 8/284 9/284

1/24 2/56 3/73 4/82 5/130
6/144 7/162 8/162 9/170

Surrey

T.H. Clark c Leary b Brown	20	b Halfyard	50
M.J. Stewart c Leary b Page	24	b Halfyard	10
D.G.W. Fletcher run out	0	b Halfyard	10
P.B.H. May c Prodger b Pettiford	99	b Pettiford	36
B. Constable c Cowdrey b Page	38	b Halfyard	10
E.A. Bedser c Brown b Page	4	c Prodger b Halfyard	12
A.J. McIntyre b Page	0	b Halfyard	25
G.A.R. Lock st Evans b Pettiford	5	c Evans b Page	57
J.C. Laker b Pettiford	0	c Evans b Pettiford	4
A.V. Bedser not out	8	not out	3
P.J. Loader c Pretlove b Page	8	b Pettiford	0
L-b 5	5	B 1, l-b 4	5
	211		222

1/30 2/30 3/91 4/177 5/182
6/182 7/191 8/191 9/195

1/26 2/54 3/105 4/121 5/129
6/148 7/181 8/188 9/221

Surrey Bowling

	O	M	R	W	O	M	R	W
Loader	23	8	54	0				
A. Bedser	18	6	24	0	12	4	35	0
Lock	44.2	16	99	8	29	11	83	7
Laker	38	14	64	2	16	5	35	0
E. Bedser	8	2	17	0	6.5	3	12	3

Kent Bowling

Brown	12	4	26	1	8	0	31	0
Halfyard	14	2	48	0	22	3	102	6
Smith	9	4	17	0	5	1	19	0
Page	20.4	6	78	5	1	0	6	1
Pettiford	14	6	37	3	10.3	2	59	3

Umpires: A.E. Pothecary and R.S. Lay

I also enjoyed scoring my first first-class hundred at Fenners in 1954. As a freshman they give you three matches and the third game was against Essex. It was a bit soft and Mike Bushby elected to bat. I strode to the wicket at twenty to twelve when we were about 8–2 and played out the over. Mike came up to me and said, 'Just stick it out, this is going to be a beautiful track.' I got my head down and one over later we were 10–3 as Mike was out! Fortunately I hung around, was supported by Vincent Lumsden, and scored 137, which was my highest score in first-class cricket. I actually think the innings that gave me the most pleasure was at Gravesend against Leicestershire in May 1957 when I scored a century [101 – first hundred for Kent]. It was one of those days when everything I tried to do seemed to come off and I felt it was my most accomplished innings. I bowled a lot at school and club cricket and occasionally for Cambridge and Kent. We played Middlesex at Fenners in 1955 and I took five wickets in the first innings, four in the second and scored runs in both innings [44 in first and 111 in second, the university's first century of the season]. That was my best all-round performance in first-class cricket.

Proudest Moment

This was when Kent won the Championship for the first time in 1971 under Colin Cowdrey. With six weeks to go they were bottom, but had a fantastic run. For me, having played for the county and still in close touch with the players, I was very proud of their feat. Les Ames called them in at the end of the first week in July and gave them a real rip-snorter when they were playing badly – to come back from that was terrific and as if out of a *Boys Own* comic!

Another proud moment and lifetime ambition for me was realised when I was appointed president of Kent CCC in March 1999 for a 12-month period. I had previously served on the Kent committee for a number of years, until it became impossible when I had my own business. I have also achieved another ambition, that of being president of my Old Boys club, which I have enjoyed and has got me back into the school in many ways.

A determined middle-order left-hand bat and slow left-arm bowler, Pretlove scored 5,115 runs (27.78), took 43 wickets (30.67), 70 catches and 1 stumping.

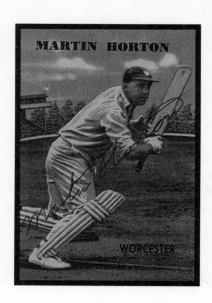

–10–

Martin Horton (b. 1934)

Worcestershire, Northern District and England

1959 was my most successful year as a batsman [2,468 runs, average 44.87] and a season when batsmen generally did well, a hot summer playing all the way through on uncovered pitches.

I also played my two England Test matches that season against India, which came right out of the blue as none of the papers had picked me. On the Saturday the selectors met I scored 161 at Cambridge. Then we were playing a benefit match on the Sunday when somebody told me I had been picked for England, which I didn't believe. Sharing a room with Len Coldwell, I couldn't sleep after that and got up at three in the morning to walk the streets of Cambridge! We reported to Nottingham on Wednesday lunchtime and had a net in the afternoon when the newcomers were made very welcome. Ken Taylor and Tommy Greenhough were also making their debut in the first Test. In the evening we had a team dinner to discuss the opposition and on the evening of the first day John Arlott invited three or four of us out to dinner. We just chatted away, purely to give him information for his commentary for the following day. He didn't take any notes, but that was the way he operated. He chose the dinner and I remember duck à l'orange, even though it was nearly 40 years ago! I also remember Peter May the captain telling me it was just another game of cricket.

Trent Bridge was a good batting pitch but even so we lost three reasonably quick wickets, the two openers and Colin Cowdrey. Then Ken Barrington and Peter May came together and, batting at number six, I sat with my pads on for three hours when we lost our second wicket. Ken and Peter put on a big partnership (125 runs) with me sitting, waiting and a bag of nerves! When Ken was out I went in with quarter of an hour to go to tea. At tea I hadn't got off the mark and Colin Cowdrey said later my face was as white as a sheet! In the first over after tea I hit a couple of bad balls from Gupte, the Indian leg-spinner, for four and was 58 not out with Godfrey Evans by the close of play. I proceeded to get out in the first over of the next day, caught in the slips off Desai at the second attempt. I only had one innings in that Test and bowled 24 overs. We bowled them out and won by an innings. In the second Test I was bowled by Desai for two, took a couple of wickets, caught Umrigar in the gully and we won by eight wickets so again I didn't get a second innings. We had won two Tests easily and, looking at options for the West Indies tour the following winter, they dropped six of us!

1961 was also a good season for me when I did the 'double'. I had achieved that in 1955, which was my first full season, after I had come out of the Services, although I scraped the 100th wicket in the last match, a festival game at Torquay. I was an opening bat and number five bowler in 1961 and understand it is the last time that an opening bat managed to achieve the 'double'. I scored 1,000 runs quite early on and completed the 'double' with ten wickets in the last home match against Lancashire – it was nice to take my 100th wicket at Worcester. We had such a good bowling attack in those days that I often went through games without having to bowl too many overs unless it was a turning pitch. That was the time we started to develop as a team which won the County Championship in 1964 and 1965.

I remember playing the last match of the 1961 season for MCC against Yorkshire at the Scarborough festival. Yorkshire had beaten Sussex the day before to win the County Championship and break Surrey's monopoly. They travelled back overnight to a heroes' welcome. The ground was packed out and everybody was cheering as the players came on. I was pleased to meet the great Wilfred Rhodes during the match.

In 1962 I hit my highest score in first-class cricket, 233 against Somerset at Worcester. The stand of 314 for the third wicket with Tom Graveney was also a record that remained until the 1997 match at Southampton which, by an incredible coincidence, Tom and I both watched as it was broken by Tom Moody and Graham Hick. The night before the Somerset match, the Worcester secretary Joe Lister, who was also captain of the second XI, got the second XI to come out of the nets and walk up and down the pitch a few times in their studded boots to scrape it, which of course a groundsman today would never stand for. We were looking for the ball to turn a bit, won the toss and batted and Don Kenyon scored 91 by about 1.10 p.m. Ron Headley came in and I ran him out for nought and remember to this day him swearing as he crossed me! I was 73 not out at lunch and Tom had just got in. In the afternoon we piled on the runs before Tom ran me out. He snicked one into slips which was unusual and it rebounded onto the leg side. I called for a very easy run, got virtually down his end, but he was watching to see where the ball was instead of responding to my call. I almost got back but was run out by two feet and then we declared having scored over 500. They were 70–2 overnight and we bowled them out. We scored a few runs ourselves, then declared and bowled them out comfortably in their second innings.

1965 was my benefit year but my worst season! In 1964 I was the first batsman in the country to score 1,000 runs, but didn't make it in 1965. I don't know whether it was the demands of the benefit that made me struggle a little, but it raised £5,800, which was a lot in those days – enough to buy a house and have some left over. During the winter of 1965–6 we went on a tour of Jamaica with quite a few supporters. We stayed in Miami *en route* and played five matches on various grounds around Jamaica. Our last game was against the full Jamaican side at Montego Bay on a magnificent batting wicket with no grass at all. They brought in Gary Sobers to strengthen the team. Ron Headley just got his finger tips to a catch off Jack Flavell at short leg before he had scored, he took 20 off the next over and scored a century. I came on for my first bowl of the innings when he was on 84 and one ball later he was 90 not out! He just hit me straight back over my head, over the sightscreen and some trees and they are probably still looking for the ball! It was a perfect shot straight out of the ground.

Hugo Yarnold, who used to keep wicket for Worcester, advised me early on in my career when I came out of the Forces to obtain my coaching qualifications. I did so and used to coach with him at Lord's in April and had undertaken some other coaching from time to time. I broke my kneecap back in 1960 but played on – they called me Jeg the Peg because I limped round the boundary when I got tired. I wanted to stay in cricket on retirement and was sent a circular from Lord's advertising for a National Coach in New Zealand for the first time. We were playing at Lord's towards the end of the 1966 season and it was arranged for me to have an interview with Donald Carr and a fellow from New Zealand. When I returned from holiday, from a shortlist of six I received an invitation from Gordon Leggat, chairman of the New Zealand Cricket Board to take up the appointment before Christmas. I still had a year of my contract with Worcester and arranged to be released. We sold the house within a month and went out on a five-year contract. It really came about five years too early for me as I would have liked to have played on, but it was too good an opportunity to miss and in the end I stayed 17 years.

I arrived just before Christmas of 1966 and didn't play the first year. The second year I played a bit of club cricket and at the age of 33 accepted an invitation to play first-class cricket for Northern Districts, who were the weakest side by far. The awkward thing was that I played all my club cricket in Auckland, so only saw my team the night before the first match when we all met up together. I made some really good friends though including Bert Sutcliffe, who I had some very enjoyable times with.

The major part of my job for 15 of the 17 years was to run all of the coaching courses for the coaches. Virtually all the coaches in New Zealand have therefore now gone through the national scheme. I was pleased with the improvement in the general standard of cricket and the fact that we went ten years without losing a home series. By 1984 our daughter had married a New Zealander and they came over to England for work purposes. I was a little tired of the travelling I was doing every other week. At the age of 50 I felt I wouldn't manage to get a job back in England if I didn't return then, even though I was offered a further five years as national coach.

Roly Jenkins had seen an advert that Eton wanted a coach and contacted the bursar, who actually wrote to me in New Zealand before I left. We wanted to come back to Worcester though and there was a piece in the local paper publicising my return to the city and the headmaster of the grammar school, Tom Savage, who was a cricket fanatic invited me to take a job there. Roger Dancey, the senior master recommended me to him and I joined in April 1984. I did nothing else other than coach cricket and thoroughly enjoyed coaching the youngsters that came through including Dean Headley. We also went on three tours including Zimbabwe, which Dean went on, and I retired in July 1996, although still do a little coaching in the school holidays.

My hobby is still skittles and I play for the same side, a team called The Albert Hall, which originated from a pub in Worcester called the Forester's Arms, which my father kept. It's the long nine-pins alley, not the table skittles. I was only nine or ten when I started and I think I am the only founder member of the Worcester Skittle League which started in 1945 still playing. I obviously missed playing when I was in New Zealand but had a phone call within two weeks of my return signing me back on! I also still read a lot and am now very keen on opera and classical music.

My favourite sportsman has always been Denis Compton. I wrote to him when I was a schoolboy asking for his autograph and received a signed picture. I played against him later on and was the last bowler to take his wicket as a professional when he played his last match against us at Lord's in 1958. He scored 100 in the first innings before being bowled by Jack Flavell and was caught off my bowling on the boundary in the second innings for 48. I always say that I got him in the leg trap, albeit 100 yards away! My wife Margaret and I went to his memorial service at Westminster Abbey in 1997.

Gradually as the years progressed I succeeded in my aim to become a better batsman although didn't bowl so much. When Basil D'Oliveira appeared on the scene my bowling opportunities were reduced and I concentrated more on batting.

Memorable Game

One of the most memorable matches I played in was the Somerset game in 1962, mentioned earlier, as I took three wickets in each innings as well as scoring the 233 runs.

16, 18, 19 June 1962. Worcester won by 264 runs

Horton struck 36 fours in his innings and was at the wicket for four and three-quarter hours. With Graveney and Kenyon also making notable contributions, the exhilarating batting was too much for Somerset, who found the bowling of Coldwell especially troublesome.

Worcestershire

D. Kenyon b Palmer	97	b Palmer		31
M.J. Horton run out	233	c Stephenson b Palmer		38
R.G.A. Headley run out	0	c and b Palmer		14
T.W. Graveney not out	164	b Palmer		15
D.W. Richardson not out	10	c Palmer b Alley		10
R.G. Broadbent		st Stephenson b Alley		0
R. Booth		not out		25
J.A. Standen		c Greetham b Alley		18
L.J. Coldwell		not out		1
N. Gifford did not bat				
J.A. Flavell did not bat				
B 10, l-b 6	16	B 2, l-b 1		3
	(3 wkts dec) 520		(7 wkts dec) 155	

1/167 2/167 3/481

1/62 2/73 3/90
4/98 5/99 6/111 7/144

Somerset

G.G. Atkinson lbw b Coldwell	3	lbw b Flavell	1
B. Roe c Booth b Flavell	42	c Richardson b Horton	11
P.B. Wight c Booth b Coldwell	45	b Coldwell	0
W.E. Alley c Booth b Coldwell	8	b Coldwell	0
M. Kitchen b Coldwell	7	c and b Horton	19
C. Greetham b Standen	28	lbw b Horton	9
J.G. Lomax c Graveney b Coldwell	65	c Kenyon b Gifford	22

C.R. Atkinson c Richardson b Horton	2		b Gifford	10
B. Langford b Horton	45		not out	7
H.W. Stephenson c Coldwell b Horton	0		b Gifford	45
K.E. Palmer not out	8		c Headley b Gifford	9
B 12, l-b 3, w 1, n-b 1	17		B 3, l-b 5	8
	270			141

1/4 2/81 3/95 4/106 5/113 6/143
7/150 8/233 9/237

1/2 2/25 3/26 4/26 5/75
6/84 7/97 8/118 9/123

Somerset Bowling

	O	M	R	W	O	M	R	W
Palmer	19	4	87	1	21	1	92	4
Alley	16	0	72	0	21	7	60	3
Langford	34	5	140	0				
C. Atkinson	16	1	81	0				
Greetham	16	1	97	0				
Wight	5	0	27	0				

Worcester Bowling

	O	M	R	W	O	M	R	W
Flavell	21	5	67	1	8	1	21	1
Coldwell	18.1	4	47	5	11	4	27	2
Gifford	16	7	41	0	16.2	9	29	4
Horton	24	7	68	3	15	4	51	3
Standen	13	0	30	1	1	0	5	0

Umpires: C.S. Elliott and L.H. Gray

I always felt my best innings was against Surrey at the Oval in 1958 when I scored 117 out of 230 against Loader, Bedser, Lock and Laker. I remember hitting Jim Laker for four fours all along the ground in consecutive balls. My best bowling was probably 6–40 in 1961 against Middlesex at Worcester when they needed 137 to win and were all out for 121. Against Somerset at Bath in 1956 I took 13 wickets in a match, 7–29 and 6–33, which was my best bowling that year, although nine wickets against the South Africans in 1955 at Worcester were my best figures. The Yorkshire match mentioned earlier was also certainly a memorable one.

Proudest Moment

The proudest moment for me was when we won the Championship in 1964. Worcestershire had never won the County Championship before and it started to get quite tense towards the end of the season, with so many variables in terms of weather, pitches, etc., and Warwickshire were pushing us hard. Don Kenyon kept us on an even keel though, and we felt that whatever pitch we played on, we had the bowling attack to win. There was also an added incentive insofar as Ron Roberts suggested whoever won the Championship should do a short tour in the winter instead of the usual select team. In the end we went to several countries in two months, places as far apart as India and Los Angeles. We were billeted in a lot of places, stayed in hotels in Rhodesia and America and never had trouble in getting a side on the field with just 12 players. In some ways 1965 was a better Championship-winning side as Basil D'Oliveira came into the team. In the first half of the season we were out of the running with games rained off and players having lost form, then we won 10 of the last 11 matches outright, and it was unusual to have the weather to achieve that number of results.

Proudest Moment

At the time I wasn't particularly proud to be picked for England, as I was too shell-shocked to take it in – I am now, of course.

A strongly built and effective all-rounder, Horton scored 19,944 runs (29.55) including 23 centuries, took 825 wickets (26.94) and 166 catches. In two Test matches he scored 60 runs (30.00), took 2 wickets (29.50) and 2 catches.

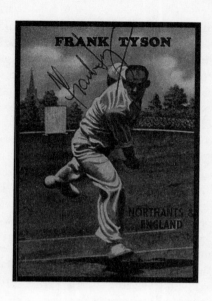

–11–

Frank Tyson (b. 1930)

Northants and England

At the beginning of 1959 I played in the Australian Test series, albeit really by default. Jim Laker was scheduled to play in the fourth Test at Adelaide and the fifth at Melbourne, but turned out to be unfit so I took his place. We were thrashed in both Tests, although it was the best England bowling side I ever toured with in terms of ability. The actual pace-bowling in the series was in the main Loader and Statham, even Trueman didn't get a regular place. He had a back injury right at the outset of the tour and played in the final three Tests. I was very surprised we didn't do better but our luck wasn't terrific. It was an ill-fated tour, as not only were there the throwers' and managerial weaknesses, but also we had injury problems reflected by the fact that Mortimore and Dexter were flown out as reinforcements. In addition to Trueman's injury, Statham and Loader were in a car crash which automatically ruled them out of consideration for the last Test, together with the New Zealand trip. We struggled with our batting as our openers never really put anything together and Subba Row was out for some time with a broken wrist. We did have May and Cowdrey though, who were undoubtedly two of the best players in the world at that time.

It wasn't an easy party to manage or captain as there were great differences of personality in the side. We weren't very well handled managerially, in my opinion, largely because it was the year of the 'chuckers', Meckiff, Rorke, Burke, Slater, Trethewey and Hitchcox and nobody made a protest about it – it was diabolical. An example was when Peter May, who scored 100 in the second Test at Melbourne, was on 113 when Meckiff bowled him out just as May was picking his bat up! Rorke was dragging through both the bowling and the popping crease, so he was throwing from about 17 metres. He was the man Colin Cowdrey referred to when asked why he didn't play forward, 'I daren't, he would have trodden on my toes!' The Press were continually saying we should have made some objection about it, as it was quite blatant and the general dissatisfaction about throwing was transferred onto the pitch. We were managed by F.R. Brown, who I always got on well with. He was very much an establishment man though, who insisted you call the captain 'Mr May' or 'Skipper' but never Peter. It's hard to imagine a side bonding with that sort of thing going on. Peter May was a wonderful player but as a captain I don't think he communicated very well. He didn't transmit a lot of his own determination, fixation and motivation, of which he had plenty, to his side. We also had lost people like Wardle shortly before setting sail, as he had written a series of articles criticising the Yorkshire establishment and, after being selected, he was withdrawn from the touring side, which was stupid. He would have been our best spinner in Australia with his wrist bowling. We were more successful when we moved on to New Zealand (winning the first Test and drawing the other), though I didn't realise the second match at Auckland was to be my last Test.

I had made up my mind to retire and start teaching when I was 30, so knew 1960 was to be my last season. My wife Ursula is Australian and whilst over there, I had been lining up prospective jobs and knew there was one on offer at Carey Baptist Grammar School in Melbourne. I knew my contract with Northampton expired in 1960 and I wasn't going to renew it. David Larter, who was a good natural fast bowler, was coming into the side and I subsequently offered to help him in 1961. I wasn't going to Australia until the end of that summer, as I had to sell my house and do various things with my family etc. Northants said 'don't bother' so in 1961 I played in the Lancashire league for Todmorden at the weekends, which was enjoyable. The director of education for Northampton was on the county committee and, knowing I had a degree, had secured me a job teaching at Bective Secondary Modern in Northampton during my previous fallow seasons. It was there that I spent the last summer teaching before we left England towards the end of 1961 and reached Australia in the new year.

My highest first-class score of 82 against Sussex at Hove in 1960 was towards the end of the season. I enjoyed that innings and met former selector Harry Altham coming off the pitch. He said, 'I didn't know you could bat like that'. I said it was a bit late to find out as it was pretty well my last game! Northants had started to falter a little, as we lost Dennis Brookes,

Jock Livingston and George Tribe, and Jack Manning came back to Australia on the same ship as me. In 1957 we had finished second in the Championship and had a very good run, so the county was undergoing a period of transition.

I had a testimonial in 1960 and bought a house with the proceeds. Northampton refused to allow me to have a benefit committee, so it was not terribly well organised. I had a friend called Cliff Senior who acted as a liaison man and organiser – what a contrast between now and then! However, when the average man was earning £5 a week at that time, £2,380 was a lot of money.

I wrote *A Typhoon called Tyson* in 1961 which largely came about because of John Arlott. As there had not been any cricketers of note who had written a subjectively orientated book themselves, he suggested that I should write not so much an autobiography, but one that expressed opinions on issues like making a living out of county cricket. I also wrote about what it felt like to bowl fast on a cricket ground and the emotive side of cricket. It was my first book and I think the best book I wrote. I used to go back and work on it in the evenings in the chemistry lab at Bective Secondary Modern! I think a lot of what I wrote still holds true today e.g. living on the razor's edge and the insecurity of making a living out of county cricket. I had previously written for a number of years for *Empire News* and went on to write 16 books in all. I started to write a bit more, particularly for a magazine called *Cricketer* in Australia, and my second book, *Cricket – all the Diversions*, was a collection of all my writings for that magazine. I am still writing in my retirement and have just finished a work on Tom Horan and the first Australian tour of England in 1878 – I have his original cuttings book which I have summarised and put together. I was also a television broadcaster with ABC from 1964 to 1977, then worked for Kerry Packer from 1979 to 1987. It was a handy arrangement as I could fit in my broadcasting and writing in my school holiday periods.

I was at the Carey Baptist School for 14 years and became a housemaster. I coached the first XI and during my time we produced Graham Yallop, an Australian captain. We won the Premiership three times and I acquired a reputation as a coach in Victoria. When the Victoria Cricket Association and the Australian Cricket Board decided they were going to instigate a National Coaching Accreditation Scheme, they asked me on to the Victorian committee to make suggestions as to the format. When we drew up what we thought should be the terms of reference for a coaching system they were sufficiently impressed to ask me to become the inaugural Director of Coaching for the Victoria Cricket Association. I left Carey in 1975 on very good terms and still go back there. The thrust of the scheme was to train enough coaches to teach youngsters throughout the length and breadth of Victoria which we did, much in the same way as the NCA, although ours was a little more innovative in that it had a lot more sports science content e.g. psychology etc. We ran about 200 coaching courses a year and established a cadre of coaches which still exists in Victoria today and operated in both the country and metropolitan areas. I remained with the VCA for another 14 years until about 1989, when it got to a stage where it was virtually running itself.

Ursula and I then decided to go back to England for two years and I taught at Denstone College in Staffordshire near Uttoxeter. I was there for one academic year and one winter until Ursula's father became ill in Australia so we returned via South Africa, where I spent two months coaching. I was subsequently four years at Ivanhoe Grammar School, another independent associated grammar school in Melbourne as senior French master. I coached the first XI until I was 62, which is the age of retirement for teachers in Australia. I then received an offer to coach in India and Sri Lanka, so for the next three years spent about three months over there. In India I was involved in a coaching scheme sponsored by Mafatlal, an industrial company. It produced quite a few good players and was an enjoyable experience. In Sri Lanka I coached the national squad and the development side.

We moved to Queensland in 1994 when I fully retired. I am now 69 and have no desire to get involved in a full-time sense in cricket any longer, although I still do some consultancy cricket coaching. My knees are no good whatsoever, my cartilages are worn out and I get arthritis very easily. That's why we live up on the Gold Coast, as I don't want another Melbourne winter. We have three children and four grandchildren, a son in Brisbane and two daughters, one living in Canberra the other in Melbourne.

I have enjoyed everything I have done in cricket and have no regrets. Lancashire offered me terms when I was 17, but my father said I was to go to university. Then in 1951 Lancashire were no longer interested. I have kept the letter that they sent me – 'Dear Tyson, there will be no opportunity for you this season'.

The nickname 'Typhoon' comes from a strip across the top of a national newspaper paper showing Keith Andrew 25 metres behind the stumps and me 27 metres behind the other stumps, so there was 70–80 metres dividing us! The headline read 'It takes a Typhoon!'.

My hobby in 1959 was reading, which I still enjoy. I read cricket coaching magazines and a lot of cricket history, which comes from my involvement with John Arlott. I have also become a very great fan of Dick Francis, which is a great diversion from the normal books I read.

Memorable Game

The most memorable game I played in was the second Test at Sydney in the 1954–5 series. I took 10 wickets for 130, we won by 38 runs and it turned the series upside down. We had lost the first Test in Brisbane and after

Sydney we won comfortably in Melbourne and again in Adelaide. I have bowled much better than that, for example when I took 13 wickets against Surrey at the Oval in 1957, when they were winning the Championship every year. I also still think I bowled quicker sometimes in university cricket than in county cricket, as I wasn't playing so much and was fitter. By the time I was playing Test cricket I was 25 – I was quicker when I was 21!

17, 18, 20, 21, 22 December 1954. England won by 38 runs
Tyson, having been knocked out by a Lindwall bouncer, bowled with terrific speed and stamina to win a palpitating victory for England. He became only the fourth bowler this century (after Larwood, Farnes and Voce) to take 10 wickets in an England v Australia Test.

England .

L. Hutton c Davidson b Johnston	30	c Benaud b Johnston	28
T.E. Bailey b Lindwall	0	c Langley b Archer	6
P.B.H. May c Johnston b Archer	5	b Lindwall	104
T.W. Graveney c Favell b Johnston	21	c Langley b Johnston	0
M.C. Cowdrey c Langley b Davidson	23	c Archer b Benaud	54
W.J. Edrich c Benaud b Archer	10	b Archer	29
F.H. Tyson b Lindwall	0	b Lindwall	9
T.G. Evans c Langley b Archer	3	c Lindwall b Archer	4
J.H. Wardle c Burke b Johnston	35	lbw b Lindwall	8
R. Appleyard c Hole b Davidson	8	not out	19
J.B. Statham not out	14	c Langley b Johnston	25
L-b 5	5	L-b 6, n-b 4	10
	154		296

1/14 2/19 3/58 4/63 5/84 6/85 7/88 8/99 9/111

1/18 2/55 3/55 4/171 5/222 6/232 7/239 8/249 9/250

Australia

L.E. Favell c Graveney b Bailey	26	c Edrich b Tyson	16
A.R. Morris c Hutton b Bailey	12	lbw b Statham	10
J.W. Burke c Graveney b Bailey	44	b Tyson	14
R.N. Harvey c Cowdrey b Tyson	12	not out	92
G.B. Hole b Tyson	12	b Tyson	0
R. Benaud lbw b Statham	20	c Tyson b Appleyard	12
R.G. Archer c Hutton b Tyson	49	b Tyson	6
A.K. Davidson b Statham	20	c Evans b Statham	5
R.R. Lindwall c Evans b Tyson	19	b Tyson	8
G.R.A. Langley b Bailey	5	b Statham	0
W.A. Johnston not out	0	c Evans b Tyson	11

| B 5, l-b 2, n-b 2 | 9 | L-b 7, n-b 3 | 10 |
| | 228 | | 184 |

1/18 2/65 3/100 4/104 5/122 6/141
7/193 8/213 9/224

1/27 2/34 3/77 4/77 5/102
6/122 7/127 8/136 9/145

Australia Bowling

	O	M	R	W	O	M	R	W
Lindwall	17	3	47	2	31	10	69	3
Archer	12	7	12	3	22	9	53	3
Davidson	12	3	34	2	13	2	52	0
Johnston	13.3	1	56	3	19.3	2	70	3
Benaud					19	3	42	1

England Bowling

	O	M	R	W	O	M	R	W
Statham	18	1	83	2	19	6	45	3
Bailey	17.4	3	59	4	6	0	21	0
Tyson	13	2	45	4	18.4	1	85	6
Appleyard	7	1	32	0	6	1	12	1
Wardle					4	2	11	0

Umpires M. J. McInnes and R. Wright

Proudest Moment

The proudest moment for me in cricket was when we won the Ashes in Australia in 1954–5. I always thought during the post-war period we took a terrible hammering and it wasn't until 1953 that the tide started to turn. We hadn't beaten Australia in Australia since 1932–3 when the 'Bodyline' series was played out. We beat them without 'bodyline' and they were one of the strongest sides Australia had ever produced. The 1948 team was called 'The Invincibles' and the backbone was still there in 1954 with Morris, Harvey, Miller and Lindwall. So they were still a pretty good side and to beat them in their own country was a remarkable achievement.

Len Hutton, who had never beaten them in Australia until '54, always said to win in Australia you have to be 25 per cent better than they are, firstly because the conditions are foreign to you, and secondly you have to overcome disadvantages like the heat and sometimes rather ordinary umpiring. I remember the fastest ball I ever bowled was to Keith Miller in the third Test of that series in Melbourne. It rose off a length on not a very good wicket, he just managed to fend it off and was caught. In fact Hutton dived, pushed it up and Bill Edrich took it at second slip.

Unquestionably the fastest bowler in the country at his peak, 'Typhoon' Tyson scored 4,103 runs (17.09), took 766 wickets (20.92) and 85 catches. In 17 Test matches he scored 230 runs (10.95), took 76 wickets (18.56) and 4 catches.

–12–

Reg Simpson (b. 1920)

Sind, Notts and England

During my playing career I was given the job of assistant secretary at Trent Bridge and worked for Gunn & Moore during the winter, which turned out quite well. At Gunn & Moore I started as assistant to the managing director and learnt all the jobs, including willow buying and learning all about bats. Since 1959 my business activities made an increasing claim on my time and in 1960 I relinquished the Nottinghamshire captaincy to the first professional, John Clay. I continued to play for the county in most of the home games and had a good season in 1962 [at the age of 42, Simpson headed the first-class batting averages with 867 runs in 20 innings at an average of 54.18 – he also completed 30,000 runs in first-class cricket].

When I retired from county cricket in 1963, I started playing for the Lord's Taverners on Sundays, and also for Sparks. I finished playing at the age of about 65 – I was man of the match in one of my last games for the Taverners at Scarborough when I scored 60-odd against Paul Allott and Richard Hutton and was given a bottle of champagne!

I then started playing golf for charity and still play around the country, although I find the travelling hard work now. In about 1993 when I was driving back from one of the Sparks' golf dos in Bedfordshire with my wife, I unfortunately fell asleep at the wheel on the A1. I broke my neck and my wife broke her pelvis and we were in hospital for weeks. I did hear that after the accident Jim Swanton asked Alan Wheelhouse how I was. Alan replied that I was slowly recovering and Jim remarked that it was a shame as he had just written my obituary!

By the time I retired from the first-class game, I had become managing director of Gunn & Moore and remained in that position until I retired in about 1987. I am still a non-executive director and go in most days. I was also involved at committee level for a number of years with the county.

It is not true that I modelled myself on Joe Hardstaff, who certainly had all the shots, including a lovely off-drive. I didn't model myself on anyone, but always stood up straight the same way Joe did, so people likened me to him. By watching players you pick up certain mannerisms and I learnt a lot from Walter Keeton, particularly how to play strongly on the on-side.

My hobby of flying dates back to the war, which changed the course of my career. When I left school I joined the police force and played cricket, also soccer for them in midweek, and rugger on Saturdays. At the beginning of the war I was very happy in the police force – I was in the CID and very uncertain about a future in cricket. I became a qualified detective officer at the age of 18 in 1938 and was attached to the Criminal Record Office, becoming the first cadet ever to go in to that branch. The police let me off to play cricket and said I could play eight games for the county side and the rest in my own time. I wasn't actually picked until the second year of the war when they started playing one-day matches at Trent Bridge on a Saturday and I did reasonably well (including 134 not out against an RAF XI in 1940).

Then I was called up in 1941 and to begin with our chief constable wouldn't permit us to join. He did though allow about half a dozen of us to apply for a pilot job in the RAF, but if we failed to qualify, we would have to go back to the police. I managed to qualify and trained in Arizona, then came back to finish my training. Whilst I was waiting for a posting I played a bit of cricket including the Birmingham festival in 1944, where I scored quite a few runs just before I went to India. Whilst waiting for postings in India, I played quite a bit of cricket in Karachi including my first game of first-class cricket. I was picked for Sind against Maharashtra and was the only European in the two sides – it was quite an experience. Then I played for the Europeans in the Pentangular, where we had a very strong side, including Denis Compton and Joe Hardstaff. When I came back from India in 1946, having flown over 1,000 hours in the Far East for the Transport Command in the RAFVR, I started playing first-class cricket and decided to resign from the police force.

Memorable Game

My most memorable match and best innings has to be the 156 not out for England in the fifth Test against Australia in Melbourne in 1951. It was the first time we had beaten them since the war and we had been given no hope.

23, 24, 26, 27, 28 February 1951. England won by 8 wickets

Simpson reached his century on his 31st birthday and went on to score all but ten of the last-wicket partnership of 74 in 55 minutes with Tattersall. The victory ended Australia's run of 25 consecutive matches without defeat.

Australia

J. Burke c Tattersall b Bedser	11	c Hutton b Bedser	1
A.R. Morris lbw b Brown	50	lbw b Bedser	4
A.L. Hassett c Hutton b Brown	92	b Wright	48
R.N. Harvey c Evans b Brown	1	lbw b Wright	52
K.R. Miller c and b Brown	7	c and b Brown	0
G. Hole b Bedser	18	b Bailey	63
I.W. Johnson lbw b Bedser	1	c Brown b Wright	0
R.R. Lindwall c Compton b Bedser	21	b Bedser	14
D. Tallon c Hutton b Bedser	1	not out	2
W.A. Johnston not out	12	b Bedser	1
J. Iverson c Washbrook b Brown	0	c Compton b Bedser	0
B 2, l-b 1	3	B 2, l-b 8, n-b 1, w 1	12
	217		197

1/23 2/111 3/115 4/123 5/156
6/166 7/184 8/197 9/216

1/5 2/6 3/87 4/89 5/142
6/142 7/192 8/196 9/197

England

L. Hutton b Hole	79	not out	60
C. Washbrook c Tallon b Miller	27	c Lindwall b Johnston	7
R.T. Simpson not out	156	run out	15
D.C.S. Compton c Miller b Lindwall	11	not out	11
D.S. Sheppard c Tallon b Miller	1		
F.R. Brown b Lindwall	6		
T.G. Evans b Miller	1		
A.V. Bedser b Lindwall	11		
T.E. Bailey c Johnson b Iverson	5		
D.V.P. Wright lbw b Iverson	3		
R. Tattersall b Miller	10		
B 9, l-b 1	10	L-b 2	2
	320	(2 wkts)	95

1/40 2/171 3/204 4/205 5/212
6/213 7/228 8/236 9/246

1/32 2/62

England Bowling

	O	M	R	W	O	M	R	W
Bedser	22	5	46	5	20.3	4	59	5
Bailey	9	1	29	0	15	3	32	1

Brown	18	4	49	5	9	1	32	1
Wright	9	1	50	0	15	2	56	3
Tattersall	11	3	40	0	5	2	6	0

Australia Bowling

Lindwall	21	1	77	3	2	0	12	0
Miller	21.7	5	76	4	2	0	5	0
Johnston	12	1	55	0	11	3	36	1
Iverson	20	4	52	2	12	2	32	0
Johnson	11	1	40	0	1	0	1	0
Hole	5	0	10	1	1	0	3	0
Hassett					.6	0	4	0

Umpires: A.N. Barlow and H. Elphinston

We ought to have won two other Tests in the series, but our senior batsman let us down for some reason at the vital moment. Denis Compton had a very bad tour, only scoring 53 runs in eight innings, and Cyril Washbrook unfortunately had a fairly poor tour, scoring only 170-odd runs [173] in the whole series, although the bowlers were magnificent. If we had had a little more assistance in the middle order of the batting, we would have had far better results. Len Hutton had a marvellous tour but needed, and should have had, far more support. The selection for the tour was most peculiar as we had six opening batsmen and Denis Compton was really the only middle-order batsman. The opening bats were not used to batting in the middle, it was the wrong thing to do and was a great shame. However, we did win the last Test which was a great morale booster.

Proudest Moment

My proudest moment in cricket was after we had had a Test trial at Birmingham in 1948 before the series against Australia. I was waiting to catch the train on the way back from Birmingham, reached Derby station and went into a hotel near the station where the radio was on. I heard I had been picked as 12th man for the first Test match against Australia, which I couldn't believe and certainly didn't expect to be selected in any way! Just to be picked as 12th man and on my home ground at Trent Bridge was marvellous and the way I heard it was most unusual.

A beautiful striker of the ball and superb fielder, Simpson scored 30,546 runs (38.32) including 64 centuries, took 59 wickets (37.74) and 193 catches. In 27 Test matches, he scored 1,401 runs (33.35) including 4 centuries, took 2 wickets (11.00) and 5 catches.

–13–

Godfrey Evans (1920–1999)

Kent and England

Evans played in the first Test against India at Trent Bridge in June 1959 and was in good form, scoring 73 at a run a ball and at one stage was in line for the fastest century of the season. England defeated India soundly in the Nottingham Test and repeated the process at Lord's, which proved to be the last of his 91 Test matches. 'I was relieved after the second Test as I was getting towards 40 and quite rightly England were looking for a replacement, so they picked Roy Swetman. I was told that if I played for the county for the rest of the season and was fit and well, I would go to the West Indies. I was not selected so decided that my career couldn't benefit any more and retired.'

Evans played for The Rest of England against Yorkshire, the Championship winners, at the Oval in September 1959, then announced his retirement from full-time first-class cricket, having taken his 1,000th victim during the season.

During the following winter Evans went on a short Commonwealth tour of South Africa to celebrate the anniversary of the Wanderers Club in Johannesburg. 'I was asked by Denis Compton to be his vice-captain. We had a strong side and won three of our five matches, trying to play entertaining cricket for the large crowds that watched us. We called ourselves the Cavaliers, after our captain, a great cavalier.'

Evans continued to enjoy playing cricket into the '60s as captain of the Rothman's Cavaliers, who became the pioneers of one-day cricket. Great players from the past from all over the world got together on Sundays to play against county sides, often in aid of the county's beneficiary. 'We played at Lord's once when Billy Griffith was Secretary of MCC. We watched the county match there the previous day in front of about 500 people. Billy couldn't believe the attendance on the Sunday when Lord's was packed with over 20,000 for Peter Parfitt's benefit match. Basil D'Oliveira's first game in this country was for the Cavaliers and we also attracted entertainers like Charlie Drake and Eric Sykes for spectators to see – it was a delight to play.' The games proved an enormous success in terms of attendance and for the television audience watching at home.

Rothman's Cavaliers also entertained abroad, playing three matches in Jamaica in early 1964 and seven matches in the West Indies at the beginning of 1965. Their cricket undoubtedly acted as the catalyst for the introduction of the Sunday League when the John Player cigarette company was approached to spread the income potential across the counties. 'Peter Dimmock, who was in charge of television, suggested that the Cavaliers were the "18th" county, as in those days there were only 17 counties, to round up the numbers. It didn't happen and once the John Player League started in 1969, the television rights were transferred to John Player, so that was the end of the Cavaliers.'

Evans also came out of retirement in 1967 to play for Kent in one match in an emergency and his last first-class game was for the International Cavaliers against Barbados at Scarborough in September 1969. He continued though to don the wicket-keeping gloves during the '70s and '80s, playing in numerous charity matches and celebrated his 70th birthday by keeping wicket in a Lord's Taverners match at Canterbury. The first ball from Fred Rumsey went very wide of the stumps and was heading towards the slips before Evans intercepted it with a trademark tumbling dive.

On retirement, he penned his autobiography *The Gloves Are Off*, one of four books he wrote. Prior to that *Behind the Stumps* was written in 1951 and *Action in Cricket* in 1957. 'Then in the '60s Chris Sandford asked if he could write a biography of me, which I was delighted with. I also wrote for *The People* for over two years on retirement when Freddie Trueman and I both had a column. Then I joined Ladbrokes and Ron Pollard advising on their cricket betting and was with them for 22 years.' He was also a public relations officer, had a jewellery business, ran a sportsman's club, invested in a leisure complex, a dice game and a pitch drier and was also a genial pub-keeper (twice), which he combined with his work for Ladbrokes.

He married Angela in 1973 (they had one daughter) and in later years enjoyed a talent, seemingly unique to wicket-keepers (Russell, Speight, etc.), for painting. He was for many years in demand as a package trip host on England overseas tours, the last one being the Ashes series in Australia during the winter of 1998–9. He was an honorary life member of Kent CCC and MCC and a vice-president of the Cricketers Club of London, a role which kept him in touch with the game past and present as he lunched weekly with members.

Cricket in Evans's day seemed to be a pleasure, not quite so serious as today. 'It appears too much money is involved and the players have got to do well, which makes them appeal far more often from deliveries that really from an on-looker's point of view are nowhere near out.' Evans, who enjoyed his life irrespective of the money, was known for his fairness in appealing. Sadly the flame that had illuminated the world of cricket in such an irrepressible way was extinguished in May 1999, when Godfrey died of a heart attack, aged 78.

Memorable Game

One of Evans's most memorable matches was in the first Test against the West Indies in 1950 at Manchester, when he scored his first century for England after a disastrous start on the first morning when they were 88–5 with ten minutes to go to lunch. 'I joined Trevor Bailey at the wicket and he said, "Godfrey, for goodness sake stay at the wicket till lunch." We stayed until tea and it was just after tea when I got my hundred. We eventually dismissed the West Indies for 183 and won the match.'

8, 9, 10, 12 June 1950. England won by 202 runs

Evans and Bailey added 161, a record for the sixth wicket against the West Indies in England. Evans batted two hours 20 minutes in a powerful display of stroke-making to enable England to regain the initiative.

England

L. Hutton b Valentine	39	c and b Worrell	45
R.T. Simpson c Goddard b Valentine	27	c Weekes b Gomez	0
W.J. Edrich c Gomez b Valentine	7	c Weekes b Ramadhin	71
G.H.G. Doggart c Rae b Valentine	29	c Goddard b Valentine	22
H.E. Dollery c Gomez b Valentine	8	c Gomez b Valentine	0
N.W.D. Yardley c Gomez b Valentine	0	lbw b Gomez	25
T.E. Bailey not out	82	run out	33
T.G. Evans c and b Valentine	104	c Worrell b Ramadhin	15
J.C. Laker b Valentine	4	c Stollmeyer b Valentine	40
W.E. Hollies c Weekes b Ramadhin	0	c Walcott b Worrell	3
R. Berry b Ramadhin	0	not out	4

| B 8, l-b 3, n-b 1 | 12 | B 17, l-b 12, n-b 1 | 30 |
| | 312 | | 288 |

1/51 2/74 3/79 4/83 5/88 6/249
7/293 8/301 9/308

1/0 2/31 3/43 4/106 5/131
6/151 7/200 8/266 9/284

West Indies

A.F. Rae c Doggart b Berry	14	c Doggart b Hollies	10
J.B. Stollmeyer lbw b Hollies	43	c sub b Laker	78
F.M. Worrell st Evans b Berry	15	st Evans b Hollies	28
E. Weekes c sub b Bailey	52	lbw b Hollies	1
C.L. Walcott c Evans b Berry	13	b Berry	9
R.J. Christiani lbw b Berry	17	c Yardley b Hollies	6
G.E. Gomez c Berry b Hollies	35	st Evans b Berry	8
J.D. Goddard run out	7	not out	16
H.H. Johnson c Dollery b Hollies	8	b Berry	22
S. Ramadhin not out	4	b Berry	0
A.L. Valentine c and b Berry	0	c Bailey b Hollies	0
L-b 6, n-b 1	7	B 4, w 1	5
	215		183

1/52 2/74 3/74 4/94 5/146
6/178 7/201 8/211 9/211

1/32 2/68 3/80 4/113 5/126
6/141 7/146 8/178 9/178

West Indies Bowling

	O	M	R	W	O	M	R	W
Johnson	10	3	18	0				
Gomez	10	1	29	0	25	12	47	2
Valentine	50	14	104	8	56	22	100	3
Ramadhin	39.3	12	90	2	42	17	77	2
Goddard	15	1	46	0	9	3	12	0
Worrell	4	1	13	0	5.5	1	10	2
Walcott					4	1	12	0

England Bowling

	O	M	R	W	O	M	R	W
Bailey	10	2	28	1	3	1	9	0
Edrich	2	1	4	0	3	1	10	0
Hollies	33	13	70	3	35.2	11	63	5
Laker	17	5	43	0	14	4	43	1
Berry	31.5	13	63	5	26	12	53	4

Umpires: F. Chester and D. Davies

In 1952 he had a memorable match against India in the second Test at Lord's. Every cricketer's ambition was to score a hundred before lunch for their country and Evans very nearly did. 'I was two short of scoring 100 and would have been the first Englishman – three Australians had previously done it, Trumper, Macartney and Bradman. I could have got it for the slowness of the Indian captain, Hazare, in setting the field after what proved to be the last over before lunch, and Frank Chester's taste for the dramatic. Looking at the clock at the Nursery end, it was perfectly clear to me that another over should be bowled because there were at least two minutes to go and in any case Hazare was already setting his field for the next over. But he seemed to be doing it as if he had the whole morning in front of him. I don't know for certain whether Hazare was deliberate in his slowness. Then Frank Chester swung up his metal arm, pointed it at no-one in particular, jutted his jaw out under the trilby hat he always wore and stated dramatically: "And that concludes the entertainment for the morning." I managed to complete my hundred after lunch.'

Another memorable match he recalls was in Australia in 1954–5. 'We hadn't won a series over there since the "Bodyline" tour of 1932–3. It was Frank Tyson's tour when he bowled absolutely magnificently. I remember the third Test at Melbourne when Australia wanted 165 to win on the last day, with Neil Harvey batting in the morning and of course everybody coming to see Australia win. With the second ball of Frank's first over, the ball pitched outside leg-stump. Harvey flicked it round the corner and it went down to Peter May for two runs. I suddenly realised it was nearer to me than I thought and at least I should have made some effort to catch it. But I was not ready and on the seventh ball of Frank's over with the ball pitching on the same spot as the second, I could see Harvey attempting the same shot and I was over like a flash catching him quite close to Colin Cowdrey, who was fielding at leg gully. That catch I think helped us win the match, as without Neil and Frank bowling with such hostility, I didn't think they stood much chance.'

Of course, Evans hit the winning runs at Adelaide in the fourth Test to win the Ashes, England having won the second and third Tests. He remembers receiving quite a rollicking from Denis Compton, having hit a four from Keith Miller to win the series. 'Denis said, "What did you do that for? When we won the Ashes in 1953 at the Oval, I hit the winning runs and a bloke gave me a hundred pounds and told me that if I did it in Australia he'd double it!" I said "Why didn't you tell me?" Denis felt it might have put me under pressure to give my wicket away.'

Proudest Moment
During his career he held several world records of which Evans is proud, including in 1957 being the first wicket-keeper to take 200 victims and score 2,000 runs – the wicket-keeper's 'double'. In addition he took 97 minutes to get off the mark at Adelaide way back in his first Test series in 1946, a record broken in 1999 by Geoff Allott of New Zealand, who was

dismissed for a duck after surviving for 101 minutes, facing 77 deliveries.

During his career there were many catches and stumpings Evans recalled with pride. One in particular was at the Scarborough festival in a Gents v. Players match against Billy Sutcliffe, Herbert's son. 'Standing up to Alec Bedser's first over with the new ball swinging, Billy was hitting with the tide and going down the wicket. I realised it was going to be wide of the leg side and dived full length. Billy in the meantime had got an inside edge to the ball and as I landed full stretch the ball smacked into my gloves – an impossible catch!'

A wonderful character and the outstanding wicket-keeper of his day, Evans scored 14,882 runs (21.22) including 7 centuries and 1,066 dismissals (816 ct, 250 st). In 91 Test matches he scored 2,439 runs (20.49) including 2 centuries and 219 dismissals (173 ct, 46 st).

–14–

Don Shepherd (b. 1927)

Glamorgan

I played for Glamorgan throughout the '60s and particularly remember a match at Swansea in 1965 when it all seemed to happen because the wicket turned a little. We beat Yorkshire and Jimmy Presdee took nine wickets in the first innings and I took 9 for 48 in the second, which had never been done before or since.

I never thought we would win the Championship while I was playing, but it happened in Investiture year, 1969. It wasn't a year of big wicket taking for me but there were a lot of players contributing rather than any one taking the major share of wickets or runs. I was very fortunate to stay fit and my 2,000th wicket came that season [by taking the wicket that sealed Glamorgan's first Championship win for 21 years]. I was also proud to be honoured as one of *Wisden*'s five cricketers of the year. From 1968 to 1970 we were third, first and second, which was a golden period for Glamorgan cricket. It was also the start of one-day cricket, which I now feel we should have given more attention to, tactically. We didn't sit down and discuss things and there was never an occasion when there were less than four fielders in what was later to become the fielding circle, as it wasn't the way we played.

One of my proudest moments was in 1970 when we started to play fewer games in the County Championship and at the age of 43 I was the only player to take 100 Championship wickets. My first game for Glamorgan was against Surrey in 1950 at The Oval and my last was towards the end of the 1972 season, again against Surrey at The Oval, so I had a pretty good run (after 647 matches).

Occasionally I got off the mark but not very often! I had a bit of fun against the Aussies in the '50s and '60s when Glamorgan depended on the gates to help finance the county. In 1961 at Swansea, we were 8 down for 94 runs when I went in, had a swish and scored 51 not out off 11 scoring shots [in 15 minutes, equalling the world record – it was also the fastest ever 50 for Glamorgan]. With a crowd of 10–12,000 it was a great feeling. I remember Wilf Wooller saying not so much 'well played' but 'well done, you've saved the gate!'.

Although I am still the highest wicket-taker never to have played for England, it doesn't bother me. There wasn't the high-pressure coverage there is nowadays and not so much speculation. I never got up wanting to buy a newspaper to see if I was in the list. I toured Ceylon and The Far East with MCC in the winter of 1969–70 and also went on a couple of Commonwealth tours to Pakistan during the winters of 1967–8 and 1970–1. Richie Benaud, who was the skipper on the first Commonwealth tour said if I had been an Australian I probably would have been looked on in a different light. I feel because I was unorthodox and quicker than Derek Underwood when I started, the selectors had a theory that you had to get the Australians out with flight, although that didn't happen very often. With bowlers like Laker, Lock, Allen, Titmus, Mortimore and Illy, it wasn't a habit of selectors to 'cross the bridge' to come and see us. If you played in the south-east or a popular area, they would certainly come one day when you played well, so you had a better chance of being selected. They might appear in Wales once in a couple of seasons and if you didn't play well then you had had your chance. It would have been nice when the grandchildren ask to have said that I achieved my ambition and played for England, but I am not bitter.

I was born in a little village called Porteynon, on the extremity of the Gower Peninsular, almost as far west as you can go. My family had a village shop about eight miles away in Parkmill which Granny opened in 1896. My brother sold it only a couple of years ago, so we didn't quite make the century. When my cricket finished I felt I owed it to my family to go back, so I spent about 13 years there working very hard. With hindsight I wish I hadn't, as I wasn't able to keep closely in touch with cricket, although I did do some television work for Wales and was occasionally called up for BBC2. I commentated on possibly the last television game that Jim Laker covered. It was at the end of the 1985 season when Essex beat Yorkshire at Chelmsford to decide the Sunday League title and the last I saw of him was him showing me the way round the M25, which was under construction. I kept in touch vaguely like that, then decided with the children grown up that I would take a chance in media, see what happened and gradually got more and more work for the BBC in Wales. Edward Bevan and I have done a radio programme now for over ten years, particularly ball by ball commentary on Sundays, together with the occasional television broadcast. I have also worked for newspapers and watch Glamorgan near enough all of the time. When Tony Lewis was made chairman he asked if I would come back for three years and help coach the bowlers, which I enjoyed. I had a part to play in the development of Robert Croft which gives us all great satisfaction.

In 1994 I received a letter inviting me to become an honorary member of MCC and that is one of the greatest things that ever happened to me, having started on the ground staff there in 1948. My job in the Lord's Test match one day was to open the dressing-room door and let Don Bradman in after another big score. I received the Queen's Silver Jubilee medal in 1977, which is much rarer than an MBE or OBE being a one-off issue and I was also a J.P. for ten years.

I played a bit of golf and got my handicap down to eight at one time. I also played badminton for Swansea men, although don't play any longer. With soccer I went to Cardiff and Leeds for a trial. When I went up from Swansea the great Major Buckley, who was the manager of Leeds at that time, made the mistake of keeping John Charles and sending me back! Of course he was right as John became one of the giants of Welsh football.

Memorable Game

It is very difficult to pin down the most memorable game I played in as there have been so many. My two top memories would be against an Australian touring side beating them on two consecutive visits, which I don't think any county had ever done before. The match in 1964 at Swansea was on a pitch which helped the spinners a bit. We won the toss and scored enough runs. Jimmy Presdee and myself bowled through the match and finished up with 19 of the wickets between us, he took ten and I took nine. To win a mini Test match in Wales was very memorable and I certainly enjoyed that.

1, 3, 4 August 1964. Glamorgan won by 36 runs

A crowd of 10,000 witnessed a thrilling climax to the last day as Australians suffered their first defeat of the tour. Shepherd, despite suffering from cramp in a marathon spell, maintained his length and line to bowl immaculately as victory was secured amongst exciting scenes in the last hour of the match.

Glamorgan

A. Jones c Simpson b Martin	33	c Connolly b Martin	15
E. Lewis c Simpson b Veivers	7	b Hawke	11
A.R. Lewis c Hawke b Veivers	0	c Connolly b Veivers	36
P.M. Walker b Hawke	41	c and b Veivers	9
J. Presdee b Martin	6	st Jarman b Simpson	24
A. Rees c Simpson b Hawke	48	c Jarman b Simpson	47
W. Slade not out	14	c Connolly b Simpson	9
E. Jones c Connolly b Veivers	0	b Veivers	4
A.E. Cordle c Sellers b Veivers	6	c Potter b Simpson	6
D.J. Shepherd c Martin b Veivers	24	not out	9
O.S. Wheatley c Redpath b Hawke	11	c O'Neill b Simpson	1
L-b 6, w 1	7	L-b 1	1
	197		172

1/42 2/46 3/50 4/62 5/130
6/147 7/150 8/156 9/182

1/13 2/49 3/67 4/74 5/126
6/152 7/152 8/162 9/171

Australia

W.M. Lawry c Slade b Shepherd	7	c Rees b Presdee	64
I.R. Redpath c Walker b Presdee	6	lbw b Shepherd	5
N. O'Neill st E. Jones b Presdee	0	c A.R. Lewis b E. Lewis	14
J. Potter c E.Jones b Presdee	2	b Shepherd	0
R.B. Simpson b Presdee	2	c Walker b Shepherd	32
B.N. Jarman c Slade b Shepherd	4	c E. Jones b Presdee	34
T.R. Veivers c E. Lewis b Presdee	51	b Presdee	54
J.W. Martin b Shepherd	12	c Presdee b Shepherd	6
N.J.N. Hawke c E. Jones b Presdee	0	c E. Jones b Presdee	1
R.H.D. Sellers lbw b Shepherd	4	c Slade b Shepherd	4
A.N. Connolly not out	0	not out	0
B 9, l-b 1, w 1, n-b 2	13	B 12, l-b 4, n-b 2	18
	101		232

1/15 2/15 3/17 4/21 5/21 6/39
7/65 8/90 9/95

1/59 2/80 3/88 4/92 5/169
6/207 7/217 8/228 9/232

Australia Bowling

	O	M	R	W	O	M	R	W
Connolly	6	1	22	0	3	2	6	0
Hawke	26.1	8	51	3	15	3	30	1
Veivers	28	11	85	5	28	6	65	3
Martin	7	0	31	2	8	2	25	1
Simpson	1	0	1	0	14.1	4	33	5
Sellers					13	6	12	0

Glamorgan Bowling

Wheatley	4	3	1	0	5	1	11	0
Cordle	5	1	7	0	7	1	14	0
Shepherd	17	12	22	4	52	29	71	5
Presdee	15.2	5	58	6	28.1	6	65	4
E. Lewis					26	13	51	1
Slade					1	0	2	0

Umpires: W.H. Copson and F. Jakeman

Then in 1968 when they came back, skipper Tony Lewis was injured, so I captained the team against a good Australian side. It was a different type of surface, which perhaps people don't realise from 100 yards away and we beat them on a pretty good wicket that spun a bit. We scored plenty of runs [224 and 250] and I used myself sparingly as the Australians were challenged to score 365 runs on the final day and I didn't want them to clam up and feel they didn't have a chance. We just got enough from it to think that we could get them out but keep them interested in chasing for the runs, as often happened in the old days.

Proudest Moment
Captaining the side in that match was a wonderful occasion for me and one of my proudest moments in cricket, together with winning the County Championship in 1969.

Glamorgan used to be the junior side in the Championship. By tradition the other counties had their holiday fixtures against the Australians but we had them twice, at Whitsun in Cardiff and August in Swansea, both enormous occasions. When you look at crowds now, Cardiff Arms Park was not considered big enough as it would only take 16,000 spectators. It is amazing to think now that there were 25,000 on the Saturday and Monday of the game at Swansea against Australia in 1953 and 32,000 spectators in a day against the same opposition at Swansea in 1956.

The leading wicket-taker of all-time not to be selected to play in Test match cricket, 'Shep' scored 5,696 runs (9.68), took 2,218 wickets (21.32) and 251 catches. He took 5 wickets in an innings over 100 times.

–15–

Maurice Tremlett (1923–1984)

Somerset, Central District and England

As told by Mrs Lee Tremlett

Maurice was a very quiet but affable person. I remember when Somerset were playing at Bristol one year and I travelled on the train to meet him at the station – we were going to stay with Horace Hazell. We sat on the top deck of a bus and I asked Maurice, 'How did you do today?' He said, 'All right,' which was a typical answer he gave – he would not elaborate. I said, 'How many runs did you score?' He said, 'A few'. There was a man sitting in front of us reading the cricket news and I saw Maurice's name headlined in the paper. He had hit another century that day and that was the kind of man he was. Maurice was a natural cricketer and the first sportsman in the family. He did start writing a book but stopped as at that time people wanted sensational news about people's private lives, so he didn't continue with it.

Maurice never really altered at all, he was just contented with his lot. He was a happy and sociable person – a very humorous man – very funny at times. Maurice actually retired from county cricket in 1960 before he felt the committee might push him out. He didn't come home with any troubles but I think he was pleased to finish at that time, even though 37 was a relatively young age to retire in those days. There was also the consequence

80

of a bad eye accident fielding close in, way back in 1953 in a county match against Kent, which affected his sight. We used to have a padre Williams who was with the county and I remember him driving me to the hospital to see Maurice. His eye was in a bad way but he was lucky insofar that it hit a bone that came out. Had it gone in, it would have killed Maurice. It also happened at Bath, where they had one of the best eye surgeons in the country and he was in hospital for two months.

After retirement he then played quite a few friendly matches and charity games, even when we moved from Somerset to Hampshire. Maurice took an interest in the local cricket club, Deanery in Southampton and was also made an honorary life member with Hampshire CCC. He took a great interest in Tim, his son's progress at Hampshire – he didn't interfere, but would be there to watch Tim play and talk to him later on. Our other son was also a good cricketer as we are a sporty family.

He was one of the first cricketers to join Guinness in 1960 on retirement from cricket – most were colonial types before. We were very friendly with John Arlott at the time, who introduced Maurice to the firm and they gave him a job as a sales rep in Hampshire. We moved to the county in 1961 when our daughter Julie was 12 – we were lucky to get Hampshire as we could have gone anywhere. It was a super firm and he enjoyed working there, but I ended up having to drive him to a few places when he became ill. He wasn't capable and didn't want to carry on with his job, so took early retirement in early 1983, about nine months before he died at the age of 61.

He hadn't been feeling well for a while which I knew – you could tell when things weren't quite right after the length of time we were married. I took him to the doctor one day, who couldn't work out what was wrong with him. He was sent to hospital and had tests. I was told he possibly had Parkinson's disease, might have had a stroke or could be senile, which he definitely wasn't as he was very together. I made a note of everything he was doing – for example his handwriting was always very neat and I noticed it was getting smaller. In the end I took him privately to a consultant who said he might have a thyroid problem. He went into hospital but they couldn't find anything at all. Then one evening when we were playing cards, he started choking and we called the ambulance. He was taken into hospital but they still didn't know what was wrong and he was given a scan. I was told he had one month to live and he died five or six weeks later of a tumour. It was terrible and what annoyed me was that I gave them so many facts but they still couldn't diagnose what was wrong. We were married for 36 years and had a wonderful life together.

Maurice's hobbies were golf and he loved to watch people fishing. We used to stay at South Moulton when we went to the Lynmouth/Lynton charity events, and Maurice would get up at five o'clock in the morning to watch the great fishermen down there. He was a keen golfer who holed in one seven times, including three times in a month! He taught me and in later years golf

81

became his main hobby. He played off a handicap of 5 for about 20 years and in his early twenties was runner-up in the West of England Championships. We played at Stoneham Golf Club but he also played at various courses with the cricketers. He also used to play table-tennis in a league in Taunton when he was in his twenties. He loved horse-racing as well and got that from Arthur Wellard. He also played snooker in later years and watched a lot of television. He used to like his home very much and loved chatting about cricket and socialising. From his cricketing days, he used to love playing cards – I didn't even like playing but we played for about 30 years. We used to play crib twice a week – two ladies took on the men, which he loved – and he also played bridge. We had a lot of fun with a game called Black Bess where we only lost about ten pence per evening, so it lasted quite a long time!

Memorable Game

The most memorable game Maurice played was on his Somerset debut in 1947 against Middlesex, when he took eight wickets including that of Denis Compton and scored the winning runs. It was also Somerset's first victory at Lord's for 20 years.

10, 12, 13 May 1947. Somerset won by one wicket

Tremlett had a sensational start to his first-class career when he almost beat Middlesex on his own, taking five wickets for just eight runs in five overs of the second innings. He then scored the winning runs soon after lofting a typical straight drive into the Members Stand and was applauded off the field by the Middlesex team.

Middlesex

J.D. Robertson b Tremlett	39	b Buse	30
S.M. Brown lbw b Wellard	7	b Wellard	0
W.J. Edrich c Luckes b Buse	102	c Lawrence b Wellard	3
D.C.S. Compton c Woodhouse b Buse	6	b Tremlett	25
J. Eaglestone b Buse	0	c Lawrence b Tremlett	4
F.G. Mann b Buse	27	b Tremlett	0
A. Thompson c Wellard b Tremlett	5	b Tremlett	0
L.H. Compton b Tremlett	11	b Tremlett	0
J. Sims c and b Buse	3	not out	6
J.A. Young not out	6	c Luckes b Wellard	1
L. Gray c Hazell b Buse	5	run out	4
B 19, l-b 1	20	B 1, l-b 4	5
	231		78

Somerset

F.S. Lee c D. Compton b Young	28	c Robertson b Young	38

H. Gimblett b Edrich	25	b Edrich	13
H.T.F. Buse lbw b Gray	1	c L. Compton b Gray	3
G.E.S. Woodhouse b Edrich	7	b Edrich	21
R.J.O. Meyer c Robertson b Sims	1	b Gray	4
J. Lawrence c Mann b Sims	30	b Young	19
E. Hill b Edrich	0	c Edrich b Young	17
W.T. Luckes c Edrich b Gray	9	c L. Compton b Gray	26
A.W. Wellard b Edrich	17	b Edrich	5
M.F. Tremlett c Gray b Sims	5	not out	19
H. Hazell not out	0	not out	8
B 1, l-b 9, w 1	11	B 4, l-b 1	5
	134	(9 wkts)	178

Somerset Bowling

	O	M	R	W	O	M	R	W
Buse	33	8	52	6	4	2	14	1
Wellard	22	4	49	1	16.3	7	20	3
Tremlett	24	5	47	3	14	3	39	5
Hazell	4	0	13	0				
Lawrence	12	2	40	0				
Meyer	4	1	10	0				

Middlesex Bowling

	O	M	R	W	O	M	R	W
Gray	24	10	25	2	29.2	7	51	3
Edrich	16	3	46	4	22	8	47	3
Young	11	6	12	1	34	14	48	3
Sims	15.4	4	40	3	7	0	27	0

Umpires: A.R. Coleman and J.J. Hills

Proudest Moment

Maurice's proudest moment in cricket may well have been when he was appointed captain of Somerset in 1956. Bob Moore, who used to work for *The Express* was a cricket enthusiast and friend of Maurice. Bob came round to us one evening and said to me, 'Aren't you proud of your old man, then?' I looked at him and said, 'Well I suppose I am, yes. Why?' He said, 'Because he's been made captain of Somerset' [the first professional Somerset captain] and that was the first time I had heard of it! He did a very good job too getting the county to third place in the Championship in 1958 and was very popular as a captain, but he didn't say a lot about it at all.

An attacking middle-order right-hand batsman and right-arm medium-fast bowler, Tremlett scored 16,038 runs (25.37) including 16 centuries, took 351 wickets (30.63) and 257 catches. In 3 Test matches he scored 20 runs (6.66) and took 4 wickets (56.50).

–16–
Eric Bedser (b. 1918)

Surrey

My last season playing county cricket was 1961. I then played my MCC qualifying matches in 1962–3 so that I could get straight in as a member. I was subsequently president of Surrey in 1990. It is not true that I acted as my brother's 'svengali' in his assessment of players. We talked to each other about players, but not officially. Since retiring from cricket, most of my time has been spent trying to earn a living. My brother and I started an office equipment business in 1955 when we were still playing and carried on until we were 74. I still enjoy golf and my handicap is now 13, although we were both on 5 at one time. I also enjoy gardening and we grow all our own vegetables.

Memorable Game

One of my most memorable matches was my highest score of 163 against Notts at The Oval in 1949. Opening the innings, I was out before five o'clock, so I must have scored quickly.

30 July, 1, 2 August 1949. Match drawn

Bedser's driving was a joy to watch, as his last 63 runs came in 55 minutes. Unfortunately, rain caused the game to be abandoned, the only Surrey match in

1949 to be ruined by the weather.

Surrey

L.B. Fishlock st Meads b Sime	95
E.A. Bedser c Butler b Harvey	163
H.S. Squires b Jepson	25
M.R. Barton b Sime	6
J.F. Parker not out	119
D.G.W. Fletcher c Sime b Notley	12
A.J. McIntyre b Butler	36
J.C. Laker not out	21
A.V. Bedser did not bat	
W.S. Surridge did not bat	
G.A.R. Lock did not bat	
B 6, l-b 6, w 1, n-b 1	14
(6 wkts dec)	491

Nottinghamshire

W.W. Keeton c McIntyre b Laker	31
R.T. Simpson c McIntyre b Laker	60
C.J. Poole b Lock	22
J. Hardstaff b Surridge	19
C.B. Harris not out	58
B. Notley c Surridge b A. V. Bedser	0
A. Jepson c Lock b A. V. Bedser	0
W.A. Sime b Laker	2
P.F. Harvey b Laker	8
H.J. Butler not out	0
E.A. Meads did not bat	
B 7, l-b 1 n-b 5	13
(8 wkts)	213

Nottinghamshire Bowling

	O	M	R	W
Butler	29	5	93	1
Jepson	30	3	96	1
Harvey	23	5	73	1
Sime	19	5	55	2
Notley	28	3	90	1
Harris	11	3	32	0
Simpson	10	2	38	0

Surrey Bowling

A. V. Bedser	23	2	64	2
Surridge	10	2	29	1
Parker	4	2	4	0
Laker	28	11	55	4
Lock	25	12	35	1
E. A. Bedser	11	8	7	0
Squires	6	3	6	0

Umpires: J. J. Hills and F. Chester

I also remember my best bowling of 7–33 against Leicestershire at The Oval in 1955 as a highlight. As an all-rounder I enjoyed both batting and bowling, although probably bowling slightly more and took 833 wickets in my career for Surrey [in 443 matches].

Proudest Moment
My proudest moment was when I first joined the Surrey playing staff at the age of 19½. We left school at 15 and had worked as clerks for Lincoln's Inn solicitors until joining the county.

A middle-order right-hand batsman and right-arm off-break bowler, Bedser scored 14,716 runs (24.00), took 833 wickets (24.95) and 236 catches.

–17–

Brian Boshier (b. 1932)

Leicestershire

Throughout the whole of my career I opened the bowling for Leicestershire and was injury-prone with sore shins, probably as I was so tall. Both 1958 and 1961 were good summers for me, though, as I played all year [taking 107 wickets in both seasons]. I recall odd incidents from those years such as the game against Surrey in August 1958 at Leicester, when Peter May was in full flight and looking for a century. Terry Spencer, who wasn't slow, hurled the ball down and Peter hit it like a rocket straight over Terry's head and I was looking towards the boundary. Terry, who had a pair of hands like buckets, leapt up in his follow through and it stuck, as some do. You could sense the feeling of relief in the team as we had got him out! There were batsmen you didn't like bowling to like Roy Marshall, who would slaughter you if you were off line. I remember one game when in the last half an hour he scored 50 very aggressively against us. Dickie Dodds was another who would either 'prop and cock' or suddenly let loose.

If I had played all the time I might have done a lot better and by 1961 I was bowling off-cutters like Don Shepherd, rather than seam bowling. It was a very wet summer that year and I opened with Terry Spencer, who was the mainstay at the time, and had a good season with a number of five-wicket hauls. I was also having quite a successful season in 1964 when we played against Somerset in July at Hinckley and again my legs let me down in their second innings. Willie Watson, who had stood by me for three or four years, despite being injury-prone, took me to one side during the season and said, 'If this committee have half a chance, you'll be gone.' It was to be my last season.

I played at the start of the one-day game in the Gillette Cup but it didn't appeal to me. Even if you bowled line and length, you would still be knocked all over the place. I played 12 years for Leicestershire and never had a benefit, neither did Jack van Geloven, who had also given them good years and performed well. My final salary was £800 plus win bonuses! However if I had the chance, I would do it all again tomorrow and have no regrets at all about playing county cricket. It was always my desire to play cricket from my first memories of standing on the crossbar of my bike and looking over the fence at Grace Road to see Don Bradman score a century until the local bobby chased us off.

For three or four years during the winter months I worked for Bill Bentley, the chairman of Leicestershire CCC in the drawing office of Bentley engineering works. When I finished with Leicestershire, I went back to work there until one glorious sunny morning in the spring of 1965, when I sat and thought, 'This is not for me, I want to be outside.' I had played a lot of friendly cricket in Lincolnshire for the editor of *Angling Times*, as I did a lot of fishing. He got me a job selling fishing tackle on the road for a firm called Edgar Sealey, a subsidiary of Dunlop. I progressed from Sealey's into the Dunlop empire in the sports division, who moved me to Leeds, and in 1965 I started playing for Harrogate, where I had my happiest years playing cricket. We had in the team Bill Sutcliffe, Brian Stott and Peter Chadwick, who I think was the best player not to play regular county cricket let alone for England, a superb all-round cricketer, a typical Pateley Bridge man. He only played half a dozen times for Yorkshire in the '60s and they batted him at about eight or nine.

I played about four very good years for Harrogate just once a week on a Saturday. The legs were fine but eventually I was stiff on a Friday night from the week before and knew it was time to pack up. We had some wonderful games and finished top or near the top every year and also won the Yorkshire Cup. We played Elsecar in the final and I took eight wickets in that match. It was the first time in my life that I had a collection and it raised £52 pounds. We drank so much that night that I stood the bill and had to give them a fiver!

I was with Dunlop until 1985 when I went on my own in the selling game for a couple of years. In 1988 we took a pub in Winksley for two years but my back collapsed on me and put me in hospital where I had an operation, although it's been fine since. We came to Masham in North Yorkshire in

1990 and opened the Mad Hatter teashop, which has thrived ever since. I decided to retire in February 1997, the decision once again being influenced by my ill health. I take an interest in the local cricket club and enjoy art from my drawing office days. I have collected pictures all my life and now have a roomful of cricket memorabilia.

John Savage was a particularly good pal of mine who lived in Lancashire. One weekend, when we stayed at his mother's house we went to a dance in the evening. He said 'Grab that one in white' as he wanted her pal, but I grabbed the wrong one, Margaret. We have now been married for 44 years and have three girls and a boy.

I have enjoyed fishing ever since I was a child and progressed though course fishing to trout and salmon. I have had a wonderful time and we have superb trout in the Ure. As a boy we fished in the local canal in Leicester but it blossomed when we came north and we often went fishing with friends to Scotland. I took Margaret salmon fishing 15 years ago and she caught a 20-pounder, quite a feat. She was a beginner and it had taken me ten years to catch a fish that size!

The card series picture comes from a photo from the *News of the World* with the middle stump about 20 yards back, as Alan Moss had knocked it out – I think I scored nought that day! I can't think why I was featured as a batsman as I couldn't bat to save my life. They used to queue up to grab the ball as I walked out to bat! I got nine noughts on the trot at the beginning of the 1955 season, which equalled the world record and is my claim to fame. I did top-score, though, in a game at Hinckley against Lancashire in June 1955 when we were all out for 32. Brian Statham was taking all the wickets with shooters and I scored 13 not out with three swipes!

Memorable Game

The most memorable game I played in was my eight-wicket haul at Brentwood in 1957. It was a sweltering hot day, and as we came off I was dripping but there were no showers. It was a game we looked so much like winning. Maurice Hallam and Gerry Lester put on nearly 100 for the first wicket, yet we lost the match so easily. It was a typical Leicester performance lacking consistency, in the ascendancy one day and down the next. We had a very good side with no real stars and there was no reason for it to be like that, but we never seemed to gel.

15, 17, 18 June 1957. Essex won by 181 runs

On the first day Boshier bowled at a brisk pace on a very fast wicket to achieve career-best figures, as the Essex batsmen found conditions difficult to defend. By the final day the pitch had become worn and Leicester were dismissed in just 75 minutes.

Essex

T.C. Dodds c and b Spencer	1	run out	57
G. Barker b Spencer	5	b Palmer	44
B. Taylor c Firth b Boshier	10	c Firth b Boshier	31
D.J. Insole c and b Boshier	65	c Hallam b Munden	43
T.E. Bailey c Firth b Boshier	0	c Firth b Munde	5
M. Bear c Spencer b Boshier	8	st Firth b Palmer	13
G. Smith c Hallam b Boshier	0	c Palmer b van Geloven	59
W.T. Greensmith lbw b Boshier	1	lbw b van Geloven	40
R. Ralph c Firth b Boshier	31	not out	17
K.C. Preston c Palmer b Boshier	25	c Diment b Boshier	6
I.M. King not out	2	not out	5
L-b 1	1	B 6, l-b 12, n-b 1	19
	149	(9 wkts dec)	339

1/4 2/7 3/31 4/43 5/67 6/67
7/73 8/100 9/138

1/88 2/130 3/139 4/164 5/193
6/211 7/304 8/311 9/324

Leicestershire

G. Lester c Taylor b Ralph	67	c Greensmith b Bailey	1
M.R. Hallam b Greensmith	39	c Ralph b Bailey	4
L.R. Gardner c King b Preston	14	lbw b Preston	13
C.H. Palmer not out	102	c Taylor b Bailey	0
R.A. Diment c Ralph b Greensmith	0	c King b Bailey	4
J. van Geloven b Greensmith	1	c Greensmith b Preston	8
V.S. Munden c Insole b Preston	8	b Bailey	0
J. Firth b Preston	12	c Ralph b Preston	9
C.T. Spencer c Bailey b King	13	c King b Bailey	1
J.S. Savage c Barker b Greensmith	0	not out	4
B.S. Boshier run out	0	b Preston	0
B 1, l-b 1, w 1, n-b 3	6	N-b 1	1
	262		45

1/92 2/120 3/120 4/127 5/135
6/181 7/206 8/236 9/237

1/5 2/5 3/5 4/9 5/30 6/31
7/37 8/41 9/45

Leicestershire Bowling

	O	M	R	W	O	M	R	W
Spencer	17	1	93	2	27	1	61	0
Boshier	19.2	4	45	8	31	6	71	2
Palmer	3	0	10	0	13	2	25	2
Munden					26	7	85	2
Savage					20	8	58	0
van Geloven					8	4	15	2
Lester					2	0	5	0

Essex Bowling

Bailey	11	3	15	0	10	1	28	6
Preston	29	6	83	3	9.2	4	16	4
Ralph	18	4	59	1				
Greensmith	32.5	9	85	4				
King	13	5	14	1				

Umpires: R.S. Lay and T.W. Spencer

Proudest Moment

This was when I received my cap in 1958 – it is the one thing you play for in county cricket. It was awarded at Ashby-de-la-Zouch and, whilst I had a hint it was being awarded, on the actual day it was still quite a surprise.

A right-arm medium-fast pace bowler, Boshier scored 579 runs (4.32), took 510 wickets (23.02) and 56 catches.

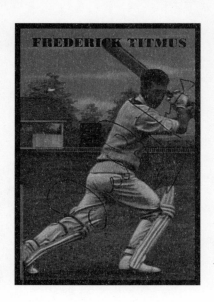

–18–

Fred Titmus (b. 1932)

Middlesex, Surrey, Orange Free State and England

One thing I do recall about 1959, the year of the cards, was winning a car in a draw for Jack Robertson's benefit, which in those days was worth quite a lot. Not only that, but I was helping to draw the numbers out so it was a bit embarrassing!

I was coaching the boys of Christian Brothers' College in Kimberley, South Africa during the winter months at that time, which I did for three years. I played with them in the men's league, as I think you can teach people much more that way than playing in the nets. Then I went to Cape Town for two years with Northerns, an Afrikaan side. They were new to the league and I was a bit worried about it when I got there, but I had a really good time. I met Peter van der Merwe and we became great friends. I did a lot of work with him on how to play off-spinners, which wasn't to my advantage when he got into the South African Test side! Then in 1975 when I was 43 years of age I went to Bloemfontein and played for Orange Free State. I enjoyed that very much and we won the 'B' section of the Currie Cup. I have a great affinity with South Africa, having been there about 20 times.

Having achieved the 'double' for four consecutive seasons, by 1962 I felt I couldn't play much better, but knew what the problem was in breaking through to the England team. Gubby Allen, who was chairman of the Test selectors, thought I bowled too quickly for an off-spinner and we had a bit of an argument about it. I said, 'Mr Allen (as it was in those days), I am getting 100 wickets a year bowling as I am and I am not going to change.' He was a pretty hard man but when R.W.V. Robins was appointed as chairman in 1962, I got in and played a couple of Tests against Pakistan. I also played in the Gents v Players game at Lord's in July and managed to score 70. Fred Trueman at the other end was getting on with it and when I went in Walter Robins said, 'You were a bit slow. If your captain says to you in Melbourne this winter you've got to get on with it, you had better get on with it.' He said that to me ten days before the MCC side to Australia was selected!

When I was chosen I was getting more runs than some of the batsmen and were it not for the little argument with Gubby Allen I think I would have been selected earlier. I have to say that on my return he apologised to me and admitted that he had made a mistake, which coming from him was fair praise. All you said to yourself in those days was, 'Get on with it and show people that you could play' – you didn't write about it in the papers. You have to have breaks at the right time and in the end they came along for me.

It was a good tour for me and I felt it helped me to establish my place in the England side. I remember my highest first-class score of 137 at Adelaide which was on a very good wicket – if you could play at all, you could play with your eyes shut on that wicket. When I got a few edges off Neil Hawke during the innings, he came down the wicket, looked at me and said, 'The way you're playing you might as well turn the bat upside down and play with the handle.' I said, 'The way you're bowling, I think I'll do that.' It was friendly banter in those days. I also bowled on it and didn't do too well though. We squared the series and I was pleased with taking seven wickets at Sydney, (best Test analysis), although we lost the game. The Australians at that stage were not particularly good players of off-spin. However it was difficult to get lbw decisions, as they were very much 'theory' umpires.

I remember taking nine wickets against Lancashire at Lord's in 1964, as I never liked bowling at the Nursery end where I bowled from that day. I got used to bowling with the slope from the Pavilion end as I knew where the ball was going to pitch. From the Nursery end the ball used to go too far down the hill for me, so I didn't particularly like it.

The 1964–5 tour of South Africa was one of the great tours as we weren't given a lot of chance, but in fact we went through South Africa beating everyone in sight, all the States and Provinces. We played Natal at Durban early on, which I didn't play in, on a green wicket, bowled them out twice and won by ten wickets. So the first Test match at Durban was played on a dusty wicket. We scored nearly 500 with centuries from Ken Barrington and Jim Parks, then bowled them out twice. David Allen took five wickets in the first innings and I took five in the second. From there on the wickets turned, we played each Test for a draw and won the series.

The next summer we beat New Zealand in a three Test series and I remember in particular the second Test at Headingley. It was quite funny as the weather was a bit overcast, heavy conditions and on the fourth day Fred Rumsey said, 'Come on we need some wickets, let's get them out.' I said, 'No, we want to stay the night – if we win today we will have to go home.' It got to about ten to six, I hadn't had a bowl, said to Fred that now was the time and managed to take four wickets in an over. Everything went right and I think the only bad shot was from Bruce Taylor, the left-hander, who slogged it up in the air, the others were genuine shots although from tail-enders. We finished the game after a quarter of an hour on the last morning. John Edrich scored 300 against them in the Test and I'm not sure they were a great side.

I remember one of Clive Radley's early games when he scored his maiden century [138] against South Africa at Lord's in 1965. He was a great worker of the ball and we added a county record of 227 for the sixth wicket and I got one of my very few centuries. He was such a quick runner between the wickets, you had to slow him down sometimes.

I had three and a half years as captain of Middlesex in the '60s. I always thought I was a better Sergeant-Major than a captain, as I worried about everybody else. I gave it up as I thought we ought to be doing better and I wasn't getting the best out of some of the young players.

It was on the West Indies tour of 1967–8 that I had an accident to my left foot when we were about to play the third Test. The worst thing about having the accident was when we came back the selectors didn't risk playing me in Tests, they picked Ray Illingworth. Give Ray half a chance and I knew I was never likely to get back in. Then they made him captain and that made it more difficult for me, but that's the way life goes sometimes.

Having said that, when you play cricket and know you have a certain amount of ability, irrespective of whether or not you are playing for England, you must always think that you are good enough to keep going. The people I played with like Peter Parfitt and John Murray were very determined, they all wanted to keep going. Some people nowadays don't want to play, they are frightened of playing. Somehow the attitude seems to have changed, I don't know why. Perhaps they just don't want it badly enough.

By the 1974 season I was bowling with Phil Edmonds for Middlesex. It was the first time I had a class spinner down at the other end, we had some good wickets to play on and were doing pretty well. John Murray said, 'If you keep going like this you will get back into the England side.' I think he put a few words around and I was picked to go to Australia, although I felt Phil Edmonds ought to have gone, as he was much younger.

In the second Test at Perth, I stood out there facing Jeff Thomson and Dennis Lillee when the ball was flying everywhere and kept saying to myself, 'What are you doing here at 42 years of age? Get yourself out!' Then Brian Luckhurst said, 'No, no, stay for a little while longer,' [which Titmus did to top-score with 61]. My wife and our very young daughter were sitting in the stand concerned for my well-being as it was the quickest bowling I ever faced. I think Lillee bowled the odd faster ball but Thomson was actually quicker – Frank Tyson was probably faster than both of them though.

In 1976 we had the best bowling side I ever played with, apart from when I came back for a few games in 1980, and we won the Championship in my last full season. When I was captain my two opening bowlers were medium pacers and then I got John Price, one of the nicest, kindest men, but who could be very frustrating, since trying to get him to bowl bouncers was virtually impossible. By 1976 we had Mike Selvey and Allan Jones, who came from Somerset, Philip Edmonds, myself and also Norman Featherstone, who could come on to bowl. When I came back in 1980 we had a superb attack in Wayne Daniel and Vintcent van der Bijl, supported by John Emburey and Philip.

I am known as a bit of a talker but it is not true what John Warr wrote that I took slip catches in mid-sentence! We never did talk once the bowler turned to bowl, although we were accused of it. Once the bowler was back on his mark the talking stopped. I think we were very fair and certainly never sledged anybody. There was more banter in our day; you would talk and joke with the batsmen – they were your friends. Some batsmen liked to talk back so you wouldn't talk to them and vice versa. The game was played very hard but in a much better atmosphere. At Middlesex we had Murray keeping wicket, Parfitt at first slip, me at second and Eric Russell in the gully and we were all deaf in one ear on the same side. We put it down to the blast that came along the line!

On retirement I had two years as Surrey coach (1977–8) but it was not a happy time as the Oval was a totally different environment from Lord's. I originally signed a contract for three years and asked for that time to do it my way, then we would look again. I think I did a pretty good job and brought along quite a few youngsters but we weren't winning anything. So towards the end of the second year there was a meeting where I was told we might have to change things and I said, 'No, you told me I had three years, I am not going to carry on,' and I left the same day. I think I left possibly the best young side in the country which went on to do very well in limited-overs cricket. I also recommended Micky Stewart to Surrey as the only man who could do the job and that it would be silly to replace me with someone from outside the county.

It was just before my 50th birthday in 1982 that I played my last game for Middlesex against Surrey. I walked into Lord's just before they went down to toss up for an 11.30 a.m. start, having just been down to get a permit to play cricket in America with MCC. Philip Edmonds hadn't arrived and I think Mike Brearley was getting a bit fed up, so he asked me to play. I made every excuse not to, including not having any kit, but Clive Radley lent me his boots and I was in the side. It was our last match of the season at Lord's and Mike Brearley's last match as captain of Middlesex there. I took three wickets, including the last chap and we got Surrey out to win in the final hour – it was an important victory as it helped us to win the Championship. I actually played with Mike Brearley's father Horace, in the first match he played in 1949 and then with Mike in his last as captain at Lord's. I am very proud of that.

I played with a lot of very sensible people who all started young like John Murray, Peter Parfitt and Don Bennett. I learnt quite a lot about strong opinions from Gubby Allen, one of the great committee men, although I'm not saying he was my favourite man, as I have already pointed out. To bowl with John Murray keeping wicket was marvellous, as he always knew what was going on. If I started to go a bit wrong, he would tell me in no uncertain terms what he thought and I would never take offence. I wished he played a bit more for England, it's a shame he didn't. John was a better wicket-keeper than Jim Parks but Jim scored hundreds. He kept well to me but it wasn't like talking to him as it was to John. Where I would get an answer out of John, Jim was more likely to agree with me all the time. If someone who knows the game is being critical, you do well to listen to him, though I don't suffer people who don't play the game and yet give me their opinions.

The biggest change I have seen over the years has been the introduction of one-day cricket. In 1974 I remember Alec Bedser saying in Australia that it would ruin our cricket and he was right. Year after year Gubby Allen tried to get it cut down but they increased the one-day competitions – it was just crazy. We have too many people running our counties who don't know enough about it, people who like to get on to committees as it helps them in other ways of life. They do it for status, but for us it is our way of life. You have to keep quiet though sometimes about these things, as people accuse you of saying cricket was better in our day.

In 1976 my wife Stephanie and I went into the post office business. I wanted to live in the country next to a golf course and fairly near London. When I heard the post office in Potten End was being sold, we went over and found it was next to a golf course. We finally shut it and fully converted it into a house when I retired in November 1997. It's an ideal place to live in a beautiful part of Hertfordshire. I have been married for 28 years to Stephanie and we have one daughter Amanda, who is known universally as Tandy. I also have a boy and a girl, Mark and Dawn, from my first marriage.

I get invited to coach from time to time and for quite a number of years

Keith Fletcher at Essex has asked me to watch some of the younger ones in the nets and talk to them. Micky Stewart got me involved in some of the England teams, which I enjoyed but each time it was not for very long, just a couple of weeks out of choice. My current cricketing involvement is as a committee member at Middlesex.

I love dogs – we've always had a dog and still have one. I still enjoy photography and used to do my own developing but not any longer. My main hobby now is golf, which I took up on my first or second trip to South Africa in the late '50s when Peter Sainsbury, who played for Hampshire, and I started playing tennis and golf. The golf improved but the tennis didn't. For about 30 years I played off 8, but I am now 9.6 – however much I play I don't get any better!

Memorable Game

Having played so many matches it is difficult to highlight the most memorable game I played in, but certainly one was the second Test at Bombay in 1964 when we struggled but saved the match and I batted rather than bowled. We had Edrich, Sharpe, Mortimore and Barrington out injured and Micky Stewart fell ill 20 minutes after the game started. We even had an Indian in the field at one stage as we didn't have anybody else. We weren't initially doing too well but needed to draw the game as we had Peter Parfitt and Colin Cowdrey coming out to reinforce us. I must say I enjoyed it, especially playing for three or four hours against Chandrasekhar, which in itself was a great delight.

21, 22, 23, 25, 26 January 1964. Match drawn

A superb performance by England, who gave debuts to Binks, Jones and Price because of injury problems. Titmus showed a true fighting spirit and revelled in the situation. He batted commandingly for 98 overs in five hours to reach his highest Test score as England displayed great determination and resolve to draw the match.

India

V.L. Mehra lbw b Knight	9	lbw b Titmus	35
B.K. Kunderan c Wilson b Price	29	c Titmus b Price	16
D.N. Sardesai b Price	12	run out	66
V.L. Manjrekar c Binks b Titmus	0	not out	43
Nawab of Pataudi jr c Titmus b Knight	10	b Price	0
M.L. Jaisimha c Price b Titmus	23	c Larter b Knight	66
C.G. Borde c Binks b Wilson	84	c Smith b Titmus	7
S.A. Durani c Binks b Price	90	c Knight b Titmus	3
R.G. Nadkarni not out	26	lbw b Knight	0
Rajinder Pal lbw b Larter	3	not out	3

B.S. Chandrasekhar b Larter 0
B 2, l-b 9, n-b 3 14
300
1/20 2/55 3/56 4/58 5/75 6/99 7/252
8/284 9/300

L-b 4, w 1, n-b 5 10
(8 wkts dec) 249
1/23 2/104 3/107 4/140
5/152 6/180 7/231 8/231

England

J.B. Bolus c Chandrasekhar b Durani	25	c Pataudi b Durani	57
M.J.K. Smith c Borde b Chandrasekhar	46	not out	31
J.M. Parks run out	1	not out	40
B.R. Knight b Chandrasekhar	12		
F.J. Titmus not out	84		
D. Wilson c and b Durani	1	c Pataudi b Chand'har	2
J.G. Binks b Chandrasekhar	10	c Borde b Jaisimha	55
J.S.E. Price b Chandrasekhar	32		
J.D.F. Larter c Borde b Durani	0		
I.J. Jones run out	5		
M.J. Stewart absent ill			
B 4, l-b 7, n-b 6	17	B 12, l-b 7, w 1, n-b 1	21
	233	(3 wkts)	206

1/42 2/48 3/82 4/91 5/98 6/116
7/184 8/185 9/233

1/125 2/127 3/134

England Bowling

	O	M	R	W	O	M	R	W
Knight	20	2	53	2	13	2	28	2
Larter	10.3	2	35	2	5	0	13	0
Jones	13	0	48	0	11	1	31	0
Price	19	2	66	3	17	1	47	2
Titmus	36	17	56	2	46	18	79	3
Wilson	15	5	28	1	23	10	41	0

India Bowling

	O	M	R	W	O	M	R	W
Rajinda Pal	11	4	19	0	2	0	3	0
Jaisimha	3	1	9	0	22	9	36	1
Durani	38	15	59	3	29	12	35	1
Borde	34	12	54	0	37	12	38	0
Chand'har	40	16	67	4	22	5	40	1
Nadkarni	4	2	8	0	14	11	3	0
Sardesai					3	2	6	0
Mehra					2	1	1	0
Pataudi					3	0	23	0

Umpires: H.E. Choudhury and A.M. Mamsa

Because of the amount of bowling I did, after the Bombay Test I didn't go up in the order, I went down to keep me going! I bowled well at Green Park, Kanpur in the fifth Test, where John Mortimore and I were having a contest to see who could bowl the most number of maidens [Titmus bowled 37 maidens out of 60 overs for 73 runs in the first innings and Mortimore 31 in 48 overs, conceding 39 runs]. It kept us going and you remember games like that. We drew the series and I bowled 400 overs in the Tests and most of them were not hit.

Another game I recall is the third Test at Leeds against Australia in 1964. Norman Gifford and I bowled all afternoon and got us back in the game in the first innings [Titmus bowled from 1.20 p.m. to 5.05 p.m. on the second day with figures of 29–17–27–3]. Then we took the new ball when maybe we shouldn't have and ended up losing the match.

Proudest Moment

My proudest moment in cricket was getting re-picked for England in Australia in 1974–5. When you are first picked you are too nervous and young to appreciate it all. When you are older and think you should be playing, to be re-selected was important to me. I was also proud to be nominated as one of *Wisden*'s Players of the Year in 1963 – I was making up for lost time!

A master right-arm off-spinner with a long and distinguished career, Titmus scored 21,588 runs (23.11) including 6 centuries, took 2,830 wickets (22.37) and 473 catches. In 53 Test matches, he scored 1,449 runs (22.29), took 153 wickets (32.22) and 35 catches.

–19–

Ray Illingworth (b. 1932)

Yorkshire, Leicestershire and England

I played the odd game for England in 1958 and came back in 1959. From my point of view, I always had to fight for my place with two or three other people who were good off-spinners like Fred Titmus, David Allen and John Mortimore. It was fairly tough competition, but Fred and myself felt that we were the better two and that whoever was in the best form should have played, and I still feel that way. I felt reasonably all right when Peter May was captain but from 1959 on never had a proper opportunity or felt I was part of the system. I played a Test then was left out and always felt whatever I did I would not be playing in the next match. That's why I never performed as well at Test level as I should have done. I played in five Tests in the West Indies in 1959–60, bowled 200 overs for 400 runs and had 11 catches dropped off me! I also had two of the plummest lbws with Frankie Worrell back on his stumps that you have ever seen in your life. Walter Robins, who was manager, came up to me and said, 'I thought you controlled your temper very well, young man. You would have been well within your rights to say something to the umpire!'

I remember playing in 1961 at Lord's against Australia when I scored runs in the first innings and took 1–16 in 12 overs in the match. I missed out in the second innings, got one that took off and was left out of the next Test

– you can't play in those circumstances. Then I was opening the batting in the MCC tour of New Zealand in 1962–3 but didn't bat in between the Tests. I went in low in the order to let other people have a knock and was fed up with the whole system, as it was crazy for me to be opening in the Test match. When I became captain in 1969, people said they didn't realise I could bat like that, but I just felt more secure of my place and my ability.

The Lord's Test in 1967 when I took my 6–29 against India was on a slightly helpful wet wicket. Before lunch it skidded then dried just sufficiently to turn and I bowled pretty well. In the 1969 Test match against the West Indies (again at Lord's) when I hit my biggest England innings (113), we were in a lot of trouble with the score 61–5. The West Indies didn't quite have the bowling line-up they have now, but to make a Test match hundred was very pleasing. I always felt I was good enough provided I had the opportunity and was just playing to my county form at Test match level. I remember Trevor Bailey writing that a lot of people were amazed by my batting, but I played three of my first hundreds against his bowling, so he knew how well I could play and it didn't surprise him at all.

I enjoyed every minute of my England captaincy – it was never hard work for me although it was tiring, but my concentration was right all the time. As a slow bowler, I enjoyed having to work people out as it was the way you were brought up, modelled on players like Wilfred Rhodes. The best captain I ever played under without a shadow of doubt was Richie Benaud, who skippered a Commonwealth tour of South Africa in 1960–1 that I went on. It was a good side with Fred and Brian Statham, who opened the bowling plus Alan Moss, Tommy Greenhough and Bobby Simpson. Richie's enthusiasm was tremendous as he made you believe you were better than you were. Richie's attitude and enthusiasm rubbed off on everybody and I remember getting more bounce than I ever did in my life. Closey was a good captain when things were going for us and he was interested, but on a slow flat wicket when nothing was happening he switched off, which you can't do as captain. You have to be on the ball all the time, which was what Richie was – Peter May was a good captain as well. I didn't need a computer to work out the opposition like now – it was in my head!

Concerning county cricket, 1959 was a magnificent summer with beautiful weather, especially after the first couple of months of the season. I think it was the first year back on uncovered pitches but it didn't make any difference. The last match against Sussex at Hove in August is my abiding memory – everybody will say that as it was such a fantastic game. If I hadn't scored a century [122] in the first innings, we wouldn't have had a chance of winning the game [and the County Championship]. We were really struggling to get them out and I remember saying to Closey towards the end that if the captain Ronnie Burnett put Fred Trueman on, it would take so long to bowl his overs we wouldn't do it. If he bowled two spinners, and we hoped for the best and crowded them a bit, we would have a better chance, which he went along with. Myself and Don Wilson [each with four wickets] managed to just get them out but by that time we wanted 215 in 105 minutes. We got them and as a young side together for the first time – there was only Closey, myself and Fred of the older ones and we were only in our twenties, it was a wonderful feeling to know that we had done it. Like Closey and Fred I played in the '50s when we were runners-up a few times, but we had never won the Championship.

Of the five centuries I scored that season the one in the Sussex game was the most important as it decided the Championship. The main reason why it went so well for me with the bat was that all through the second half of the season I batted at five, which was to the credit of Ronnie Burnett. Ken Taylor was a very gifted, talented sportsman, but it hadn't gone too well for him as opener and Ronnie moved him down the order. I said I was playing well at number five and Ronnie agreed to move Ken down the order below me, which was the first time a captain had done that. The only other season I batted five for Yorkshire was in 1957 when I was third to Willie Watson and Frank Lowson in the batting averages. In 1960 I asked Vic Wilson if I could stay at five but he wanted me to do a lot of bowling. I said if I get out at five, I get a rest, if I bat at seven and bat until the end, I would go straight out in the field, but he didn't agree, so I was pushed down again.

From a team point of view our success in the '60s was down to the collective effort. I played through the '50s when Yorkshire weren't a happy team, which was one of the reasons why we didn't win the Championship at least twice when Surrey won it seven times. If results had been the most important thing, we would have won championships. Great credit for the change goes to Ronnie Burnett, who took over in 1959 and got a good team spirit together again. We became a side in the true meaning of the word as we went out on a Saturday night for a meal together and became a happy team. People who played against us said we used to argue amongst ourselves which we did, but it was over cricket points and if anyone from outside tried to criticise, we would close ranks. It was all constructive stuff as we all wanted to win – that was the great thing about it.

All the Championship wins for Yorkshire in the '60s were similar – the one thing we knew was that nobody was going to give us a chance – we had to earn it. There were no silly declarations like when Hampshire won in 1961 with 16 declaration matches – we had none that year but got within two points of them. Towards the end of that season we played at Warwickshire and bowled them out for 310, we scored 318–4 and declared to put them back in the game. When they eventually declared, they left us about 270 in two and a half hours and everybody was on the edge. I told Brian we were throwing wickets away, giving them bonus money and wins, which they didn't deserve. From then on we said if we didn't bowl them out the game was dead, as we knew we wouldn't get anything out of the game otherwise.

From a personal point of view I remember in particular when we beat Kent in 1964 at Dover. I scored 135 (out of 256) and nobody else in the match scored above 40, then I took 14 wickets the next day (for 101 runs). Then in 1966 they put a limitation on the first innings of 65 overs and that blew it for people like me batting in the middle order and bowling slow. I remember one match against Lancashire when they batted first, Statham and Higgs bowled for most of the day and then nearly all next morning. After about 50 overs Don Wilson and Fred were sent in to have a slog – it was a poor rule.

We had no contracts at all with Yorkshire and in 1968 I asked for a three-year contract. I was brought up to give my right arm to play for Yorkshire and agonised over whether or not to make the move away from the county, as it was a big decision. I had three offers in my back pocket though, one of them offering double what Yorkshire were paying me, so knew I was on good ground from that point of view, but was willing to sacrifice all that if they gave me a contract. When I went to see Mr Nash, the secretary, at Bradford he said, 'They won't offer you a contract, Raymond.' I said, 'If that's the case, then here's my letter.' Even then I didn't want to go. Then in no time at all Bill Bowes, the former Yorkshire bowler who was writing for the *Yorkshire Evening Post*, came to see me and said 'Are you leaving the county?' I asked who had said that and he told me that Mr Nash had rung Brian Sellers, whose words were 'I can **** off and so can everybody else who wants to go with me!' It never even went to committee and Sellers got pulled over the coals as Ronnie Burnett, who was on the committee, said if it had gone to the committee it would not have been allowed to happen. It was probably the best thing to happen to me in my career. I also wanted to have a go at captaining a side, felt I could do the job and Leicestershire could give me the opportunity. Northants had just appointed Roger Prideaux and so couldn't do anything until the year after, Notts had just appointed Gary Sobers and Lancashire, Jackie Bond or they would have given it to me. In all I had about six good offers with Notts, then Northants, financially the best. Leicester was possibly the least lucrative, so it wasn't the money.

What also annoyed me was that Closey felt Geoff Cope would be playing soon in place of me. That was Sellers's influence again, after I had just taken more wickets than anyone in the country in addition to scoring 1,000 runs and being near the top of the batting averages – it was ridiculous. What really annoyed me was when I was in Australia in 1970–1, they held an extraordinary general meeting at Leeds town hall, as Closey was leaving. Sellers stood up on the stage and said that I was allowed to leave as I had asked for more money than anyone else and was causing the trouble.

Money had never at any time been mentioned, although Closey, myself and Fred had many times discussed finances. Closey and Fred felt we should be paid more on individual contracts. I always said we should all be paid the same – when I came in I was not worth the same as Len Hutton, but over a ten year period it evened itself out. I thought it was disgusting for Sellers to stand on stage and say that, a complete lie. He was covering his own back again and it was well over a year before I found out.

It took us a little while to get going at Leicestershire, as I played all six Test matches for England in 1969 and the odd one-day internationals as well. Then in 1970 Graham McKenzie was picked for the Rest of the World side and I played in the Test matches against them. We steadily improved and did better in the one-day cricket, winning the Benson & Hedges at the first attempt in 1972, and finishing runners-up in the Sunday League. The B&H final was for me a very nervous occasion, but it wasn't so much playing Yorkshire I was nervous about, more that we had worked so terribly hard getting Leicester into a decent side. I felt that if we could win something then we would become stronger, whereas if we lost we would have had to start again. As it happened we became the best side in the Championship and it gave the young lads like Jeff Tolchard and Paul Haywood a lot of confidence. I finished with England in 1973 and in 1974 we had a full side at Leicestershire where I was ever-present.

1975 was again a wonderful summer. We were the first side to win the Benson & Hedges and the Championship in the same season. The B&H had given us a bit of confidence in 1972 and we were back winning the final in the early part of the 1975 season. Of the last six championship matches [all won], we played four of them away from home. The wickets were as hard as nails and didn't offer much turn, so it was a great advantage for us to play away and that was very satisfying. I remember John Steele saying to me, 'They were great days, walking on the field knowing that sides were frightened of us.'

The biggest problem at Leicester was when Tony Lock played they made wickets that used to turn 'square' – I remember I took 14 wickets in a game for Yorkshire in those days. They got reported so often that Trevor Bailey once brought up a deckchair on the pitch, as there was so much sand on the wicket! They were frightened after that to make a pitch turn, so we got the fastest wicket the groundsman could make and then took some grass off it to make it turn a bit, then you had the best of both worlds. If we could have got the wicket to turn a little more, we could have won the Championship four or five times on the trot, but they were just too good to finish on, and sides by then were a bit more wary of us. People sometimes said we made Leicester wickets to suit us but they were the best in the country, good three-day pitches – if anything they were a bit too good.

Mike Turner, the Leicestershire secretary, and I used to have a meeting in

April every year where I would outline my plans for the season – he ran all the sponsorship and it worked well. The only time we would argue was when he put his tents on the ground and affected my boundaries! We got over that by him telling me when he would have a big sponsor and the groundsman would put the wicket over the right side of the square.

The only injury problem I had was with my back, which started in the last match of the 1962 season when Vic Wilson was captain. I had never had a day off for anything and when I told Vic my back had gone, he thought I was taking the 'mick'. I left it until almost Christmas before seeing the specialist in case it settled down, he manipulated it and it was right as rain the next day. I wish he had done it earlier as it messed up my golf! I had it manipulated twice at Yorkshire and a couple of times at Leicester. When it came on I could do anything but bowl, as soon as I got into that position to bowl, it was like someone sticking in a knife. That was one reason why I didn't bowl so much latterly, we had plenty of bowlers there. I remember in May 1976 I had hardly bowled for two or three weeks, we went to Swansea on a slightly wet wicket and Barry Dudleston said, 'I hope you are going to bowl today,' and took 8–38 against Glamorgan. He said it was bloody marvellous how I could do that after not having bowled for a fortnight! I could close my eyes and bowl which you can't do as a youngster. It was second nature, though I have suffered for that since and five years ago a disc went.

It was a difficult decision for me to return to manage Yorkshire in 1979, although stopping playing wasn't really a problem, as I would have been 47 at the start of the following season. I could have played one-day cricket, but Mike Turner offered me another three-year contract which I thought was unrealistic. I would have stayed at Leicester if they had offered me a similar contract to that offered by Yorkshire.

I didn't play at all whilst managing Yorkshire for a couple of years, then half-way through the 1982 season they had a problem with Chris Old's drinking. The committee gave him three weeks to sort himself out, otherwise he would be relieved of the captaincy, so when he didn't the committee asked me to play again. I had been bowling in the nets with the boys and knew I could come back even though I hadn't done any training, so played in the second half of the year [first game being at Ilford 15 days after his 50th birthday].

In 1983 we went to Carnegie College in Leeds for pre-season training, where they did a number of tests, including a reaction test and there was only one other player with quicker reactions, which pleased me! We won the John Player League that season and I was delighted to finish top of the one-day cricket averages at the age of 51 with 36 wickets at 12 apiece. I remember sadness, though, from the 1983 season with Geoff Boycott playing mainly for himself. There were three matches in particular where he made big hundreds but took a long time over them, which in three-day cricket you could not do. One of them was at Notts where they just saved the follow-on with nine wickets down. If we had got the tenth wicket we might even have won the match. The same thing happened at Cheltenham against Gloucestershire when he batted on again for a third of the match and I had a real go at him. He was always very keen to explain that he hadn't had all the bowling etc. I actually checked with the scorer and he had had 53 per cent of the bowling, so he had no argument there, and had scored 140 out of 360-odd. Anybody who bats through the innings should always score over half the runs and another 60 would have made all the difference. We could have declared that night or put them in a follow-on position and that did annoy me. We sent some news out via the 12th man to say what we wanted and his message was 'I'm playing my own way'. You can't have that in a team and that's where it all blew up – it was sad, he had too much power. He probably had two or three thousand members who were Boycott fanatics which split the membership and committee down the middle. At the end of the day, it is a team game which unfortunately Geoff didn't always remember.

My departure after the 1983 season came about when Boycott's 'cronies' got into power on the committee and took control. I told Yorkshire that if they didn't fight dirt with dirt they would lose the meeting – they took control and I was sacked. By that time the BBC had already spoken to me and said there was a job with them so I wasn't worried. When Boycott won the day I knew there was no future for me. I had about ten marvellous years from 1984 with the BBC. We had a happy commentary box with Tony Lewis, Tom Graveney, Jack Bannister, Richie and Peter West when I started. Then when Boycott came on the scene again I remember one of them saying to the producer that wherever he had been involved there was trouble, and he was right.

When I was with the BBC and also writing for *The Daily Express*, Sir Lawrence Byford asked me if I would be interested in this England job (as manager and chairman of selectors, starting with the New Zealand Test series in 1994), as it was being rubber-stamped down the 'old boys network' again and M.J.K. Smith was going to take over. There were quite a few against two or three people still making all the decisions. I discussed it with my wife Shirley who said if I didn't go for it I would kick myself for not having tried it, so agreed subject to being compensated for loss of other earnings. I was on a salary of about £20,000 per year and came in when we were getting bowled out and losing matches too easily. To quote one of Brian Bolus's sayings, 'We have got to stop the bleeding!'

In England we couldn't continue playing on fast bowlers' wickets all the time, so I wanted a slighter, slower wicket which encouraged spin a bit later, and to get a balanced side in with two quickies, an all-rounder and two spinners. We did that, and I thought we were going in the right direction with a lot of runs coming from late order batsmen like Cork, Watkinson and Illingworth. The 1995 summer we played the West Indies was wonderful – the grounds were full and they were excellent Test matches. Then we went to South Africa (in the winter of 1995–6) where things went right until the last Test where we made an absolute mess of it. We won every one-day series when I was chairman and didn't lose a Test series until the second half of the 1996 summer against Pakistan when I was finished anyway and had more or less washed my hands of it by then [stood down as manager in March, although Illingworth remained as chairman of selectors, albeit by summer he was disillusioned by the TCCB and cricket and became more of a peripheral figure]. What we didn't do was win away from home, which was annoying as we were a better side than the results suggest. I had my own way at home but on tour someone else went as manager like M.J.K., which I thought was a mistake, but it was too late. I should have gone on tour as manager at that time to keep the system going – now there shouldn't be any excuse.

When I left school I worked with my father, who was a cabinet maker, for four years in the village before I went into the Forces. I then worked during the winter at Fulneck Golf Club for a year and found it interesting, before working for a golfing friend of ours called Fred Barlow of Barlow Mills from Queensbury, who wanted me to learn the trade. I also worked for a fellow in the village who had a chemical factory – they mixed all the dyes and chemicals for the mills, which I didn't enjoy as it was a messy job. Then in 1962 I was introduced to the fireworks and greeting cards business by Brian Bolus, who worked for a fellow called Eddie Joyce on a commission-only basis. The first year he guaranteed me a minimum sum as I was worried I might not meet his targets and just make what he guaranteed me. Then I doubled it the next two years as I worked very hard. I used to start in Scotland and he would ring me at the end of the first week and base his whole sales for the year on what my figures were for the first week. If I was up, he would order up, if I was down, he would order down. I did so well it affected the commission of the other lads as he paid them 12.5 per cent and knocked it down to 10 per cent plus a little bonus! He would show my figures to the other reps and say if I could do it, so could they. I worked for about 16 years through the '70s during the winter while I was England captain. When I was on tour others did it for me like Neil Hartley and I paid them commission, but they didn't earn as much as I did.

Now we spend the winter months on the outskirts of Torremolinos – we have had a property out there for 20 years, which I bought at the back end of the Leicester days. We have lived in Farsley, which is in the borough of Pudsey, for just over six years, but are now in what is termed LS28. When I was awarded an honorary degree at Leeds University, I said in my speech,

107

'LS28 doesn't sound like Pudsey!' We would still like to be on our own instead of being swallowed up by Leeds.

I was president of the local Farsley club for quite a few years and put in a lot of work up there, but found others were not prepared to do their bit which saddened me, plus the back problem restricted me. I remember when I played there in 1949, I got a £21 collection – what's that worth now? I think league cricket is sadly dying.

My hobbies have always been golf and bridge. I still play golf at the local club and also in Malaga when we are in Spain. My handicap is about 12 but I have been down to 8. The interest in bridge goes back to the '50s when we had two bridge schools and Willie Watson and Johnny Wardle were good players – on rainy days it was a godsend. When I went to Leicester we also had two full schools going on at one time. One or two played before I came like Micky Norman and Norman McVicker, but it was really my influence that others started. Then when I went to Pakistan with the England side, the Doc (Philip Bell), Malcolm Ashton, Peter Martin and Mike Atherton played a bit and we played for hours there. When I was officially fined [£2,000 by the TCCB following a breakdown in relations with Devon Malcolm, although it was subsequently overturned], I got a letter from the Doc to say that at least you could pay for it out of all your bridge winnings! I don't play much bridge now.

My hero in 1959, Tom Finney, was everything I think a sportsman should be. He played the game absolutely the right way and was a brilliant footballer. I played a lot of football when I was younger and he was the type of player I would have liked to have been. You never saw any dissent, he got on with the game and I thought he was the perfect footballer and more direct than Stanley Matthews. I have met him many times since and he is a very nice man, everything I thought he was, which has pleased me. My only regret is not playing professional football. I did have the opportunity but my dad put me off as he said I would get injuries and muck both careers up. I had a chance to go for trials to Huddersfield, Bradford City and Aston Villa when I was about 18. The Aston Villa man said I was the best two-footed player he had seen, which was rather nice. I loved the game and played a lot in the RAF, which was to a good quality as every station side had four or five pros, which I enjoyed and knew I could live with them and was up to their standard. We were paid more playing for Yorkshire than professional footballers in those days and it became near impossible to carry on when I started going on tours.

Memorable game

The most memorable game I played in was the last Test match in Sydney in 1970–1 when we won the Ashes. On the last morning, they only wanted about 80 with five wickets down and Greg Chappell still there. It was a very tense time and you thought after six months over there if it goes wrong, you left with just a share of the Ashes. Everything hung on that last morning and there was tremendous tension, a wonderful atmosphere and big crowds, who were booing you. I said to John Snow as we walked out, 'When they're booing Snowy, we're winning!' Richie Benaud wrote that it was one of the best Test matches ever seen, it had everything, good batting and bowling and the Lou Rowan incident [cautioning Snow for felling Terry Jenner with a bouncer] added to the excitement of the game.

The greatest achievement for me as England captain was winning that Ashes series. People don't realise how hard it is in Australia and we had a tough tour with seven Test matches, five in the last six weeks, which was a hell of a finish. We also lost Alan Ward, one of our main bowlers, early on, which was disappointing, but the others came through well. Frank Tyson wrote at the end of the tour that Lever and Shuttleworth, the other seam bowlers, would return home far better bowlers due to my careful advice and handling. Peter Lever will tell you he came back a yard quicker and a better bowler than when he went. Both the Sydney matches were super Tests on good wickets where you could finish the game naturally without declarations, which is what a Test match should be all about. It is a great place to play and outside Lord's, Sydney was my favourite ground.

12, 13, 14, 16, 17 February 1971. England won by 62 runs

Under the astute captaincy of Illingworth, England regained the Ashes on the fifth day of this six-day Test after the longest rubber in Test cricket.

England

J.H. Edrich c G. Chappell b Dell	30	c I. Chappell b O'Keefe 57
B.W. Luckhurst c Redpath b Walters	0	c Lillee b O'Keefe 59
K.W.R. Fletcher c Stackpole b O'Keefe	33	c Stackpole b Eastwood 20
J.H. Hampshire c Marsh b Lillee	10	c I. Chappell b O'Keefe 24
B.L. D'Oliveira b Dell	1	c I. Chappell b Lillee 47
R. Illingworth b Jenner	42	lbw b Lillee 29
A.P.E. Knott c Stackpole b O'Keefe	27	b Dell 15
J.A. Snow b Jenner	7	c Stackpole b Dell 20
P. Lever c Jenner b O'Keefe	4	c Redpath b Jenner 17
D.L. Underwood not out	8	c Marsh b Dell 0
R.G.D. Willis b Jenner	11	not out 2
B 4, l-b 4, w 1, n-b 2	11	B 3, l-b 3, n-b 6 12
	184	302

1/5 2/60 3/68 4/69 5/98 6/145
7/156 8/165 9/165

1/94 2/130 3/158 4/165 5/234
6/251 7/276 8/298 9/299

Australia

K.H. Eastwood c Knott b Lever	5	b Snow	0
K.R. Stackpole b Snow	6	b Illingworth	67
R.W. Marsh c Willis b Lever	4	b Underwood	16
I.M. Chappell b Willis	25	c Knott b Lever	6
I.R. Redpath c and b Underwood	59	c Ham'shire b Illingworth	14
K.D. Walters st Knott b Underwood	42	c D'Oliveira b Willis	1
G.S. Chappell b Willis	65	st Knott b Illingworth	30
K.J. O'Keefe c Knott b Illingworth	3	c sub b D'Oliveira	12
T.J. Jenner b Lever	30	c Fletcher b Underwood	4
D.K. Lillee c Knott b Willis	6	c Hampshire b D'Oliveira	0
A.R. Dell not out	3	not out	3
L-b 5, w 1, n-b 10	16	B 2, n-b 5	7
	264		160

1/11 2/13 3/32 4/66 5/147 6/162
7/178 8/235 9/239

1/0 2/22 3/71 4/82 5/96 6/131
7/142 8/154 9/154

Australia Bowling

	O	M	R	W	O	M	R	W
Lillee	13	5	32	1	14	0	43	2
Dell	16	8	32	2	26.7	3	65	3
Walters	4	0	10	1	5	0	18	0
G. Chappell	3	0	9	0				
Jenner	16	3	42	3	21	5	39	1
O'Keefe	24	8	48	3	26	8	96	3
Eastwood					5	0	21	1
Stackpole					3	1	8	0

England Bowling

	O	M	R	W	O	M	R	W
Snow	18	2	68	1	2	1	7	1
Lever	14.6	3	43	3	12	2	23	1
D'Oliveira	12	2	24	0	5	1	15	2
Willis	12	1	58	3	9	1	32	1
Underwood	16	3	39	2	13.6	5	28	2
Illingworth	11	3	16	1	20	7	39	3
Fletcher					1	0	9	0

Umpires: L.P. Rowan and T.F. Brooks

Proudest Moment

The proudest moment in cricket for me was when I was awarded my Yorkshire cap at Bradford in 1955, more so than my England cap. I had waited five years and still had to ask for it! When I came out of the Forces in 1953 I only just missed the 'double' playing behind seven England batsmen, then in 1954 Appleyard and Close came back so I didn't get much of a chance.

By 1955 two counties, Worcester and Warwickshire, were asking about me but it wasn't easy to move like it is now. In the end I said to Norman Yardley that if he felt I was good enough to play for Yorkshire, he should cap me. In those days, if you didn't play you didn't get paid anything, so if he didn't want me, it was unfair to keep me. I said he should let me go and I got capped the next home match! I had played for the second team in 1949, 1950 and 1951. I also played for the first team while I was in the Forces, every game in 1953, was with the team for every game in 1954 and they should have made their mind up by then, you shouldn't have to tell them!

A shrewd captain, accurate right-arm off-spinner and sound batsman, 'Illy' scored 24,134 runs (28.06) including 22 centuries, took 2,072 wickets (20.28) and 446 catches. In 61 Test matches, he scored 1,836 runs (23.24) including 2 centuries, took 122 wickets (31.20) and 45 catches.

–20–
Brian Taylor (b. 1932)

Essex

My most successful season was 1959, with over 1,800 runs, my highest score of 135 at Lord's against Middlesex and 80-odd victims. I feel I should have been picked to go to the West Indies at the end of the season but missed out and was very disappointed. Keith Andrew and Roy Swetman were selected and as wicket-keepers I had no argument about that, but I thought my batting would get me selected. As it was both of them failed and Jim Parks, who was coaching out there was called up and played in the last Test match. He was effectively a fielder who was a wicket-keeper and that situation stayed the same until Alan Knott's days.

I remember playing the Aussies in 1961 and looking back also remember them scoring 721 against Essex in 1948. During that game the Australian scorer drew charts where every shot was made and on two occasions the scoreboard was 30 runs ahead of the book and he reckons they actually scored nearer 780 odd that day! It was Don Bradman's last tour and he was run out by a yard and a half, but as there was a big crowd the umpire gave him not out and he went on to score 187! In 1961 at Southend we scored 470–6 when we had to come off for bad light with an hour to play. We managed to turn the tables on them though and went on to win by six wickets.

In 1962 I had 91 dismissals which was a record at the time, but didn't quite make my ambition of the wicket-keeper's 'double'. As a wicket-keeper/batsman, though, I have the all-time record of both victims and runs – there is no one with more. People like Jim Parks and Les Ames have far more runs than me but they haven't anywhere near the number of victims, just short of 1,300 and scored 20,000 runs. Had I known I was that close to 20,000 I might have played another season but I never played for statistics! I always thought that if I was playing well the bar takings would go down as people would come out to watch me! I liked to hit the ball and had a lot of fun. The spectators liked to watch me, and from that point of view I like to think I was reasonably successful.

When I was appointed captain of Essex in 1967, we played Worcestershire two or three games into the season at Worcester. Gordon Barker and I were having a drink with Don Kenyon, the Worcester skipper after the game and I asked for some time to talk with him about his views on captaincy and he declined! He said, 'You do the job as you think you should – be your own man and if you are still in the job in two years' time I will talk to you about captaincy.' It was the finest bit of advice I ever had. Later when Don became president of Stourbridge Cricket Society, I asked if he went to the meetings and was told because of his angina he rarely ventured out in the winter. When he heard I had been invited, though, sure enough he attended. One of the questions I had was about captaincy and I pointed to Don and told the story about my meeting with him. Don looked at me and was amazed I still remembered that discussion.

I had always been upset when we played Yorkshire and Surrey as we found it difficult to compete against them, so when I was appointed captain I was determined to overcome that. We had no money, but experience in Gordon Barker, Trevor Bailey and Michael Bear plus nine youngsters in the side – Fletcher, East, Hobbs, Boyce, Lever, Acfield etc. The committee offered to bring in a couple of players released from other counties but I said there was only one way we could go and that was up with what we had. I wanted to get those youngsters into our way of playing and thinking so that we could move forward. You had to be patient, though; I bullied the young players into believing in themselves. Tom Pearce, Doug Insole and Tiny Waterman, our treasurer played a tremendous part in the development of the club. David Bradford and John Welsh on the committee also worked really hard behind the scenes. With the introduction of the Sunday League people gave us no chance but we talked for hours about how we would go about this game as a lot of other counties weren't interested. We won seven of our first eight matches and that success started to gather momentum and rub off into the three-day games.

I remember my very last match, which was in 1973 at Chelmsford against Notts. On the second day we couldn't get Mike Smedley and Basharat Hassan out. John Lever asked for the ball with 40 minutes to go and from the top end he knocked those two over and took three wickets. It was the quickest he ever bowled for me and I told him if he bowled like that in every game he would make the England side, which of course he did. In every Test match he played he took five wickets, which is a tremendous achievement. We still play as an old boys team in testimonial games locally, which is a reflection of the team spirit we had in the '70s.

I was nominated by Essex to be a Test selector in 1972 and I'm still one of the few selectors who have won more games than lost – we won 11 and lost 7 over a period of four years. I played 301 consecutive games between 1961 and 1972. We just wanted to play, irrespective of how the team was doing, and I took a personal pride in keeping fit. You used your common sense about when to have a few beers and when not to. When I look back I find it difficult to believe I played in that many consecutive games.

When I retired from first-team cricket in 1973 I put myself up for election on the committee. I captained the Essex second team from 1975 to 1981 then Mike Denness took over. I went on tour in 1976–7 with the MCC 'A' team to Bangladesh once devolution had arrived. The team was captained by Ted Clark and made up of a number of club cricketers and some retired cricketers. It was an interesting tour but never again!

I started a business in sports goods in 1974 and finished up with a partnership in a retail shop in Romford, which unfortunately went in the recession of 1989–90.

I was coaching a little but came back full-time to the county in 1990 as youth development coach to work with Alan Lilley, who I had brought into the side earlier. We developed a schools programme with the Board money which has come into the game and I enjoyed the involvement until fully retiring in 1997. We held five-week courses during the winter in 180 primary schools introducing the game. The teachers were very enthusiastic about the project, as were the children.

So many aspects of cricket have changed since I played. Players don't seem to be so interested in talking to the senior pros as they used to. Peter Smith, the great leg-spinner, was the senior pro when I first went to Essex and I learnt from him. When we went away you never saw the captain or the amateurs who lived out. We went to dinner and Peter always sat at the head of the table and in seniority you went down the table. I always remember the first time I played at Cambridge we stayed at the University Arms Hotel. The residents dressed for dinner but we went in our lounge suits and ties, sat down and everyone looked at us!

Sledging is so different now – it used to be funny without the obscenities. You would make a remark if you beat the bat two or three times like, 'Would you like to put a bell on the ball?' I remember during a match against Northants when the wicket was taking spin, George Tribe and Jack Manning were making the ball 'talk'. Les Savill was battling away against them, playing and missing about four times an over, when Jock Livingston came across from first slip and said to Les, 'Try and keep your bat still and I will get George to hit it!' Those remarks became universal in the game and that clever humour is missing now.

Another change is how you could talk to the Press and make off-the-cuff remarks that wouldn't be repeated in the papers. The players can't be so liberal now with what they say as the Press today seem only capable of regurgitating quotes and don't always understand what they are watching. If you go back to journalists like Michael Carey, Crawford White, Michael Melford, Jim Swanton and Alex Bannister they would watch the game, write about it and make you feel if you hadn't been at the game that day you had missed something.

I signed as a professional footballer for Brentford in 1950 and spent three years there when Tommy Lawton was the player-manager. With the overlapping of the seasons, it was normal to see the football season out, but as cricket was my main sport I forewent football at the start and end to have a full season of cricket. I went to Deal for a couple of years, then Bexley in the Kent league for five or six seasons and, after 17 years as a pro, finished in 1967 with Dover in the Southern League. It was financially very profitable as you were paid per match. When I first started in the Football League I was paid eight pounds in the first team, seven pounds in the reserves, six pounds in the summer and a pound a point bonus. It was not until about 1960 that Jimmy Hill raised the minimum wage. In the non-League I was paid seven pounds per match and with two matches a week it was more profitable playing as a part-timer.

My favourite player was Willie Watson who combined both sports and was a double international at cricket and football. I had a problem batting to spin bowling at one time but not keeping wicket to spin. By the time I read the chinaman and googly I had lost the length of the ball whereas when you kept wicket it didn't matter. I spoke to Willie about this at Colchester once when we were playing Yorkshire. He said, 'Very simple – don't look at the ball, look for the length. Don't worry about whether it is a leg-spinner or a googly, just play the length of the ball.' From then on I came to read the ball and that simple bit of advice proved very effective.

Memorable Game

There were so many memorable games I played in. I do remember playing at Leyton in 1964 against Leicestershire when the game ebbed and flowed until the last afternoon by which time it was virtually dead. There was a little friction within the committee about the way the game was being played and Tom Pearce was irate. The members were shouting at Leicester's captain Maurice Hallam to declare and make a game of it – I had never heard that on an Essex ground before. It finished up that he did set a target for us and left us with 167 to score in 50 minutes plus the half-hour at the end of the game. I suggested to Gordon Barker – the acting captain – that we have a go for it. I offered to go in with Michael Bear, two left-handers to start, then Gordon at three, Fletch at four and Knighty at five. If four of us were out on the flat wicket the rest could bat it out as there wasn't much time to play with and he agreed.

Trevor Bailey, the usual captain, was injured and watching from the dressing-room. He wanted to bat it out but on this occasion we took over and told him the score! Michael Bear scored eight off the first over and I hit Jack van Geloven's first ball out of the ground for six! Don Watt came running over to Tom Pearce and explained what we were doing. Tom said, 'What are you standing here for, get back in the office and get some more balls to throw to them out there!' We put on 70 in the first seven overs before I was out and we won the game with three minutes to spare. Tom was happy as Larry!

12, 13, 14 August 1964. Essex won by six wickets

Responding to the challenge, Taylor and Bear began with a partnership of 74 in 26 minutes. Taylor thrilled the crowd with three sixes and seven fours in his 54 as Essex secured an unlikely victory in entertaining style.

Leicestershire

B.J. Booth c Hilton b Knight	45	c Knight b Hilton	0
H.D. Bird b Bailey	22	lbw b Edmeades	31
S. Greensword c Taylor b Bailey	0	b Knight	1
C.C. Inman lbw b Bailey	2	b Bailey	57
S. Jayasinghe b Phelan	61	c Fletcher b Edmeades	20
M.R. Hallam lbw b Knight	4	b Hilton	21
J. Birkenshaw c Taylor b Hilton	85	c Knight b Phelan	11
J. van Geloven b Bailey	0	not out	10
P.L. Pratt c Taylor b Hilton	21		
R. Julian c Taylor b Hilton	38		
C.T. Spencer not out	1		
B 4, l-b 4, n-b 9	17	B 1, l-b 6, n-b 5	12
	296	(7 wkts dec)	163

1/45 2/45 3/69 4/73 5/77
6/171 7/172 8/221 9/293

1/0 2/1 3/99 4/106
5/119 6/151 7/163

Essex

M.J. Bear lbw b Spencer	77	not out	64
G. Saville c Julian b Spencer	2		
B. Edmeades lbw b Greensword	66	not out	6
G.E. Barker c Julian b Spencer	69	c Julian b van Geloven	35
K. Fletcher b Spencer	32	c Julian b Pratt	1
B. Taylor c Spencer b Pratt	1	c Birkenshaw b Spencer	54
B.R. Knight c Booth b Spencer	6	c van Geloven b Spencer	1
T.E. Bailey not out	20		
J. Wilcox lbw b Spencer	11		
P.J. Phelan b van Geloven	6		
C. Hilton c Julian b van Geloven	0		
L-b 1, n-b 2	3	B 1, l-b 4, n-b 1	6
	293	(4 wkts)	167

1/9 2/126 3/175 4/249 5/250
6/250 7/256 8/280 9/289

1/74 2/139 3/140 4/154

Essex Bowling

	O	M	R	W	O	M	R	W
Knight	22	7	70	2	10	3	33	1
Hilton	22	2	80	3	10	4	40	2
Bailey	25	5	49	4	6	1	13	1
Edmeades	10	2	39	0	10	5	32	2
Phelan	12	6	41	1	11.2	2	33	1

Leicestershire Bowling

	O	M	R	W	O	M	R	W
Spencer	38	10	94	6	7.3	0	70	2
Pratt	26	6	79	1	3	1	18	1
van Geloven	36.1	15	53	2	10	0	73	1
Booth	8	0	36	0				
Greensword	15	6	28	1				

Umpires: A.E.D. Smith and F. Gardner

I also remember beating Surrey at Clacton when we scored 256–8 in the last innings. We were the only side to beat Surrey batting fourth in 1957. They only had Peter May out for England – the rest were playing. Doug Insole hit a century including an eight! He hit Tony Lock for three and ran for the fourth. The ball was thrown in wide of the wicket, Tony picked it up, had a shy, missed and the ball went for four overthrows!

Proudest Moment
The proudest moment for me was when I was awarded my Essex cap at Colchester in 1956. Doug Insole the captain presented it to me. I knew I

had scored over 1,000 runs that season and felt I was a bit overdue for it! I also remember with pride receiving my second XI cap and being the first professional to be appointed Essex captain.

A tremendously enthusiastic cricketer, as a middle-order left-hand bat and wicket-keeper 'Tonker' scored 19,094 runs (21.79), took 1 wicket for 30 runs and 1,294 dismissals (1081 ct, 213 st).

–21–

Derek Shackleton (b. 1924)

Hampshire and England

Since 1959, the highlight for me was of course helping Hampshire win the County Championship in 1961 for the first time ever. I also took 9–30, my best bowling figures, against Warwickshire in 1960 at the United Services ground at Portsmouth [12–85 in the match]. I will always remember that day, Friday, 13 May – certainly not an unlucky one for me! Warwickshire were 196–4 and with 50 minutes left to play had an outside chance of getting about 90 to win. Then Colin Ingleby-Mackenzie brought me back at the Southsea end and after Fred Gardner had hit my first delivery for four, I took the new ball. I captured the last six wickets in 26 deliveries without having a run scored off me [Leo Harrison caught four] and we won by 82 runs. One of the first people to congratulate me, on what a reporter described as 'the most lethal spell of bowling seen on the ground in 63 years', was Jack Newman, the famous old Hampshire bowler who was on holiday that summer from Cape Town. My performance won me a second Brylcreem Cup and a one hundred guinea cheque, as the season's best, and the club presented me with the ball, duly mounted and engraved, to add to my collection of souvenirs. Then in 1962 I took my highest number of wickets in a season, 172 at an average of 20.15. I also bowled more overs than ever before at the age of 37, a total of 1,717!

When I was selected to play again for England against the West Indies in 1963 after a break of 11 years, it was a surprise and a great thrill. I had wondered what I had to do to get back in the England side. Hampshire were a bit off the beaten track compared with Surrey etc. and the England selectors went through a phase of going for pace bowlers such as Tyson, Trueman, Statham.

I had a testimonial in 1967 (raising £5,000) and played for the county until 1969. I had five seasons for Dorset after I left Hampshire, which was harder work than playing three-day county cricket. Over two days, if batting first you had to push on and declare at around four o'clock, otherwise if you carried on the game would be 'snookered'. Being the professional there, they expected and got a lot out of me. It was funny if I wasn't bowling, but I loved every minute of it.

When I retired from Hampshire I also coached at Canford School, where I remained until 1979. I then became a first-class umpire for three seasons until 1981 and since then have been fully retired. I don't go to Southampton to watch Hampshire a lot nowadays, other than for the players' annual reunion. I keep up with cricket now through the papers. I still like gardening and doing a bit of decorating. My wife is keen on gardening as well and we lead a quiet life in Ferndown, nothing hectic.

Memorable Game

The most memorable match I played in was the second Test at Lord's in 1963 against the West Indies. It was the way everything went – either side could have won but as things turned out a draw was a good result. It was one of those games where the batsmen played and missed so many times to my bowling.

At the end of the match Colin Cowdrey, the skipper, had to come in with a broken wrist to save the game when I was run out. David Allen and I suggested that if either of us played and missed when Wes Hall was bowling the last over, we would go for a single because Deryck Murray was keeping wicket so far back. I played at the third ball, missed it and he caught the ball. I went for a run and Deryck threw the ball to Frank Worrell at short leg. Frank daren't throw at the wicket with me running because there was no-one backing up, otherwise it would have been four runs and we only wanted six at that time. He whipped the bails off and whilst I had the bat down as I was taught, I think I was out and never looked at the umpire. We were playing the West Indies at Southampton the match after and, travelling down by train, I bumped into George Duckworth, the West Indian scorer. He asked me, 'Do you reckon you were out?' I said I never looked but thought I was. With the scorers at square leg, George said, 'We didn't give you out,' but that's water under the bridge.

20, 21, 22, 24, 25 June 1963. Match drawn

This match is universally considered as one of the most exciting in Test history as it ebbed and flowed from start to finish. Shackleton was recalled to the England side after an absence of over 11 years and did not let the side down. Carrying his county form into the Test, 'Shack' took seven wickets, including the last three wickets in four balls to end the West Indies' first innings.

West Indies

C.C. Hunte c Close b Trueman	44	c Cowdrey b Shackleton	7
E.D. McMorris lbw b Trueman	16	c Cowdrey b Trueman	8
G.S. Sobers c Cowdrey b Allen	42	c Parks b Trueman	8
R.B. Kanhai c Edrich b Trueman	73	c Cowdrey b Shackleton	21
B.F. Butcher c Barrington b Trueman	14	lbw b Shackleton	133
J.S. Solomon lbw b Shackleton	56	c Stewart b Allen	5
F.M. Worrell b Trueman	0	c Stewart b Trueman	33
D.L. Murray c Cowdrey b Trueman	20	c Parks b Trueman	2
W.W. Hall not out	25	c Parks b Trueman	2
C.C. Griffith c Cowdrey b Shackleton	0	b Shackleton	1
L.R. Gibbs c Stewart b Shackleton	0	not out	1
B 10, l-b 1	11	B 5, l-b 2, n-b 1	8
	301		229

1/51 2/64 3/127 4/145 5/219
6/219 7/263 8/297 9/297

1/15 2/15 3/64 4/84 5/104
6/214 7/224 8/226 9/228

England

M.J. Stewart c Kanhai b Griffith	2	c Solomon b Hall	17
J.H. Edrich c Murray b Griffith	0	c Murray b Hall	8
E.R. Dexter lbw b Sobers	70	b Gibbs	2
K.F. Barrington c Sobers b Worrell	80	c Murray b Griffith	60
M.C. Cowdrey b Gibbs	4	not out	19
D.B. Close c Murray b Griffith	9	c Murray b Griffith	70
J.M. Parks b Worrell	35	lbw b Griffith	17
F.J. Titmus not out	52	c McMorris b Hall	11
F.S. Trueman b Hall	10	c Murray b Hall	0
D.A. Allen lbw b Griffith	2	not out	4
D. Shackleton b Griffith	8	run out	4
B 8, l-b 8, n-b 9	25	B 5, l-b 8, n-b 3	16
	297	(9 wkts)	228

1/2 2/20 3/102 4/115 5/151
6/206 7/235 8/271 9/274

1/15 2/27 3/31 4/130 5/158
6/203 7/203 8/219 9/228

England Bowling

	O	M	R	W	O	M	R	W
Trueman	44	16	100	6	26	9	52	5
Shackleton	50.2	22	93	3	34	14	72	4
Dexter	20	6	41	0				
Close	9	3	21	0				
Allen	10	3	35	1	21	7	50	1
Titmus					17	3	47	0

West Indies Bowling

	O	M	R	W	O	M	R	W
Hall	18	2	65	1	40	9	93	4
Griffith	26	6	91	5	30	7	59	3
Sobers	18	4	45	1	4	1	4	0
Gibbs	27	9	59	1	17	7	56	1
Worrell	13	6	12	2				

Umpires: J.S. Buller and W.E. Phillipson

Proudest Moment

My proudest moment in cricket was being selected for England at Trent Bridge in the third Test match against the West Indies in 1950. My particular memory from my England debut in that game is being top-scorer in the first innings with 42 [out of 223].

A model professional and tireless right-arm stock bowler of uncanny accuracy, 'Shack' scored 9,561 runs (14.69), took 2,857 wickets (18.65) and 223 catches. In 7 Test matches, he scored 113 runs (18.83), took 18 wickets (42.66) and 1 catch.

–22–

Derek (Dick) Richardson (b. 1934)

Worcestershire and England

During 1959 and 1960 Worcestershire were going through a period of transition under Don Kenyon, with Roly Jenkins having retired and George Dews about to. The great thing was that Jack Flavell and Len Coldwell were bowling well and Norman Gifford was also starting to assert himself. From being a reasonable side we became a very good one, which paved the way to winning the County Championship in 1964.

I always enjoyed fielding close to the wicket but in the '50s when I started there were a lot of 'elderly statesmen' in the side like George and Roly, who couldn't throw. I could run and throw so I was banished to the outfield for a couple of years 'chasing leather'. When they retired I came into the close catching area at slip or short leg, as I had good reflexes [which enabled Richardson to take 65 catches in 1961]. The ball seamed and turned a bit at Worcester and, with Jack and Len bowling well, supported by a good spin attack, you had a number of catches, much in the same way as Peter Walker had at Glamorgan at the same time.

My best bowling of 2–11 v Lancs in 1963 wasn't a prolonged spell! I bowled Harry Pilling and had Kevan Tebay caught by Graveney at slip. It was probably a last-ditch effort or because four of our bowlers had broken various parts of their anatomy! I would describe myself as a very average bowler but I do also remember trapping Bob Barber lbw at Worcester in George Dews's benefit match against Lancashire in 1960. Norman [Buddy] Oldfield, who used to open for Northants, was the umpire. He blinked a lot and I think I must have caught him on the blink as this one was missing leg-stick but I shouted anyway. I was very pleased about it but Bob wasn't. [Richardson actually finished top of the Worcester bowling averages in 1960 with 2–38 from 13 overs at an average of 19!]

I remember Tom Graveney playing so well in the second half of the 1964 season when we won the County Championship. He gave us enough runs and we were lucky to play on wickets where a result was possible. A lot of counties struggled to bowl a side out twice on good wickets, but because we were a good side with an all-round balanced attack, we didn't mind what sort of wickets we played on.

Joe Lister, the secretary, organised a world tour at the end of the season [February–April 1965 in seven countries covering 34,000 miles]. It was a memorable trip that started in Nairobi, then went to India, the Near and Far East, Hong Kong, Hawaii, ending in the USA, where it rained for four days in Hollywood, so we didn't play.

We were confident of doing well and finishing at least in the top three in 1965, although it was more of a struggle to retain the Championship. Half way through the season we were languishing in mid-table then had a marvellous run-in, winning 10 of the last 11 matches and we pipped Northants on the last half-hour of the final day. We received a nice telegram congratulating us from Keith Andrew the Northants skipper, which was a lovely gesture.

We then went on tour after the 1965 season [March 1966] to Jamaica for about a month, playing in Kingston, Montego Bay, and a lovely ground up in the hills in a beautiful wooded location, where there was a big aluminium factory. We had a great time and Gary Sobers was flown over to play for Jamaica in the match at Montego Bay. He of course scored a hundred and played very well indeed – he was the greatest all-rounder there has ever been.

My memories of the Gillette Cup and one-day cricket are very disappointing, especially the first year, when we lost to Sussex in the 1963 final by 14 runs in the dark. It was nearly nine o'clock and I remember going out to face John Snow in the dark from the Pavilion end and I couldn't see him! Then we lost to Warwickshire in the 1966 final. The one-day game suited my style, as I was never one for hanging around, so didn't have to change the way I played.

For many years I went abroad in the winter months after I saw a circular advertising for coaches in South America. I coached cricket from 1959 to 1963 in Brazil, Argentina and Chile, which were all part of the South American Cricket Association. I had a wonderful time and was looked after very well. When Argentina were admitted to the World Cup in 1982, six or seven of my boys came through to play for their country, which was very gratifying. I met them at Lord's and it was wonderful to see the boys that I coached at the age of ten playing there.

In 1966 a 65 over limit was introduced in the first innings of the first 12 matches played by each of the 17 counties on a home and away basis. So I had about eight or nine first innings matches where, batting at five behind Kenyon, Headley, Graveney and D'Oliveira, I came in for three or four overs or less and was slogging to score 20-odd runs. After a few years learning how to play the game, it was something I didn't enjoy in the early part of the season. It was designed to obviate the draw on the third day, but it was rescinded shortly after as it didn't work. The obvious thing was to make them four-day matches and let people bat properly. I am a great believer in a firm technique of one step forward or backward – the present-day players seem to 'scuttle' all over the place. I lost a lot of interest in the game and didn't feel that situation would produce good players and 1967 was my last season in first-class cricket.

After retiring from the county game I moved to London and played half a season for South Hampstead Cricket Club, scoring a couple of hundreds along the way. I still had a cottage in Worcestershire and wanted to visit at the weekends, so I agreed to play one game in three for the club. They were pushing for the League at the time and asked me to play more regularly, which I declined. I didn't think it fair on the players being dropped for me, there were no harsh words though – I still see the then captain. I enjoyed it at the time but they were more professional than the professionals!

After cricket I went into public relations with Standard Life from 1967 to about 1973 – they owned several motor groups and hire car companies. I then went into the advertising world, then had an industrial agency with a friend. I was doing a lot of print broking and finally bought into the baby market and bought a title, *You and Your Baby*, published it and sold all the advertising. I sold the business in about 1995 and now do a bit of consultancy work for a promotional company two or three days a week.

I still enjoy jazz music but more the big bands like Basie, Ellington, etc. – I don't follow the avant-garde jazz, I like the good solid swing. I still love golf and during my cricketing days was down to a handicap of four. Tom Graveney and I used to have some great games on the Sundays, especially when playing away matches we had the opportunity to play at the local 'track'. The other lads who were not golfers couldn't understand why we wanted to walk 36 holes on a Sunday when we could have put our feet up! I don't play very often now so am off a handicap of about 12.

Memorable Game

This would have to be my one and only Test match in 1957 against the West

Indies at Trent Bridge. I played well that year and had scored four hundreds in the previous two weeks. On that burst of form I was worth a look. Tom Dollery, who was one of the selectors, saw me score a career-best 169 against Derbyshire at Dudley in about three hours and I played pretty well. I was sharing a room with Roy Booth at the Grand Hotel in Eastbourne on the Sunday when I heard the news I had been selected, and we had a few drinks to celebrate.

I was of course disappointed not to get another chance but there was no MCC tour that winter which might have given me the opportunity to establish myself. In the Test itself Trevor Bailey broke down and we were left with three and a half to four bowlers. I don't think that helped either as after that Test the selectors would never go in with less than five bowlers, which is fair enough. Then Kenny Barrington came into the England side and it was difficult for me to get back in.

4, 5, 6, 8, 9 July 1957. Match drawn

A Test where batsmen dominated in perfect conditions and on a firm wicket. Brilliant innings from Graveney, Worrell and O.G. Smith entertained the crowd of over 60,000. Richardson showed promise with a confident knock, sharing a stand of 63 with Cowdrey.

England

P.E. Richardson c Walcott b Atkinson	126	c Kanhai b Gilchrist	11
D.V. Smith c Kanhai b Worrell	1	not out	16
T.W. Graveney b Smith	258	not out	28
P.B.H. May lbw b Smith	104		
M.C. Cowdrey run out	55		
D.W. Richardson b Sobers	33		
T.G. Evans not out	26		
T.E. Bailey not out	3		
J.C. Laker did not bat			
F.S. Trueman did not bat			
J.B. Statham did not bat			
B 1, l-b 10, w 1, n-b 1	13	B 7, l-b 2	9
	(6 wkts dec) 619		(1 wkt) 64
1/14 2/280 3/487 4/510 5/573 6/609		1/13	

West Indies

F.M. Worrell not out	191	b Statham	16
G. Sobers b Laker	47	lbw b Trueman	9
C.L. Walcott c and b Laker	17	c Evans b Laker	7
R.B. Kanhai c Evans b Bailey	42	c Evans b Trueman	28
E.D. Weekes b Trueman	33	b Statham	3

O.G. Smith c Evans b Trueman	2	b Trueman	168
D. Atkinson c Evans b Trueman	4	c Evans b Statham	46
J.D. Goddard c May b Trueman	0	c Evans b Statham	61
R. Gilchrist c D. Richardson b Laker	1	b Statham	0
A.L. Valentine b Trueman	1	not out	2
S. Ramadhin b Statham	19	b Trueman	15
B 5, l-b 10	15	B 2, l-b 10	12
	372		367

1/87 2/120 3/229 4/295 5/297
6/305 7/305 8/314 9/317

1/22 2/30 3/39 4/56 5/89
6/194 7/348 8/352 9/365

West Indies Bowling

	O	M	R	W	O	M	R	W
Worrell	21	4	79	1	7	1	27	0
Gilchrist	29	3	118	0	7	0	21	1
Atkinson	40	7	99	1	1	0	1	0
Ramadhin	38	5	95	0				
Valentine	23	4	68	0				
Sobers	21	6	60	1				
Goddard	15	5	26	0	1	0	2	0
Smith	25	5	61	2				
Walcott					1	0	4	0

England Bowling

	O	M	R	W	O	M	R	W
Statham	28.4	9	78	1	41.2	12	118	5
Trueman	20	8	63	5	35	5	80	4
Laker	62	27	101	3	43	14	98	1
Bailey	28	9	77	1	12	3	22	0
Smith	12	1	38	0	15	5	23	0
Graveney					5	2	14	0

Umpires: F.S. Lee and J.S. Butler

Two other memorable games were firstly winning the Championship in 1965 at Hove when we were in trouble and John Snow was bowling fast. We were 4 down chasing 132 when Roy Booth and I added 51 for the sixth wicket. I scored an undefeated 31 on a difficult wicket and with Douggie Slade hit the winning runs well into the last half hour.

Secondly, scoring my first hundred was quite memorable. We were playing Gloucestershire in August 1955 and at tea I was in my nineties. When I was on 99 the late Frank McHugh, who was bowling pretty fast, suddenly let one go on a beautiful wicket and hit me straight on the end of the thumb. The masseur came out and said I had broken a bone, but I managed to score the necessary one run, although I couldn't hold the bat. I ended on 126, but was ever grateful to the masseur for not dragging me off, as I might never have scored a hundred!

Proudest Moment

My proudest moment in cricket was when I walked out with the three lions on my sweater and England cap. That was very important to me and it saddens me that so much sport is geared to money nowadays. I was proud to have played once but would love to have fulfilled my ambition and gone on an MCC official tour, although the wonderful tours with Worcestershire go some way though towards compensating for that.

An attractive left-hand, middle-order batsman and fine close fielder, 'Dick' scored 16,303 runs (27.40) including 16 centuries and 419 catches. In his one Test match he scored 33 runs and held 1 catch.

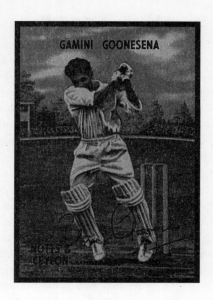

GAMINI GOONESENA

–23–

Gamini Goonesena (b. 1931)

Ceylon, Notts, Cambridge University, and New South Wales

My last season playing for Nottinghamshire was in 1958, although I played half a season for the county in 1964. I joined the Ceylon diplomatic service working in London for the first couple of years, so I played for Hampstead Cricket Club. Then I was transferred to Canberra and left England for Australia in 1960.

I played seven matches for New South Wales between 1961–4. I was with the Ceylon diplomatic service working in Canberra and drove down in time for the final nets on Thursday afternoon with the match starting on Friday. They were a very powerful side at that stage and had half a dozen regular Test players in the team. So every time Australia had a Test they would lose these players, including Richie Benaud and they invited me to play in the State games. Despite the six being out, in 1960–1 we retained the Shield under Ian Craig in the absence of Richie. We had to beat Western Australia outright in the final match to win the Shield and did so at about four o'clock on the last day. We had fellows like Graham Thomas, Brian Booth, Gordon Rorke, Frank Misson and Billy Watson, so had a cracking side despite losing the big six. It was a very happy period for me and I still consider the Sheffield Shield the most competitive tournament I ever played in, as everyone is trying for the 'baggy green' [Australian cap]. When I

129

played for Notts, Bruce Dooland and I used to bowl in tandem, two leg-spinners and when I went to NSW I bowled with Peter Philpott, another 'leggie'. So I am thrilled to see Stuart MacGill and Shane Warne playing together for the present Australian side – it takes me back to my days.

I was then seconded to the Tea Board in Sydney and started playing Grade cricket for Waverley. Jack Fingleton, who I had known in Canberra, introduced me to the club. He was a correspondent and a political writer and Waverley was his old club. I captained the first Grade side and was also president for a couple of years. I am an honorary life member of the club which is now known as Eastern Suburbs District Cricket Club.

In 1964 I was transferred from Sydney to London with the Ceylon Tea Board so I took four months leave. I spent a month in Ceylon, reaching England in early July and played for Notts for the rest of the season. After playing four matches for the county the secretary came into the dressing-room and handed me an envelope with a cheque inside. I told the secretary I was an amateur and he informed me there weren't any amateurs any more and that I was a cricketer! It was quite a pleasant surprise to be doing something I very much enjoyed and find out that someone was paying me for it! I remember the last game I played was against Worcester when we scored 305. I scored 70 but dropped Tom Graveney caught and bowled and he went on to score 164. The match ended in a draw but I think if I had got Graveney's wicket we would have won the match.

In 1964–5 I went on an International Cavaliers tour to the West Indies and in early 1968 with an International XI to Ceylon. We went through Sierra Leone, Uganda and Kenya in Africa, then on to Pakistan and India. We beat Pakistan in Karachi with their full side and also beat India in Madras then drew against them in Bombay. It was a very happy tour as we had a good side with Micky Stewart as captain and Tony Greig, Harold Rhodes, Billy Ibadulla, Roger Tolchard and Jackie Birkenshaw in the team. I was fortunate enough to pick up ten wickets in the Test match versus Pakistan. My final first-class game was in 1968 against Oxford University for Free Foresters at Oxford when I took 10–87. It was a very enjoyable time and the Free Foresters had a pretty good side. I always enjoyed playing the game whether it was in the 'bush' in Australia or in the city. Cricket is a great game and I am disappointed the way it has gone nowadays with players accepting bribes etc. When we were at Cambridge we had to pay for our own lunch and drinks and thought nothing of it.

In 1990 I was invited by the Board to manage a Sri Lankan side to India and we had a very pleasant tour. We lost the Test match but won a few one-day games, which is what we are better at.

I worked with the Tea Board for 11 years, mainly abroad until the late '60s, early '70s. Then we decided to emigrate to Australia as my children and wife are Australian and we liked the lifestyle there – casual but competitive. I got a job with Unilever and worked for them for a few years, then joined another company in fats and oils for about 12 years. Then I returned to Sri Lanka for another company and from 1985 have lived in blissful retirement in Sri Lanka. We have been married for 26 years and have two daughters who now live in Australia, one aged 22 the other 24. I returned to Australia in 1997 to attend the graduation ceremonies of my daughters.

My hobby was motoring. I was keen on vintage cars and had a 1935 Alvis, a beautiful three carburettor car. I bought it in 1956 when I was at Cambridge – it was still doing 100 mph easily but unfortunately I had to sell it in England as Alvis didn't have an agent in Australia.

Peter May was my favourite sportsman, not merely because he was a top world-class batsman, but he was also an absolute gentleman who was a true sportsman. That I value very highly in any sport and I liked him for those qualities and played with and against him. Another person I rate equally highly is Lord Cowdrey, a fine person who I shared rooms with on two tours of the West Indies.

Memorable Game

The Varsity match at Lord's in 1957 was the most memorable game I played in. It was pretty tense in that on the first day we bowled Oxford out for 92 and we scored 108–5. By the end of the first day it was well balanced, but as it had been pretty warm, the pitch had dried out. The following day seemed so much easier and I was fortunate in that if I tried to drive the ball it hit the bat beautifully. It was one of those days which I think you only get once in a lifetime. Ossie Wheatley bowled extremely well and got a lot of wickets in the first innings. Then in the second innings Colin Smith, now Sir Colin Smith the architect, bowled superbly. We had had three dreary drawn Varsity games before and we were very happy to win by a wide margin. I remember ringing my bank manager on the afternoon of the third day to tell him there was a possibility that we were going to win. I had to ask him for an overdraft as I knew I would have to buy the champagne! 'Buy as much as you want,' he said, 'and I will honour your cheque.'

6, 8, 9 July 1957. Cambridge won by an innings and 186 runs

A number of records were broken in this resounding victory. Goonesena's score was the highest ever individual innings for Cambridge in the Varsity match. He added 289 for the 7th wicket with Geoff Cook, a record for either side in this fixture, and the winning margin was the biggest since the series began in 1827.

Oxford University

I.M. Gibson c Barber b Wheatley	8	run out	63
J.A.D. Hobbs lbw b Wheatley	0	b Smith	19

A.C. Walton run out	4	st Swift b Goonesena	7
C.D. Melville b Pieris	9	lbw b Smith	6
M.A. Eager c Dexter b Wheatley	0	lbw b Smith	2
R.G. Woodcock c Swift b Wheatley	11	retired hurt	5
R.L. Jowett c Swift b Pieris	0	lbw b Goonesena	0
M.D. Scott c Swift b Smith	0	b Goonesena	22
R. Bowman b Goonesena	17	c Swift b Goonesena	0
R.W. Wilson not out	17	b Smith	6
J.A. Bailey b Wheatley	21	not out	4
B 3, l-b 1, n-b 1	5	B 8, l-b 3, n-b 1	12
	92		146

1/0 2/12 3/16 4/16 5/33 6/33 7/36
8/44 9/60

1/56 2/82 3/89 4/93 5/104
6/123 7/123 8/130 9/146

Cambridge University

R.W. Barber lbw b Woodcock	36
I.M. McLachlan b Bowman	11
D.J. Green c Gibson b Bowman	20
E.R. Dexter b Gibson	7
R.M. James lbw b Gibson	15
G. Goonesena c Jowett b Woodcock	211
C.S. Smith lbw b Gibson	8
G.W. Cook not out	111
P.I. Pieris did not bat	
B.T. Swift did not bat	
O.S. Wheatley did not bat	
L-b 3, w 1, n-b 1	5
(7 wkts dec)	424

1/20 2/67 3/67 4/80 5/97 6/135 7/424

Cambridge Bowling

	O	M	R	W	O	M	R	W
Smith	12	3	26	1	30	13	42	4
Wheatley	15	8	15	5	13	4	17	0
Pieris	14	4	31	2	7	4	16	0
Dexter	1	0	3	0				
Goonesena	5	2	12	1	17.2	6	40	4
Barber					4	0	19	0

Oxford Bowling

	O	M	R	W
Bailey	36	5	146	0
Bowman	39	10	101	2
Melville	4	0	12	0

Woodcock	13.5	2	40	2
Gibson	17	4	48	3
Wilson	22	11	51	0
Jowett	6	0	21	0

Umpires: H.G. Baldwin and T.W. Spencer

Another memorable match for me was in 1956 when I toured the West Indies with Jim Swanton's side under the captaincy of Colin Cowdrey. When we played a West Indies XI at Port of Spain Sonny Ramadhin and I crossed paths. I happened to 'pick' his leg-break and once this happened he was easy to play. This is confirmed in Clyde Walcott's book *Island Cricketers* where he writes about the West Indies' 1957 tour of England.

> Our visit to Fenners, Cambridge University's lovely ground, did not produce the run-riot of 1950, though the wicket was still good for plenty. I noticed that Gamini Goonesena, the university captain, could 'pick' Sonny Ramadhin's leg-break every time – and he was the only opposition batsman I saw on the whole tour who could.

Proudest Moment

The proudest moment for me was when I was invited to captain Ceylon in an unofficial Test against Polly Umrigar's Indian side in 1956, which was a great privilege. They brought me down from Cambridge and fortunately it was during the vacation so I could get away for three or four weeks. I was also proud that we drew the game – even though India had their full side out. [Goonesena scored 48 runs and took 7–79.]

A middle-order right-hand batsman and leg-break bowler, 'Gami' scored 5,751 runs (21.53), took 674 wickets (24.37) and 108 catches.

–24–
Mike (M.J.K.) Smith (b. 1933)

Leicestershire, Oxford University, Warwickshire and England

I do remember from 1959, the statistic of scoring a record 1,209 runs in July, as I hit 500 runs in a week, firstly playing in the Gents v Players game, which in those days was considered a tour trial, then Worcester at Edgbaston, when I scored 200 not out. I also remember scoring my 3,000th run at Scarborough in the festival. I previously scored 2,000 runs in 1957 and 1958, had a good spell and things went for me. It was a good summer in 1959 and I played over 70 innings, but it was physically easier in those days of three-day games and no one-day cricket.

After having played for England against New Zealand in 1958, albeit not very successfully, I also played in the last two Tests against India in 1959. I scored my maiden Test hundred [in the first innings of the fourth Test at Old Trafford] and should have also scored a century in the last Test at the Oval, ending up with 98. It was a very interesting season from an England selection point of view, in that the previous winter the side had gone to Australia under Peter May and had been comfortably beaten. It was the end of a very successful side as Frank Tyson, Trevor Bailey, Willie Watson and Jim Laker never played again for England. In addition Peter Richardson was made to qualify as he changed from Worcestershire to Kent and Tony Lock went off the scene for a while with the 'throwing' business.

So the England side was comprehensively changed and Barrington, Pullar, Dexter, Allen and myself started to come through and went on to tour the West Indies in 1959–60.

The tour was a very interesting series as the West Indies had a change around as well. The previous winter they had gone to India when Frank Worrell, who was to be skipper, dropped out and Gerry Alexander took over. They replaced Frank, a batsman, with bowler Wes Hall, and he and Gilchrist terrorised the Indians, bowling beamers, bouncers and in general very fast. Roy Gilchrist was actually sent home and didn't play again for them. Sonny Ramadhin was coming towards the end of his career but Lance Gibbs was coming through. It was some time before they came round to the all-pace attack and in any case at that time they didn't have the squad of outstanding fast bowlers to play in that way. We went into most matches with four bowlers and Kenny Barrington and Ted Dexter, who weren't major Test match bowlers. Ken bowled a lot of overs quite cheaply and Ted took some wickets. In the first Test at Barbados we batted first and scored 482, Ted Dexter scoring 136 not out. We got Easton McMorris, making his debut, out for a duck when David Allen, who was fielding at mid-on threw him out back-handed. We went through two five-hour days without getting a wicket with Sobers and Worrell batting. Gary scored 226 and Frank, who hadn't played Test cricket for some time, was totally shattered on 197 not out. He couldn't get it off the square and we couldn't get it past the bat and in the end Gerry Alexander declared.

In the second Test at Trinidad when we scored 382, I scored 108. They were six-day Tests in those days and their supporters came down on Saturday, the third day, to see the West Indies smash us about. Fred Trueman and Brian Statham bowled them out for 112 and the day finished with a riot! They were so fed up, with a lot of betting and boozing, that they came over the fence when Trinidadian Charran Singh was run out. Trinidad had not had a major Test hero since Sonny Ramadhin and Sonny had spent most of his time away. It was Singh's first Test match after he took wickets in the island match against us. Rohan Kanhai got a century in their second innings before I caught him out at mid-wicket off a full toss from the bowling of Ted Dexter. There was quite a lot of short stuff from Wes Hall and Chester Watson but Colin Cowdrey, Geoff Pullar and Ken Barrington handled it well. I batted at five and remember taking a first ball off Wes at Jamaica in the third Test, then seeing David Allen and Brian Statham blocking it out for a long time to save the game. The fourth Test was Charlie Griffith's debut and the century Jim Parks scored in the last Test with me was the real start of his Test career. I remember getting out to Conrad Hunte, who was not a regular bowler, for 96 after the record partnership of 197 [for the seventh wicket] with Jim.

My highest first-class innings was on Ron Roberts's Cavaliers tour in

1960–1 when I scored 204 against Natal at Durban on a flat wicket. Richie Benaud skippered a side including Norman O'Neill, Bobby Simpson, Ken Barrington and Alan Moss.

I also scored my highest Test innings [121 in the third Test] at Cape Town in a high scoring draw in 1964. It was a very good tour that started in Rhodesia and we went through unbeaten despite being second favourites and won the series 1–0. We managed to get Graeme Pollock on one or two turning wickets early on and dominated him until the last Test match when he scored 214 for once out.

From an England captain's point of view the highlight for me was always to skipper a winning side. The stiffest opposition when I was captain were the two away trips, South Africa in 1963–4 and Australia in 1965–6. We won in South Africa and had every opportunity in Australia, which would have been the highlight for me if we had won from a position of one up and two to go. We played very poorly though to lose the fourth Test match in Adelaide. I hadn't been getting enough runs and was dropped after the first Test the following season against West Indies.

When I look back to the advent of the one-day game in the '60s, I do remember Sussex murdered us in the second Gillette Cup final in 1964 when we batted first. What is interesting though when you look back is that this year [1997] for the 11th time out of 12, the side batting second has won the final. It is accepted that this final has got to be brought forward as there is an unacceptably high percentage of finals that have gone with the toss.

My time with Warwickshire was characterised by playing on ultra-flat wickets which became a bit boring in three-day cricket, as you could come along on the third day and see a declaration game. It was not good for the game and hard work for bowlers. I thoroughly enjoyed playing on wet wickets and in those days given the choice I used to hope it rained so we could play on a wet wicket. It was more interesting although I wouldn't advocate its return.

I played for Warwickshire the season I came back from Australia in 1966, then missed the next two [1967–8]. I returned under Alan Smith's captaincy and played in the Championship-winning team in 1972 which is always the highlight for a player. We had come second in the past and in 1971 ended on equal points with Surrey, but on a countback on outright victories they won. I was pleased at getting a recall for England in 1972, I was in my late thirties, I had scored a few runs that season and there was speculation in the press. I carried on playing for Warwickshire until 1975 when I retired.

When I was captain of the club I was also on the committee at Warwickshire so have been a member since then. I was originally cricket secretary when I played as an amateur but effectively I was a professional. When it all went 'open' I toured three winters on the trot. I have been involved with the club on the administration and management side from that time on. I became chairman of the club five years ago which I hadn't anticipated doing. It is a job with as much involvement as you want, and being retired from business, I can therefore put in a lot of time to the club. There are not many days of first-class cricket that I don't appear at.

Brian Lara was the catalyst for our recent successes. Although we won the NatWest trophy under Andy Lloyd, when Lara and Bob Woolmer came and Dermot Reeve was made captain it all came together. We were very fortunate because he wasn't actually our first choice of overseas player – that was Probahar who dropped out through injury. The interest was tremendous especially after he scored the 300-plus against England. He exceeded all our expectations and raised everybody's ambitions.

I don't play any sports now, but did play rugby, which was my major sport in addition to cricket. It's impossible to combine sports nowadays to any level. I finished up in business with a squash club so I also played a bit of squash. We had a country club for about 14 years near Warwick – we bought a house in the country and turned it into a small hotel with squash, snooker and other leisure facilities. We sold it ten years ago. Since then I have been free to manage two England tours and have refereed in South Africa and Australia.

My hero was not Jack Hobbs as stated on the 1959 card, though I did meet him once. John Arlott took me to the Masters Club in the '60s, which was lunch at the Oval with Jack Hobbs. One of the regrets in my life was not seeing Don Bradman bat, although I did meet him. I am also sad I never saw Wally Hammond bat, nor Everton Weekes, although I played against him. When we went to the West Indies in 1959, a number of our players who had played against him in the Lancashire league said what a great player he was. He captained Barbados in our first game, we lost and never got him in! I played against Frank Worrell and also Clyde Walcott, who the West Indies fetched out of semi-retirement for two Tests.

Memorable Game

For me personally, this was in 1959 at Stroud for Warwickshire against Gloucestershire, who I always enjoyed playing against. It was the only time I ever played there and it is now a housing estate. We avoided the follow-on with the last two at the wicket, Ossie Wheatley and Roland Thompson. Basil Bridge, the off-spinner bowled them out in their second innings with eight wickets and then I scored a big hundred and we came back from the dead to win a tremendous game of cricket.

30 May, 1, 2 June 1959. Warwickshire won by four wickets
Smith won the game virtually single-handed as Warwickshire spectacularly came from behind. He was particularly strong on the on-side to the spinners as

he powerfully struck five sixes and 28 fours in four hours in a brilliant undefeated innings.

Gloucestershire

D.M. Young b Thompson	13	c Cartwright b Bridge	17
C.A. Milton lbw b Thompson	2	b Bridge	27
R.B. Nicholls c Thompson b Wheatley	35	c Smith b Bridge	3
T.W. Graveney b Cartwright	53	absent hurt	
D.G. Hawkins c Fox b Cartwright	13	c Thompson b Ibadulla	52
J.B. Mortimore c Fox b Ibadulla	28	c Cartwright b Bridge	13
D.A. Allen c Fox b Thompson	39	c Ibadulla b Bridge	21
A.S. Brown b Thompson	28	b Bridge	0
D.R. Smith c Fox b Thompson	29	c Wolton b Bridge	12
B.J. Meyer c Cartwright b Thompson	0	not out	6
C. Cook not out	4	b Bridge	14
B 9, l-b 2, n-b 2	13	B 1, l-b 9	10
	257		175

1/12 2/17 3/83 4/116 5/123 6/159
7/210 8/240 9/240

1/25 2/37 3/65 4/95 5/123
6/123 7/137 8/161 9/175

Warwickshire

N.F. Horner c Nicholls b Brown	1	b Mortimore	20
W.J. Stewart c Brown b Cook	43	b Smith	30
T.W. Cartwright b Smith	3	lbw b Cook	40
M.J.K. Smith c Milton b Smith	3	not out	182
K. Ibadulla c Meyer b Cook	38	c and b Mortimore	2
A.V. Wolton c Brown b Cook	4	c Milton b Mortimore	4
A. Townsend b Cook	0	c Milton b Mortimore	24
W.B. Bridge lbw b Mortimore	3	not out	3
J.G. Fox c Brown b Mortimore	6		
R.G. Thompson c Graveney b Cook	4		
O.S. Wheatley not out	4		
B 6	6	B 10, l-b 1, w 2	13
	115	(6 wkts)	318

1/3 2/22 3/26 4/80 5/96 6/96
7/100 8/100 9/107

1/43 2/66 3/131
4/144 5/278 6/288

Warwickshire Bowling

	O	M	R	W	O	M	R	W
Wheatley	34	7	75	1	10	2	17	0
Thompson	29.4	7	74	6	12	3	15	0
Townsend	9	2	19	0				
Cartwright	23	6	61	2	1	0	6	0

Ibadulla	10	4	15	1	20	7	61	1
Bridge					30	9	66	8

Gloucestershire Bowling

Smith	23	8	44	2	25	9	61	1
Brown	15	5	36	1	15	2	46	0
Cook	17.3	13	13	5	31	11	89	1
Mortimore	10	5	16	2	29	12	64	4
Allen					13	4	45	0

Umpires: J.B. Bowes and T.W. Spencer

Proudest Moment

I have always enjoyed playing at Lord's, which not all players do, and leading the England side there is probably my proudest moment in cricket.

A prolific run-scorer and brilliant short-leg field, 'M.J.K.' scored 39,832 runs (41.84) including 69 centuries and 593 catches. In 50 Test matches he scored 2,278 runs (31.63) including 3 centuries, took 1 wicket for 128 and 53 catches.

–25–

Keith Andrew (b. 1929)

Northants and England

When I was selected for the MCC tour of the West Indies in 1959–60, it was as first wicket-keeper. I had been in great form during the 1959 season and was beginning to keep wicket a lot better. However I was very ill on the boat and spent most of the time on board in bed. I was also in hospital in Barbados for some time. They wouldn't let the players see me as I had a temperature of over 103 and in a way it was incredible that I stayed, as I was never really fit. I actually played in a match in Port-of-Spain when someone nicked one, I lost the ball and it went for four – I never even saw it. I played in four first-class matches but lost two stone on the tour. Towards the end of the tour, Walter Robins, the manager brought Jim Parks in for the last Test, as Roy Swetman was labelled as not being able to do the job. Roy was a very good keeper but stood up to the wicket a few times and got a few thick edges which no-one would have caught. They hit him on the arms – I remember watching him. I was not unhappy with Jim playing as I was still far from 100 per cent and looking forward to going home. In fact I lent Jim my Gray Nicolls bat, he scored a century with it and never looked back! The Test match in Port-of-Spain had the bottle-throwing incident when the Chinese umpire Lee Kow rightly gave Charran Singh run-out. Brian Statham and a few of us went up

140

to the English pub in the afternoon as the riot stopped the game.

I played in the first Test match for England against West Indies at Old Trafford in 1963 but didn't do very well. I missed a catch I would have caught on a Sunday standing on my head. I was wrong-footed and didn't get a hand on a nick from Conrad Hunte off Brian Statham. I nearly backed out of the match with a hamstring problem and still think about whether I did the right thing. Only the year before I made a record seven dismissals in an innings against Lancashire on the same ground. I do remember going in as night watchman and batted for about an hour against Hall and Griffith with Micky Stewart, which I felt was quite an achievement. Then Gary Sobers came on to bowl spinners and 'did' me with an edge that went straight up in the air. That was the end of my Test career but it was something that I never expected and was a wonderful thing for me.

When I took those seven dismissals in 1962 against Lancashire, I received a telegram from Fred (W.F.F.) Price, who was the only other player at that time to catch seven dismissals in a first-class match for Middlesex. He subsequently became a first-class umpire. That year I set a record for Northamptonshire of 84 catches and 6 stumpings.

I used to prefer unpredictable wickets as they presented more of a challenge to me. I was actually tiring of wicket-keeping towards the end of my career, but the offer of captaining Northants in 1962 was welcome and made the last five years of my career very enjoyable. Captaincy changed my whole view of life and was the best thing to happen in terms of my own personal development and the confidence it gave me. Underneath my exterior there has always been a desire to win and it was such a great feeling to give me the knowledge and stature to progress from there in later life.

I always fancied myself as a bowler and against Yorkshire at Sheffield in 1962, as captain I decided to have a bowl when to all intents and purposes the game was over. I always say that I took a Test cricketer's wicket, Don Wilson, which nearly went for six but I beat him in the flight. I only bowled a few overs and also got the wicket of Mike Cowan, who was caught by Colin Milburn, ending with 2–9. Jimmy Binks, the Yorkshire wicket-keeper, came on to bowl in that game as well! I was also in the Players side in 1962 which was the last Players v. Gents game. I enjoyed the game and thought I had a chance of being taken to Australia but Alan Smith got the job. I did tour India and Pakistan though with the Commonwealth XIs in 1963 and 1964.

My most successful season as captain was in 1965. Towards the end of the season we played Glamorgan at Cardiff and felt whoever won that match would win the Championship. Brian Crump, Jim Watts, two fine cricketers and myself all agreed at the end of the second day that we were out of the game. We woke up the following morning though to a massive black cloud hanging over the ground and it poured for about half an hour.

When we got to the ground Wilf Wooller had rollers all over the outfield, where he got them from I don't know. By the time he had finished the grass was shining! In the first half hour the ball moved all over the place and I remember Tony Lewis coming in at 36–3. I bowled Brian Crump unchanged, we won the match and I thought the Championship was ours. I telephoned Ken Turner, secretary of Northants for 38 years, a remarkable man who was a great influence on me and told him we'd won the Championship. Worcester however, who had won their previous eight matches, still had two games to go and I remember playing golf with Laurie Johnson, our wicket-keeper, when Worcester were playing Hampshire and it was on the radio. The game was well into the second day and Worcester hadn't even got through the first innings. However Hampshire's captain Colin Ingleby-Mackenzie colluded with Don Kenyon to achieve a result when Don declared after just one ball of the second innings and Hampshire managed to get themselves all out for 31! It all was very strange-looking back as the game was heading for a draw. Worcester then went on to beat Sussex at Hove in the final match of the season and won the Championship by finishing four points ahead of us – I could say more!

I had not been involved in coaching before I retired but Freddie Brown approached me to be national coach for the north in 1975 when I was actually about to take another job outside cricket. I tried to make as professional an approach to coaching as I could and it worked. I obviously knew all about tactics and captaincy and ultimately, I feel, made the words 'national coach' mean something. In 1979 I moved into what I consider my most important job, NCA Director of Coaching. I worked with six very capable national coaches making films and writing books on coaching over the years. I also redesigned the national coaching scheme in 1983 and was manager/coach of Young England teams from 1978–84. The most fascinating part of my cricket life though was when I was appointed chief executive in 1986, a position I held until 1994. I like to think we helped develop the game at all levels with the support of some marvellous coaches during that time. I drafted the original development plan for state schools' cricket at clubs in 1991–2. Don Robson the chairman of Durham County Cricket Club, who started to develop the game at grass roots level in Durham, is in my view the man most influential in the development of cricket in this country in the second half of the century. He has made such a contribution to the structure of cricket over the last 20 years and is the principal reason why there is now an English Cricket Board. I was also a committee member of Northants from 1967 to 1974 and Lancashire CCC from 1975 to 1978. I retired in 1994 although still undertook some consultancy work in 1995–6. I am life vice-president of the English Schools Association and the National Association of Young Cricketers, honorary life member of the National Cricket Association and president of the National Association of Cricket Coaches.

I still pursue golf as a hobby. For the first time in my life in 1997 I had a net score of 64, below my age I am pleased to say. I have run the counties' Cricketers Golfing Society for the last 17 years in this region and my handicap is now down to 13. Whilst Ben Hogan was quoted as being my favourite sportsman, it is actually Arnold Palmer. I don't play squash any longer but still enjoy gardening a little.

The most important person by far in my life is Joyce, my wife and best pal for 43 years. I am very proud of my family. I have a daughter Clare and a son Neale – both very nice people. My grandchildren Christopher and Sarah are a bit special, naturally.

Memorable Game

The most memorable game for me was the first time I officially captained Northants at the beginning of 1962 at Northampton against Kent. I was apparently the youngest ever elected professional captain at 31.

3, 5, 6 May 1962. Match drawn

A declaration game was finely poised until rain brought a premature end on the last afternoon. Earlier Richardson and Reynolds both scored fine centuries on an easy-paced wicket.

Kent

P.E. Richardson run out	120	c Norman b Dilley	23
J. Prodger c Scott b P. D. Watts	47	c Prideaux b Larter	4
R.C. Wilson c and b Scott	25	c P. J. Watts b Crump	51
M.C. Cowdrey c Reynolds b P.J. Watts	52	c Norman b Larter	76
S.E. Leary not out	37		
P.H. Jones c and b P. J. Watts	17	not out	11
A.L. Dixon c Crump b P. J. Watts	0	c P.D. Watts b Dilley	20
D.G. Ufton not out	4		
D.J. Halfyard did not bat		not out	2
D.M. Sayer did not bat			
A. Brown did not bat			
B 4, l-b 4, w 4	12	L-b 4	4
(6 wkts dec)	314	(5 wkts dec)	191

1/111 2/190 3/225
4/263 5/289 6/289

1/13 2/33 3/149
4/156 5/178

Northamptonshire

M. Norman c Ufton b Halfyard	0	c Ufton b Brown	3
B.L. Reynolds c and b Jones	110	b Sayer	17
R.M. Prideaux st Ufton b Dixon	13	not out	40
A. Lightfoot b Brown	15	c and b Dixon	19

P.J. Watts c Ufton b Dixon	56	not out	20
B. Crump c Dixon b Leary	11		
P.D. Watts not out	85		
K.V. Andrew c Ufton b Halfyard	4		
M.E. Scott not out	12		
M.R. Dilley did not bat			
J.D.F. Larter did not bat			
B 7, l-b 2, w 1	10	L-b 2	2
(7 wkts dec)	316	(3 wkts)	101

1/5 2/36 3/85 4/177
5/197 6/238 7/282

1/3 2/42 3/71

Northamptonshire Bowling

	O	M	R	W	O	M	R	W
Larter	20	1	73	0	16	2	34	2
Dilley	21.2	4	56	0	17.3	2	55	2
P. J. Watts	16	6	34	3	5	0	18	0
Scott	13	4	39	1	7	0	33	0
P. D. Watts	17	3	52	1				
Crump	9	1	28	0	7	0	47	1
Lightfoot	5	2	20	0				

Kent Bowling

	O	M	R	W	O	M	R	W
Halfyard	22	9	55	2	10	1	31	0
Brown	20	3	59	1	7	2	12	1
Sayer	23	2	68	0	6	2	22	1
Dixon	28	8	78	2	6	1	27	1
Jones	15	7	23	1				
Leary	9	3	23	1	2.5	1	7	0

Umpires: F.S. Lee and J. Arnold

Proudest Moment

The proudest moment for me was putting my England cap on for the first time in 1954 at Brisbane in the first Test against Australia. I must say I had a wonderful life in cricket.

Regarded technically as the most skilful wicket-keeper of his generation, Andrew scored 4,230 runs (13.38) and 903 dismissals (721 ct, 182 st). In 2 Test matches, he scored 29 runs (9.66) with 1 dismissal.

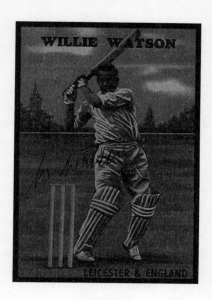

WILLIE WATSON

LEICESTER & ENGLAND

–26–

Willie Watson (b. 1920)

Yorkshire, Leicestershire and England

During the winter of 1958–9 I toured Australia with MCC but suffered an injury. Back in 1942 when I was in the army I had a cartilage operation. I came out in 1946, played soccer and cricket all those years and never had any trouble. On the ship going over I sat talking to the physio in the lounge. When I got up off the settee to get dressed for dinner, I turned round and my knee felt funny, but not painful. I found I couldn't bend my knee but could straighten it, although there was no pain. The physio tried to put it back but couldn't. When we reached Aden I saw an RAF doctor who frightened me to death as he said I had osteoarthritis, which I couldn't believe. Eventually I was flown from Colombo to Perth to see a specialist. After a couple of weeks it was manipulated under anaesthetic but I still couldn't bend it. On the day before the team arrived, I was invited to a school. As I was getting out of the taxi, my knee felt different and I could bend it right back but couldn't straighten it. When I told the specialist he identified the problem and it has been all right ever since. When I had had my initial operation in the army, where they had cut the cartilage out, there had been a regeneration of gristle which chipped off and had floated about in my knee. I was hospitalised in Perth for a while to remove the gristle and as a result couldn't play cricket until the end of December.

We were right in the midst of the series and, although I played in a couple of the Tests it wasn't a good tour from my point of view because of the injury.

I also toured New Zealand in 1960–1 with MCC, which was an England 'A' side containing seven players with Test experience and Dennis Silk as captain. However, Dennis broke his finger in the first match so I captained the side for the rest of the tour. [According to John Reid's autobiography *Sword of Willow*, Willie Watson, the old pro, became the leading light of the team. His knowledge of the game was the property of everyone, Englishman or New Zealander.]

I was captain of Leicestershire for four years from 1958–61 inclusive. It was probably the best period for me personally. When I was with Yorkshire I never had a contract – if you played you would be paid, if you didn't you wouldn't. After Yorkshire played at home to Leicestershire in 1957, I was having a drink with Charlie Palmer their captain, who told me he was retiring at the end of the season. In conversation he asked if I knew anyone who would like to come and captain Leicestershire. I was 37 at the time and knew that the next day Yorkshire could say 'Thank you very much' and I could have a five-year contract with Leicester, so told him I might be interested. They agreed terms so I went there to secure my future and felt I was the boss as I picked the side. We didn't have a good batting side as Maurice Tompkin had died and Jack Walsh the Australian and Charlie Palmer had retired, so we lost a lot of experience. Maybe I felt I had to do well but it was a struggle. My home was in Huddersfield and I travelled down and virtually lived in a suitcase and only came home on a Sunday. I enjoyed the responsibilities of captaincy though. My best performances were for Leicester where I felt more relaxed.

1959 was a good season for me in terms of runs. When I look back on figures and records I can't tell you how many runs I scored as it wasn't the reason I played – records don't mean a lot to me. I just enjoyed cricket and have always thought of it as a game. Even now when I watch a cricket match, if one side is running away with it, I lose interest. If a team is behind, my thoughts are with the underdog and how they can come back.

I remember we played Hampshire at Coalville in 1960 after Brian Statham had hit me in the ribs in the previous game – I was sore but played. We batted first and scored 285 [Watson himself made 110]. The first time though I went down to pick a ball up on my right hand side I couldn't do it, as unknown to me I had cracked a rib. They scored 367–4, declared, and I batted down the order in the second innings because of the rib injury. We were 52–8 overnight with one batsman in and myself. When we arrived on the last day, a truck was there picking up all the deck chairs and the marquees were coming down. Everyone thought the game would be over in five minutes. I was batting with a young lad called Bob Gardner, a nervous type, who didn't like facing Derek Shackleton. I said I would take him as much as

I could. I went in at 11.30 a.m. and batted through until just after tea and we saved the match. I scored 76 but not once did Derek bowl to Bob the whole day. I would play out his over and when they took him off, would always take the first ball of every over, even at the expense of scoring runs, in case they brought him back! I remember that type of innings more than big scores.

By 1962, my final season at Leicestershire, I was 42 and had reached the stage when I would go in and score 20 or 30, whereas before I felt I could bat all day. Suddenly that feeling of wanting to bat left me and I knew it was time to pack it in [even allowing for that, Watson topped the county's batting averages with over 1,000 runs].

In 1962–3, I went on one of Ron Roberts's tours to Rhodesia as captain in a team which included Basil D'Oliveira, Colin Ingleby-Mackenzie, Wes Hall and Chandra Borde, the leg-spinner. We played at Corfu, then Rhodesia, East Africa, and on to Kuala Lumpur. When we reached Athens on the first leg of the journey, we found out that Ron had left all the passports in the bus that took us from the terminal to the plane at Heathrow and they had to be sent on! The matches in Corfu started at about two o'clock in the afternoon on a piece of ground right in the middle of the town. We had a strong side and didn't know how good the opposition was, so when I won the toss we put them in and bowled them out for next to nothing. The next day we decided to bat and leave two and a half hours to get them out, which we did. On the third day, I asked the captain what he wanted to do. He didn't speak much English so we batted to about 200 when they suddenly walked off the field. They thought we had batted long enough but we hadn't declared – they had declared for us!

To reach Kuala Lumpur from East Africa, we had to stay overnight in Karachi. When I handed the tickets and passports over in Karachi, the authorities said, 'You have a South African national' [D'Oliveira]. It was about six o'clock at night and we were leaving at seven in the morning. We had to leave a deposit of £300 to allow him in – when I see him I remind him he was their most expensive tourist! You also had to have a yellow fever certificate coming from East Africa and Colin Ingleby-Mackenzie lost his. When we reached Pakistan, they put him in a house on the far side of the airport – they wouldn't let him into the country! We tried to get confirmation from the British embassy of evidence of his certificate, but they couldn't find proof. In the end he didn't travel with us but went to Kuala Lumpur in a cargo plane! I was at the airport to meet him, but as it had been in the newspapers, they sent an ambulance out and put him in another airport room, where he had to stay for seven days while we played a couple of games. He eventually came out the day we left to go on to Singapore!

I also managed and played in an MCC touring side to East Africa in the early '60s [1963–4]. Mike Smith was captain and it was fairly common for MCC to tour in those days. I was also a Test selector from 1962 to 1964.

My involvement in football management began in 1961 when a friend of mine, who was a director of Halifax Town Football Club, asked me to help them out when their manager left at the start of the season. As I lived nearby I agreed until the start of the cricket season and when I finished playing cricket, the chairman asked me to manage them [September 1964–April 1966]. Then Bradford City asked me to manage them and I joined a month before the end of the 1965–6 season when they were bottom of the Football League. I read in the paper there was a new Board there which had spent £10,000 on three players, including an old English international and an old Welsh international. That was a lot of money in those days and I thought they must have been mad. I watched three or four matches and they successfully applied for re-election to the Football League. We put all the youngsters in the next season and finished mid-way in the League.

The following season [1967–8] we started well but needed a good centre-forward and would have to spend some money. A 19-year-old lad called Paul Aimson who played for York, had been bought for £10,000 by Bury, who were at the time in the Second Division. That year they were relegated and as this lad had been in and out of the side, I asked Bury if he was available. They were looking for £8,000 but there was no way we could raise that amount, as the Bradford Board told me they only had £2,000! I went back to Bury who said they wouldn't take a penny under £6,000, which was a start. I asked if we could make a down-payment of £2,000 and pay the balance in instalments, to which they agreed, and he did well for us. At this stage, I had one or two differences with the chairman as he tried to interfere, and I told him I would only manage on the basis that I picked the side. When we were top of the Fourth Division Tom Johnston, the manager of Huddersfield, wanted to buy Aimson together with a young full-back, but was only prepared to give me older reserve players, so I declined. In the November I had a big row with the chairman and, as I was on a three-month-notice contract, told him I was finishing at the end of the season. I said I would get to February 1968 and give him my notice. We stayed top of the table through until February when the chairman, after offering me more money which I refused, told me he wanted to get someone in straight away. I picked up my things, walked out and they had to pay me for the remainder of my contract. They then sold Aimson and the full-back and finished fourth at the end of the season – stupid!

Having tasted football management, I wasn't looking for a job after that as unpredictable. In 1967 I heard about a cricket coaching job in Johannesburg and came out to have a look of my own accord. It was at one of the public schools where Athel Rowan was involved. I asked about the winter months and they said they would find something suitable, but I decided it was not on. While I was there, I went to the Wanderers Club in Johannesburg on a Sunday morning as I was asked to give a talk. I hadn't been home long when I received a letter from Doug Robinson, the Wanderers' chairman, asking if I was interested in becoming their sports manager and I saw him in London soon after. That resulted in an offer and we came out to Johannesburg, where we have lived ever since. My son was 18 and had just finished at York and my daughter was 11 having just finished junior school at Huddersfield. I decided if we were going to move, now was the right time so we sold the house and moved over.

Looking back it was a big step to take and took us a year to settle down. I was in charge of all the grounds and the groundstaff for seven years from 1968 to 1975. Tennis, squash and bowls were played, apart from the cricket so there was lots of preparation. Everything was happening at the weekends so it was a seven days a week job and very tiring. I then had a chance to go into industry with Fenners, who manufacture conveyor belts and V belts for engineering. They are based in Hull and used to sponsor the Scarborough festival so I knew them. I met the managing director of the branch in Johannesburg who offered me a job and stayed for 15 years until I retired. I started on the shop-floor and was involved in time study, stores, transport and eventually managed conveyor-belting, manufacturing of conveyor belts and the stores and transport. When I reached 65 it became too much for me, so I worked mornings only for a few years as they had so much work on.

When I was at the Wanderers I was captain of the youngsters for two or three years and continued to enjoy playing cricket. They used to run two second team sides in the same league and one of them was a side of youngsters from the public schools. Towards the end I also played social cricket on a Sunday for a while with old players like Johnny Waite. The last game of cricket I played was in 1981 at the age of 61 against a touring side from England which Geoff Pullar brought out. I still watch a lot of cricket and football and people ask me which I preferred when I played. I couldn't tell you though as, towards the end of the cricket season, I looked forward to playing football and the same thing happened towards the end of the football season.

I used to play a lot of bridge but not so much now. Music has always been part of my life. When I was about ten years old, my parents sent me to music lessons but I was too involved in playing sport. I would come home and nip out before my parents realised I had a music lesson! When I was 18, though, of my own accord, I wanted to play the piano so went to a music teacher and carried on until I went in the army at the age of 20. Now I would love to be able to play the piano again.

Memorable Game
The most memorable match I played in would have to be the second Test against Australia at Lord's in 1953. I don't think it was the best innings I played but the occasion warranted it.

25, 26, 27, 29, 30 June 1953. Match drawn

With England facing defeat on the last day, Watson batted for over five hours in a determined and resolute fashion on his debut against Australia, adding 163 for the fifth wicket with Trevor Bailey, one of the classic rearguard actions of Test cricket.

Australia

A.L. Hassett c Bailey b Bedser	104	c Evans b Statham	3
A.R. Morris st Evans b Bedser	30	c Statham b Compton	89
R.N. Harvey lbw b Bedser	59	b Bedser	21
K.R. Miller b Wardle	25	b Wardle	109
G.B. Hole c Compton b Wardle	13	lbw b Brown	47
R. Benaud lbw b Wardle	0	c Graveney b Bedser	5
A.K. Davidson c Statham b Bedser	76	c and b Brown	15
D. Ring lbw b Wardle	18	lbw b Brown	7
R.R. Lindwall b Statham	9	b Bedser	50
G.R. Langley c Watson b Bedser	1	b Brown	9
W.A. Johnston not out	3	not out	0
B 4, l-b 4	8	B 8, l-b 5	13
	346		368

1/65 2/190 3/225 4/229 5/240
6/280 7/291 8/330 9/331

1/3 2/168 3/227 4/235 5/248
6/296 7/305 8/308 9/362

England

L. Hutton c Hole b Johnston	145	c Hole b Lindwall	5
D. Kenyon c Davidson b Lindwall	3	c Hassett b Lindwall	2
T.W. Graveney b Lindwall	78	c Langley b Johnston	2
D.C.S. Compton c Hole b Benaud	57	lbw Johnston	33
W. Watson st Langley b Johnston	4	c Hole b Ring	109
T.E. Bailey c and b Miller	2	c Benaud b Ring	71
F.R. Brown c Langley b Lindwall	22	c Hole b Benaud	28
T.G. Evans b Lindwall	0	not out	11
J.H. Wardle b Davidson	23	not out	0
A.V. Bedser b Lindwall	1		
J.B. Statham not out	17		
B 11, l-b 1, w 1, n-b 7	20	B 7, l-b 6, w 2, n-b 6	21
	372	(7 wkts)	282

1/9 2/177 3/279 4/291 5/301
6/328 7/328 8/332 9/341

1/6 2/10 3/12 4/73
5/236 6/246 7/282

England Bowling

	O	M	R	W	O	M	R	W
Bedser	42.4	8	105	5	31.5	8	77	3
Statham	28	7	48	1	15	3	40	1
Brown	25	7	53	0	27	4	82	4
Bailey	16	2	55	0	10	4	24	0
Wardle	29	8	77	4	46	18	111	1
Compton					3	0	21	1

Australia Bowling

	O	M	R	W	O	M	R	W
Lindwall	23	4	66	5	19	3	26	2
Miller	25	6	57	1	17	8	17	0
Johnston	35	11	91	2	29	10	70	2
Ring	14	2	43	0	29	5	84	2
Benaud	19	4	70	1	17	6	51	1
Davidson	10.5	2	25	1	14	5	13	0
Hole					1	1	0	0

Umpires: F.S. Lee and H.G. Baldwin

Proudest Moment

The proudest moment for me in cricket was in 1951 when I made my England debut in the first Test against South Africa at Trent Bridge [scoring a half-century in the first innings]. I had already received my England soccer cap and now had both.

A natural and graceful left-handed batsman, Watson scored 25,670 runs (39.86) including 55 centuries and 293 catches. In 23 Test matches, he scored 879 runs (25.85) including 2 centuries and 8 catches.

–27–

Maurice Hallam (1931–2000)

Leicestershire

In 1959 I scored 158 at Leicester in our first match of the season against the Indians, which was the second game of their tour. It was great to be the first player to score 1,000 runs that season. I nearly scored them all in May but hit the last 16 in early June. I was never a very big guy and remember coming off the field after all those innings absolutely shattered, as I scored the 1,000 in about eight knocks. I was told to keep it going and I would be bound to get an opportunity for England! In one of the games against Glamorgan, when we lost the toss they batted and I think declared with about half an hour to go, we went in and I scored about 18 overnight. Wilf Wooller, who was an England selector at that time, had a selection meeting the next day and I thought I was in with a great chance of being selected, as England were looking for an opening batsman at that time. I was upset not to be picked, came back to play on the Monday and went berserk! I hit them all round the ground and Allan Watkins said to Wilf, 'I thought you didn't pick this guy because he didn't have any shots!' I hit 210 not out, my highest ever score, and in the second innings did exactly the same to score 157 (one of five men ever to score a double century and 150 in a match, the others being Arthur Fagg, Warwick Armstrong, Zaheer Abbas and Greg Blewett). Wilf gave me awful stick out there as I was knocking those runs, but was first in the dressing-room after the game with the champagne – that's how he was. I remember being so tired I asked Willie Watson the skipper, if I could field at third man or fine leg after we declared for the final session. He agreed and in the second over the ball went to the slips, where I normally fielded and it went down. Some wag in the crowd said, 'Oh, bloody hell, Hallam, you're at it again!' I waved at him from where I was fielding, but having watched me knock the ball all over the park, some people are never satisfied!

I did feel cheated at not being selected for England and fulfilling my ambition, particularly as just before I also scored 200 against Derbyshire and wondered what more I had to do to be picked for my country, especially as I was a reasonable slip fielder. I remember most the hurt of not being selected and it took the stuffing out of me for a while. I think that was the nearest I got to being selected for England as I was in such good nick at the beginning of the 1959 season, particularly as about 20 openers were tried around that time. It would have been nice to have gone on at least one tour, I am known as the guy who never played for England. One could equally say this about John Langridge, with 34,000 runs for Sussex and Les Berry, who scored 30,000 runs for Leicester and never even got a call up for MCC. One has to say if you played for Yorkshire in those days you either went on a tour or played for England. I do feel that element of not playing for a fashionable club is relevant to this day.

There was then a lull mid-season before I came back to make some good scores towards the end. It was a good summer and we didn't play on so many 'wet ones'. In those days we played eight games at four away grounds in Leicestershire, Ashby-de-la-Zouch, the only ground where play stopped for coal trains to pass, Hinckley, which shot along the ground, Snibston Colliery with its slagheap and Loughborough, where the groundsman just 'marled' it. So we had some interesting tracks to play on!

I remember Maurice Tompkin saying to me when I first joined the ground staff, 'If you are playing merely as a batsman, you've got to score at least 1,500 runs a season to justify your place.' That was my aim every season.

1961 was my best season in terms of consistency and runs scored [2,262 at 39.68]. I remember when we played Sussex at Worthing, Hubert Doggart came in to the dressing-room and said, 'The last time I saw you, you bagged a pair.' It was the first time I had taken my wife away with me and I told her she was never coming again! At the end of this game though I was 203 not out and 143 not out, and after the Glamorgan match in 1959 I was the first Englishman to score a double century and a single century in a match more than once. Sussex skipper Don Smith said to Hubert, 'That'll teach you to open your mouth!' It was one of John Snow's early games and Don advised him not to bounce me. He did though as he was a bit raw, which was meat and drink to me as I preferred to play off the back foot. Don came in down the order and with John Savage bowling, I fielded at slip and caught him for a duck. Having scored 200, I sympathised with him in the evening over a beer. Then in the second innings exactly the same happened off the same bowler and I really did feel for him.

Sid Hickling, who was a committee man and looked after me like a second father, came down to Worthing and took me out one evening for ham, egg and chips. When I scored the 200 he said, 'We're going back there tomorrow!' He had a big Humber and let me drive it to Scarborough, where I was playing in a Gents v Players game straight after. Dai Davies gave me out lbw to Ossie Wheatley when I was on 97 and it would have been the only time I scored three centuries on the trot. Norman Hill said I shouldn't have missed the ball after I had scored 97 runs! Peter May was skipper of the Gents team and I remember towards the end of the game it was pelting down and we wouldn't go off, as we only wanted two wickets to win when Ossie came in. I was the Players' skipper and John Edrich kept on telling me not to go off and we won it, although I'm not sure whether it was in the spirit of festival matches as I was never invited again!

I took over from David Kirby as skipper for three seasons from 1963–5. I don't have great memories as we didn't have a particularly good side in those years. I was a bit of a worrier and used to have sleepless nights about how we could win matches, particularly in 1963. We never seemed to be able to bowl sides out twice. My own form declined as well as I was too concerned about the performance of the other players. There were other problems like the outfield at Grace Road, making it very difficult to hit boundaries along the ground. My requests to improve the facilities were ignored until Illy came along and then things changed. In 1965 I do remember being the first batsman ever to score two unbeaten centuries in two matches when I followed up the 1961 game against Sussex with 107 not out and 149 not out against Worcester at Leicester. It made it all worthwhile as there were a lot of noughts in between! When you're on that kind of form, it's a pleasure just to be out there – the ball flows off the middle of the bat and the timing is good. It was nice having someone like Tom Graveney congratulating me, as when I was a boy Tom was the player I always liked to watch.

I enjoyed the one-day cricket when it started in 1963 as it suited my style. With 65 overs you could really play an innings. Then when the John Player League was introduced, I remember a match where we beat Sussex with an over to spare in July 1969 at Leicester. Peter Marner opened the innings with myself and was holding the bat like a baseball bat! While I scored 36, 'Wally' hit 99 in 53 minutes, including eight 6's. He asked me if I thought he was doing the right thing and I said I would just watch him from the other end!

I was asked to skipper again in 1968 when Tony Lock didn't return from Australia. Tony's wife wanted to stay and he decided to settle down over there as he was also playing for Western Australia. I wasn't all that thrilled about captaining again at such short notice but we had a reasonable season in the end and finished ninth. Tony was a match winner when I had him in 1965 for a few matches, but he was a bit wary of people looking at him at that time as he was going through a period of trying to straighten his left arm. He was a great character and competitor though, even more so when he became captain. You could tell him he was on the wrong line and suggest he got the ball over about another three inches and he would do it, he was that good. Bowlers today seem to be incapable of that degree of accuracy.

In 1969 Ray Illingworth came along and was appointed captain and the side gradually improved with imports like Davison, Higgs and McKenzie. I remember going to the Oval towards the end of my career when Roger Tolchard was batting with me. We put 70 runs on for the first wicket and hadn't scored a boundary – we ran the lot and I was 48 not out. As I crossed with 'Tolly' I kept shouting to him, 'stop hitting those singles'. I had to get out because I couldn't stand any more as I was so tired. It was some comfort to me that he felt the same at the tender age of 21! I came off having got out deliberately and was as white as a sheet. I was dreading fielding as well and told Ray Illingworth my thoughts – I knew then it was time to call it a day.

When I retired in 1970 I had a year off, then looked after the second XI for two or three years before working in the office promoting the membership and recruitment. I had undertaken some freelance coaching at Lilleshall and one or two other venues. When Les Berry, my predecessor retired from Uppingham, by a chance meeting I was asked if I was interested in taking over the coaching. The next thing I knew I was interviewed and offered the job, spent 19 years coaching there and retired in 1996. James Whittaker and Jonathan Agnew were two of the little 'urchins' I had.

In my playing days I turned my hand to everything bar the kitchen sink. I was a driving instructor, ironmonger, worked in a hosiery and a carpenter's. It was difficult to get a job for the winter months only. I left school at 14, went into engineering at 16 and was on the staff with no educational background to speak of.

The card series photograph is the most common one of me. It shows me hooking Frank Tyson as I used to take him on. He was certainly the quickest bowler I faced. I first played him in the second team against Northants and Percy Davis said he was the quickest thing in England – he ran from the sightscreen in those days!

My hobby is still woodwork – I recently made a wendy-house for my granddaughter. My interest goes right back to my schooldays as I have always been better with my hands than my brain!

Tom Graveney and Stanley Matthews were both to me like watching 'poetry in motion'. That's what I always call a cover drive when it looks so sweet and so elegant. Both gave you something to look at. I have obviously played with and against Tom and in the '50s it was a pleasure to watch players like him playing so gracefully. I haven't met Stan, but remember going to Wembley with my friend Sid once to watch England play Germany which we won quite comfortably. The whole stadium was shouting 'Give it to Stanley'. As soon as he had the ball the full-back was backing away and he got to the by-line, put his crosses over and England kept scoring. It was marvellous seeing someone at his peak, the likes of which we may not see again, with the game having quickened up. It was particularly interesting for me as I was on the staff at Leicester City Football Cub and played at Filbert Street as a boy.

Memorable Game

My most memorable game was when Arthur Gilligan watched Sussex play us at Hove in June 1956. He was looking more at Alan Oakman as a candidate for selection for England. I scored 80 in the first innings and Alan scored a ton in the second. Arthur came up to me and said, 'That 80 you scored was superb, but I'm sorry, I am looking at the other guy.' I scored 64 not out in the second innings and remember to this day what pleasing innings they were.

27, 28, 29 June 1956. Leicestershire won by eight wickets

Hallam dominated the Leicester batting, with over half his score in the first innings coming from boundaries. Set 126 to win, he received good support from Palmer to secure victory for the visitors after an uncertain start.

Sussex

D.V. Smith b Jackson	34		b Goodwin	4
A.S.M. Oakman c Firth b Goodwin	26		lbw b Goodwin	106
D.J. Foreman run out	5		c Hallam b Goodwin	1
J.M. Parks c Tompkin b Goodwin	15		b Jackson	48
D.J. Semmence c Jackson b Palmer	40		c Firth b Goodwin	39
K.G. Suttle b Jackson	17		b Goodwin	0
D.A. Stripp c Firth b Palmer	16		not out	8
N.I. Thomson b Smith	0		b Goodwin	0
D. Manville b Jackson	3		c Boshier b Goodwin	0
R.G. Marlar b Palmer	20		c Palmer b Goodwin	0
A.E. James not out	0		c Firth b Palmer	0
B 6, l-b 4, n-b 2	12		B 4, l-b 2	6
	188			212

1/49 2/69 3/69 4/101 5/126 6/162
7/163 8/163 9/188

1/4 2/6 3/107 4/184 5/184
6/188 7/209 8/209 9/209

Leicestershire

G. Lester run out	22		b Thomson	4
M.R. Hallam c Smith b Marlar	80		not out	64
J. van Geloven not out	67		c Oakman b Thomson	8

C.H. Palmer c Thomson b Smith	16	not out	42
V.E. Jackson c and b James	43		
R.A. Diment b Thomson	13		
J. Firth c Oakman b Thomson	0		
R. Smith c Suttle b Thomson	1		
J. Goodwin c Suttle b Marlar	15		
B. Boshier c Stripp b Marlar	2		
M. Tompkin absent hurt	0		
B 8, l-b 8	16	B 4, l-b 3, n-b 1	8
	275	(2 wkts)	126

1/74 2/117 3/148 4/201 5/226 6/232
7/234 8/268 9/275

1/4 2/26

Leicestershire Bowling

	O	M	R	W	O	M	R	W
Goodwin	18	1	80	2	27	5	81	8
Boshier	6	1	22	0	8	1	30	0
Palmer	19	12	31	3	15.2	8	25	1
Jackson	19.2	10	28	3	20	4	53	1
Smith	5	1	15	1	9	1	17	0

Sussex Bowling

	O	M	R	W	O	M	R	W
Thomson	34	8	70	3	15	2	41	2
James	28	7	60	1	4	3	9	0
Marlar	18.5	6	67	3	13	3	35	0
Stripp	3	0	10	0				
Oakman	6	2	12	0				
Smith	16	5	40	1	11	3	33	0

Umpires: J.S. Buller and F.S. Lee

Proudest Moment

The proudest moment for me in cricket is knowing I came through the ranks to be made skipper of the county I was born in – it is something that cannot be taken away from you.

An opening right-hand batsman and very good close fielder, Hallam scored 24,488 runs (28.84), took 4 wickets (35.50) and 451 catches.

Author's note: When I spoke to Maurice in the summer of 1999, he was looking forward to this book being published, but added that he hoped to be around long enough to be able to read it. Sadly this was not to be, as Maurice passed away on 1 January 2000.

–28–

Cyril Washbrook (1914–1999)

Lancashire and England

As advised by Malcolm Lorimer with assistance from The Cricketer *and*
Brian Bearshaw of the Manchester Evening News

Cyril Washbrook's last season as a player was in 1959. Captain of Lancashire from 1954, he had reason to look back on his last year of captaincy with some satisfaction as his side, although coming fifth, were just 20 points behind Champions Yorkshire. His last Roses match played early in the season also saw Lancashire beat Yorkshire for the first time since 1927. Despite injury problems, he was able to finish the season with two sound contributions: the first was top-scoring in the Old Trafford game against Kent with 50. Then against Somerset, with Ken Grieves he lifted the score from an uncertain 33–4 to 121–4 to help secure a victory by the slender margin of 41 runs. Business calls were regular and urgent though and whilst still very active, he would have been 45 at the start of the 1960 season.

I was very proud to be captain of Lancashire, but it was a position I never coveted. I enjoyed it but I'm not sure I wouldn't have been happier just to have continued opening and scoring runs. But I was a lucky captain. I had a decent set of chaps and I was the boss and they knew I was the boss. I would like to be remembered by people because I provided entertainment. You are in the entertainment business and I feel the man on the popular side has to have some pleasure watching the game, otherwise he isn't going to sit six or seven hours on a hard seat watching cricket.

Washbrook spectacularly returned from retirement to captain MCC at the age of 50 in their centenary match against Lancashire in August 1964. He opened the innings with his old colleague John Ikin and after a slow beginning they added 139 in about even time against, amongst others Statham and Higgs. Washbrook began uncertainly and the first hour produced 37 runs. The second, as Washbrook soared in full flight, produced twice that number. He pulled Greenhough classically and when Green came on to bowl his offbreaks, he drove him so straight and mightily that the umpire was still skipping aside as the ball thudded against the sightscreen. His wristy square cut came time and time again as he seemed set for another century. But at 85 Statham moved a ball across him with awkward lift. He could not keep it down and tried too late to force it higher and Greenhough at short mid-wicket pouched the ball almost apologetically. The pavilion rightly rose to him as he came in. When fielding, Washbrook was there in the covers with cap aslant and jaunty stride, captaining with authority and assurance and swooping on the ball with his old certainty. Likewise in the two matches played at Lord's between an Old England XI and the Lord's Taverners in 1962 and 1963 his batting was on both occasions the most delightful seen on either side.

Behind the scenes Washbrook became a member of Lancashire's committee in 1961 and also took on a second spell as a Test selector in 1971–2.

I found it frustrating at times. Cricket is big business and you do need solicitors, accountants and engineers on committees. But cricket knowledge is essential as well because the first-class game is totally different from club cricket. But I enjoyed my work on the committee and on the Test and County Cricket Board committees. Basically I am interested in the way the game is played and that it provides entertainment.

Apart from a two-year break, Washbrook remained on the committee until 1988, when he served a two-year spell as only the second professional to be elected as president of the county, and was also an honorary life member.

In 1964 Washbrook accepted the position of team manager to the county side, setting high standards on and off the field. He was regarded with awe by many players and could be seen standing at the front of the pub where the team were staying, making sure none of the players went out on the town.

Washbrook went into his sports outfitting business soon after his record fourteen thousand pound benefit way back in 1948 and only retired in 1986. Cyril latterly lived in a nursing home in Altrincham, Cheshire and sadly passed away in April 1999 at the age of 84.

Memorable Game
According to Neville Cardus, Washbrook's finest hour was when inspiringly recalled in 1956 after a six-year absence to the third Test match in his 42nd year against the Australians at Leeds. He was a Test selector himself at the time and was asked by the chairman, Gubby Allen, to go and order the beer while they discussed him. 'He told me I had been chosen and I said, "Surely the situation isn't as desperate as all that." But you don't refuse to play for England and I don't appreciate today players opting out of Test cricket.'

As he came to the wicket, England were struggling at 17–3 and even Peter May was in dire trouble. Washbrook magnificently took control, calm and experienced to produce a vintage innings of 98. 'The Yorkshire crowd gave me a splendid reception. There is no doubt that did help me and I got off the mark in a very short time. I was very glad to get that 98 in that Test match, but another two wouldn't have done any harm. I was beaten by a good ball but I was pleased not to have let my co-selectors down. I wasn't nervous – I loved playing cricket. I loved batting and loved a contest.' Wilf Wooller, a fellow selector, remembered it as one of the finest examples of psychological cricket he had ever seen. 'Cyril took guard quietly, then he stood back and memorised the field. He looked down again, checked his guard, and signalled he was ready. He played out the first over and the crowd settled down. It was as though he had given them a bromide!'

12, 13, 14, 16, 17 July 1956. England won by an innings and 42 runs
Washbrook's experience was invaluable as his partnership with May proved to be the turning point. England decisively went on to win the Test in front of an estimated attendance of 100,000 and in doing so levelled the series.

England
P.E. Richardson c Maddocks b Archer 5
M.C. Cowdrey c Maddocks b Archer 0
A.S.M. Oakman b Archer 4
P.B.H. May c Lindwall b Johnson 101
C. Washbrook lbw b Benaud 98
G.A.R. Lock c Miller b Benaud 21
D.J. Insole c Mackay b Benaud 5
T.E. Bailey not out 33
T.G. Evans b Lindwall 40

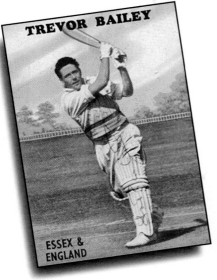

TREVOR BAILEY

ESSEX & ENGLAND

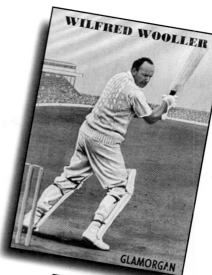

WILFRED WOOLLER

GLAMORGAN

ROY TATTERSALL

LANCASHIRE & ENGLAND

COLIN McCOOL

SOMERSET & AUSTRALIA

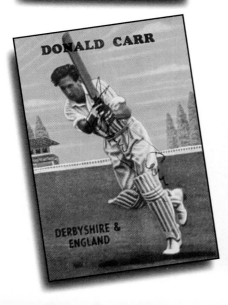

DONALD CARR

DERBYSHIRE & ENGLAND

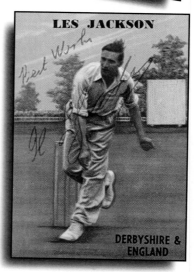

LES JACKSON

DERBYSHIRE & ENGLAND

ALAN MOSS

MIDDLESEX & ENGLAND

ROBIN MARLAR

SUSSEX

JOHN PRETLOVE

KENT

MARTIN HORTON

WORCESTER

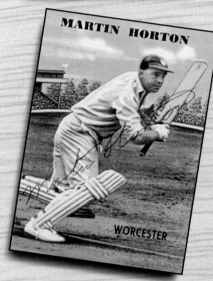

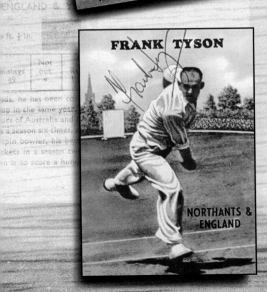

FRANK TYSON

NORTHANTS & ENGLAND

REGINALD SIMPSON

NOTTS & ENGLAND

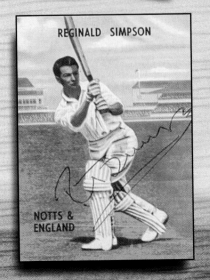

GODFREY EVANS

KENT &
ENGLAND

DONALD SHEPHERD

GLAMORGAN

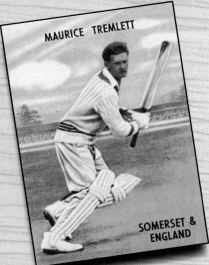

MAURICE TREMLETT

SOMERSET &
ENGLAND

ALEC BEDSER

SURREY & ENGLAND

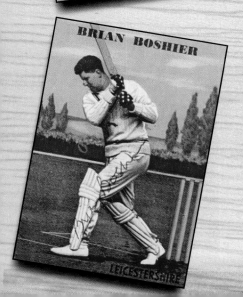

BRIAN BOSHIER

LEICESTERSHIRE

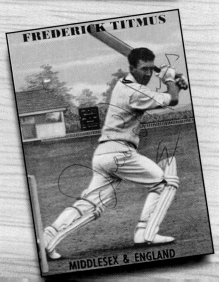

FREDERICK TITMUS

MIDDLESEX & ENGLAND

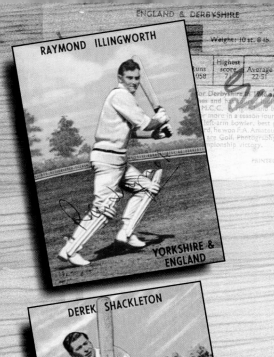

RAYMOND ILLINGWORTH

YORKSHIRE &
ENGLAND

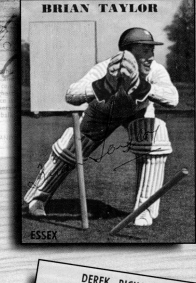

BRIAN TAYLOR

ESSEX

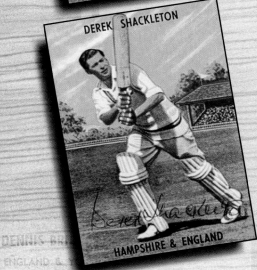

DEREK SHACKLETON

HAMPSHIRE & ENGLAND

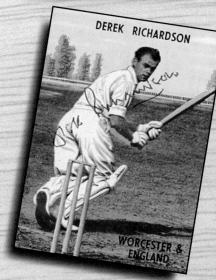

DEREK RICHARDSON

WORCESTER &
ENGLAND

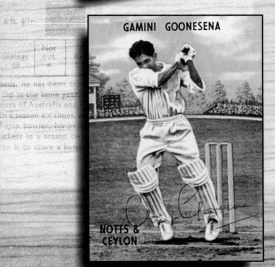

GAMINI GOONESENA

NOTTS &
CEYLON

MICHAEL SMITH

WARWICK & ENGLAND

KEITH ANDREW

NORTHANTS & ENGLAND

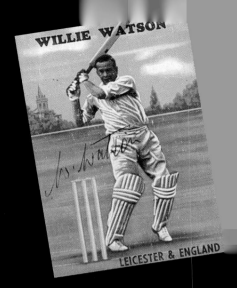

WILLIE WATSON

LEICESTER & ENGLAND

MAURICE HALLAM

LEICESTERSHIRE

CYRIL WASHBROOK

LANCASHIRE &
ENGLAND

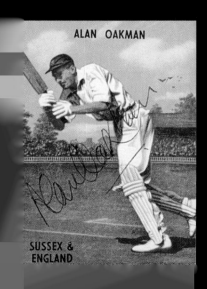

ALAN OAKMAN

SUSSEX &
ENGLAND

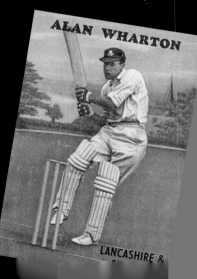

ALAN WHARTON

LANCASHIRE &

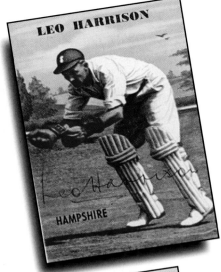

LEO HARRISON

HAMPSHIRE

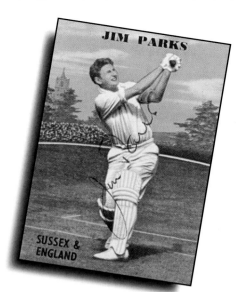

JIM PARKS

SUSSEX & ENGLAND

GEORGE TRIBE

NORTHANTS & AUSTRALIA

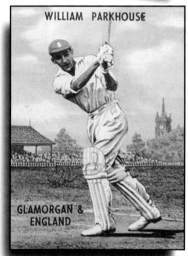

WILLIAM PARKHOUSE

GLAMORGAN & ENGLAND

DONALD KENYON

WORCESTER & ENGLAND

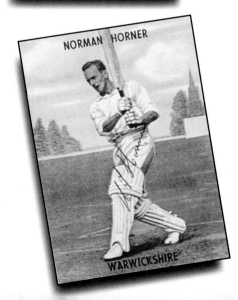

NORMAN HORNER

WARWICKSHIRE

FREDDIE TRUEMAN

YORKSHIRE & ENGLAND

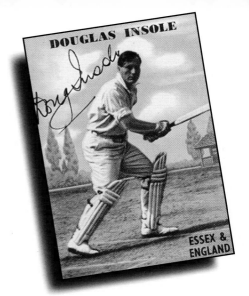

DOUGLAS INSOLE

ESSEX & ENGLAND

MALCOLM HILTON

LANCASHIRE & ENGLAND

ALLAN WATKINS

GLAMORGAN & ENGLAND

VIC WILSON

YORKSHIRE & ENGLAND

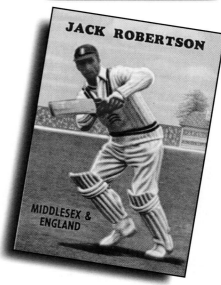

JACK ROBERTSON

MIDDLESEX & ENGLAND

ALEC BEDSER

SURREY & ENGLAND

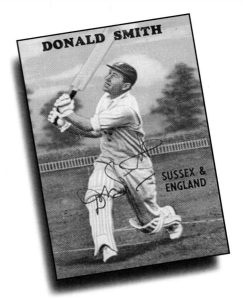

DONALD SMITH

SUSSEX & ENGLAND

COLIN INGLEBY-MACKENZIE

HAMPSHIRE

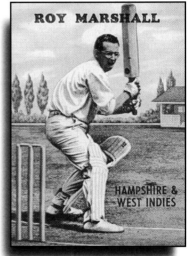

ROY MARSHALL

HAMPSHIRE & WEST INDIES

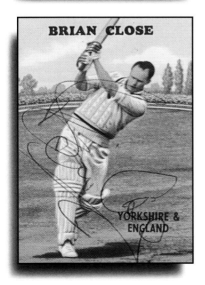

BRIAN CLOSE

YORKSHIRE & ENGLAND

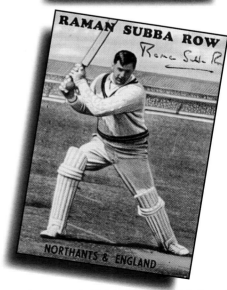

RAMAN SUBBA ROW

NORTHANTS & ENGLAND

J.C. Laker b Lindwall	5
F.S. Trueman c and b Lindwall	0
B 4, l-b 9	13
	325

1/2 2/8 3/17 4/204 5/226 6/243
7/248 8/301 9/321

Australia

C.C. McDonald c Evans b Trueman	2	b Trueman	6
J.W. Burke lbw b Lock	41	b Laker	16
R.N. Harvey c Trueman b Lock	11	c and b Lock	69
P. Burge lbw b Laker	2	lbw b Laker	5
K. Mackay c Bailey b Laker	2	b Laker	2
K.R. Miller b Laker	41	c Trueman b Laker	26
R.G. Archer b Laker	4	c Washbrook b Lock	1
R. Benaud c Oakman b Laker	30	b Laker	1
L. Maddocks c Trueman b Lock	0	lbw b Lock	0
I.W. Johnson c Richardson b Lock	0	c Oakman b Laker	3
R.R. Lindwall not out	0	not out	0
B 4, l-b 6	10	B 7, l-b 4	11
	143		140

1/2 2/40 3/59 4/59 5/63 6/69   1/10 2/45 3/108 4/120 5/128
7/142 8/143 9/143   6/136 7/138 8/140 9/140

Australia Bowling

	O	M	R	W	O	M	R	W
Lindwall	33.4	11	67	3				
Archer	50	24	68	3				
Mackay	13	3	29	0				
Benaud	42	9	89	3				
Johnson	29	7	59	1				

England Bowling

	O	M	R	W	O	M	R	W
Trueman	8	2	19	1	11	3	21	1
Bailey	7	2	15	0	7	2	13	0
Laker	29	10	58	5	41.3	21	55	6
Lock	27.1	11	41	4	40	23	40	3

Umpires: J.S. Buller and D. Davies

Proudest Moment

Washbrook regarded the high spot of an illustrious career as being asked to tour Australia – 'That is the greatest Test match to play in.' Thus he was selected to tour with Wally Hammond's team in 1946–7 which, though not a match-winning success, was a notable first trip to Australia for him. One of only three batsmen to make 1,000 runs on the combined Australia/New Zealand tour, he saved England from defeat at Melbourne with a stubborn innings of 112 in six hours, holding back the likes of Lindwall, Miller, Dooland and Toshack.

Another proud moment was being selected for England for the first time against New Zealand in 1937, although Washbrook was not initially chosen. Lancashire were playing Notts at Trent Bridge when the England side was announced and his boyhood hero and colleague Eddie Paynter was chosen. The following day however Paynter pulled a leg muscle while fielding and it soon became obvious that he would not be fit for the Test the following Saturday. Later in the week Washbrook was sitting in the Ladies Stand with his wife Marjory, at the time his fiancée, when his presence was requested in the committee room. Major Rupert Howard, the secretary had received a telephone call from Lord's advising of his selection in Paynter's place. That was a proud moment for Washbrook, particularly after having been dropped from the county side a few weeks earlier, as he dashed off to tell Marjory. Being picked to play for his country certainly gave him particular pleasure and Washbrook made his debut at the Oval in the last Test.

A determined right-hand opening bat with strong technique and an excellent cover-point, Washbrook scored 34,101 runs (42.67) including 76 centuries, took 7 wickets (44.14) and 206 catches. In 37 Test matches, he scored 2,569 runs (42.81) including 6 centuries, took 1 wicket for 33 runs and 12 catches.

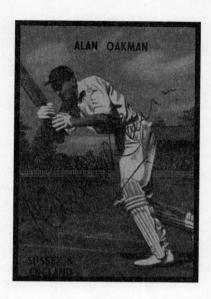

–29–

Alan Oakman (b. 1930)

Sussex and England

The 1961 season was my most successful in terms of runs (2,307) – it was a good summer with not too many rain-affected pitches, which helped. I also made my highest ever score of 229 not out on a small ground at Worksop against Notts. I don't think the county ever went back, although I did about 15 years ago with Warwickshire second XI. A chap came up to me and said, 'I remember you smashing a window over there with your double century!' It was a good pitch – Norman Hill scored a double century in the same game. Don Smith was captain and went out with the chairman of Notts on the first evening we were there. Several drinks later Don said, 'I'm going to prove you can get wickets even when you have had rather too much to drink.' He went out the next day, bowled them out and we won! He bowled left-armers that drifted in like Michael Buss, another Sussex player.

In the early '60s we knew we weren't strong enough to win the County Championship, especially with Ted Dexter, Jim Parks and John Snow on Test match duty so we turned our attention to the new Gillette Cup. Before the competition started, as there was a £50 man-of-the-match award, Ted asked the players if they wanted the winner to keep it or share it. We looked around the dressing-room and thought the only two likely to win the award were Jim or Ted, so we decided to share it!

The greatest memory for me is the very first one-day Gillette Cup final in 1963 at Lord's when Worcester were batting and going well. I hadn't bowled a lot as we were going through a phase when all the bowlers were seamers, unless you were on a dusty turning pitch. I was a bit rusty when Ted asked me to bowl. In front of a full house and against a good side, my first ball looked like being a full toss and ended up a yorker which was whipped out to fine leg for a single. I also remember bowling to Ron Headley, who kept winking at me! I thought he was trying to put me off but I think now he was giving himself confidence. Tom Graveney, an elegant stroke player, lofted me out to long-on between Les Lenham and Ted Dexter. As it went up I shouted out to the captain as I fancied him to catch it more than Les! I bowled 13 overs for 18 runs, which batsmen wouldn't allow today and we won the match.

I also remember the very first Gillette Cup game against Kent at Tunbridge Wells where they kept an orthodox field when we batted. Our policy was to bat for 20 overs, hopefully not lose a wicket and use it as a launch pad for Ted and Jim etc. When Kent batted, we spread our fielders after the first four overs. Peter Richardson wasn't happy, even though he scored a century and won the man-of-the-match award.

My last season in 1968 was a difficult year. We were not doing well in the Championship and the situation came to a head mid-season when Jim Parks relinquished the captaincy and Mike Griffith was subsequently appointed. We played Warwickshire in the Gillette Cup final at the end of the season, which we were winning until Dennis Amiss came in and batted well. Then Alan Smith polished it off and won man of the match. It was a disappointing way to end my career.

I was appointed a first-class umpire in 1969 for a season. I enjoyed it but likened it to playing as I felt the longer you umpired the harder it became.

During my career, I spent ten winters coaching in South Africa, prep school in the morning and senior school in the afternoon. It gave me great satisfaction to see good players coming through. Then I had an anonymous letter in childish pencil handwriting which said, 'Dear Mr Oakman, I do hope that you do not stay in this country because of all the problems it's going to have.' It didn't influence me, although I had a letter at about the same time from Les Deakins, who was secretary at Warwickshire CCC. Tom Dollery was retiring and they were looking for a senior coach and asked if I was interested. I had never really thought about it, as in the 20 years I was with Sussex I had six coaches, so there didn't seem much stability in terms of employment! There had only been two at Edgbaston, Tom Dollery and 'Tiger' Smith.

I was offered the job as senior coach in 1970 and held that post until a manager was appointed. Then I moved to the administration side as assistant secretary/cricket until retirement in 1995. It was an exciting time to be coach during the era of Kanhai, Gibbs, Jameson, Kallicharran and Amiss when we were a strong side. Ironically it wasn't until most of those players had retired and Andy Lloyd took over the captaincy, that we won the Sunday League in 1980. It was a brilliant fielding side and very rewarding to see Andy Lloyd go on to play for England and also Geoff Humpage in the one-day side. It was also pleasing to see youngsters like Steve Perryman come through. I am still involved at Edgbaston co-ordinating school and group visits to the ground which I enjoy.

I still like a game of snooker. I enjoy swimming and play chess now and again. My main hobby now is gardening. Harry Gregg was my favourite sportsman as I was a goalkeeper very briefly for Hastings United. I wrote asking for a trial to Arsenal around the time that Brian Close and Arthur Milton were playing for them, but nothing came of it. I got bundled in the back of the net a few times and remember Sussex secretary Colonel Grimston saying, 'Oakman, you might get injured, do you want to play cricket or football?' He advised me to give up!

Memorable Game
My most memorable game was the fourth Test in 1956 at Old Trafford against the Australians. I went to a dinner with Jim Laker shortly after the match and when he was introduced as the man who took 19 wickets, I was introduced as the chap who took five catches. He leant across to me and said, 'That was six months ago – you aren't still living off that, are you?' Forty-three years on and I am still doing so! At the time I don't think anyone really appreciated the significance of that match. Tony Lock never had a catch dropped or a stumping missed, but the harder he tried the less he looked like getting a wicket. He didn't deliberately let Jim take the wickets – in fact the more wickets Jim took the more annoyed Tony became. At the end of the game Jim picked up a glass of Lucozade and held it up to the crowd and the photographers. In that time Lockie had changed and left the ground! He was disappointed only to get one wicket out of 20 on a pitch that turned so much.

26, 27, 28, 30, 31 July 1956. England won by an innings and 170 runs
This will of course always be known as Laker's match as he broke the more significant bowling records in the history of the game. England achieved victory with about an hour to spare and, in doing so, retained the Ashes.

England
P.E. Richardson c Maddocks b Benaud	104	
M.C. Cowdrey c Maddocks b Lindwall	80	
Rev. D.S. Sheppard b Archer	113	
P.B.H. May c Archer b Benaud	43	
T.E. Bailey b Johnson	20	

C. Washbrook lbw b Johnson 6
A.S.M. Oakman c Archer b Johnson 10
T.G. Evans st Maddocks b Johnson 47
J.C. Laker run out 3
G.A.R. Lock not out 25
J.B. Statham c Maddocks b Lindwall 0
B 2, l-b 5, w 1 8
459

1/174 2/195 3/288 4/321
5/327 6/339 7/401 8/417 9/458

Australia

C.C. McDonald c Lock b Laker	32		c Oakman b Laker	89
J.W. Burke c Cowdrey b Lock	22		c Lock b Laker	33
R.N. Harvey b Laker	0		c Cowdrey b Laker	0
I.D. Craig lbw b Laker	8		lbw b Laker	38
K.R. Miller c Oakman b Laker	6		b Laker	0
K. Mackay c Oakman b Laker	0		c Oakman b Laker	0
R.G. Archer st Evans b Laker	6		c Oakman b Laker	0
R. Benaud c Statham b Laker	0		b Laker	18
R.R. Lindwall not out	6		c Lock b Laker	8
L. Maddocks b Laker	4		lbw b Laker	2
I.W. Johnson b Laker	0		not out	1
			B 12, l-b 4	16
	84			205

1/48 2/48 3/62 4/62 5/62 6/73   1/28 2/55 3/114 4/124 5/130
7/73 8/78 9/84   6/130 7/181 8/198 9/203

Australia Bowling

	O	M	R	W
Lindwall	21.3	6	63	2
Miller	21	6	41	0
Archer	22	6	73	1
Johnson	47	10	151	4
Benaud	47	17	123	2

England Bowling

	O	M	R	W	O	M	R	W
Statham	6	3	6	0	16	10	15	0
Bailey	4	3	4	0	20	8	31	0
Laker	16.4	4	37	9	51.2	23	53	10
Lock	14	3	37	1	55	30	69	0
Oakman					8	3	21	0

Umpires: F.S. Lee and E. Davies

I also remember scoring a century against Lancashire in the last game of the 1956 season at Hove when I had just been selected to go to South Africa with MCC. I thought I played Statham, Tattersall and Malcolm Hilton well and it gave me a great deal of satisfaction.

Proudest Moment

My proudest moment in cricket was when I was picked to play for England in my Test debut against Australia at Headingley in 1956. I knew I was in with a chance as Gubby Allen, the Test selector watched me score a century against Leicester at Hove. I was 50 not out overnight and when he came down the next morning I scored 100 before lunch. When I came in at lunchtime he said, 'Well played Alan, it was a good innings.'

A right-handed batsman, very useful off-break bowler and superb close fielder, 'Oakie' scored 21,800 runs (26.17) including 22 centuries, took 736 wickets (27.63) and 594 catches. In 2 Test matches, he scored 14 runs (7.00).

–30–
Alan Wharton (1923–1993)

Lancashire, Leicestershire and England

As told by Mrs Margaret Wharton with assistance from Brian Bearshaw of the Manchester Evening News, *Noel Wild and Gerry Wolstenholme.*

Wharton's best season was in 1959, when he scored 2,157 runs as one of the most reliable batsmen in the country and averaged more than 40. In a drawn game at the beginning of June against Sussex at Hove he hit a career-best score, before being run out for 199.

> I hit a ball to cover and, as it looked as though it was being stopped I had no intention of running. Then I saw the fielder let it go behind him but apparently Jack Dyson didn't. I called for the run and got halfway up the wicket with Jack, who had also come out but then he suddenly turned back. As I turned round I slipped and finished up on my hands and knees trying to scramble in. The lads in the pavilion were killing themselves laughing and somebody said that it was a tragedy. It wasn't because plenty of folk have made 200 but not many have a top score of 199.

Wharton then scored over a thousand runs in 1960, yet it was suggested to him that he captain Lancashire's second XI in 1961. The committee request was presented by the chairman, Dr Bowling Holmes and two pre-war players, Frank Sibbles and George Duckworth.

I was uncertain and discussed it with my wife. She said that they obviously wanted to bring on some youngsters and use my experience in doing so and if that was the case, I should ask for first team pay. The committee refused. I left and wept in my car in the car park. I discussed the possibility of my going to another club and was able to do so because Leicestershire, in the form of Willie Watson, had asked me to join them, but the committee were not too keen on my knowledge and experience being used elsewhere. As I also had an offer to write a series of articles on Lancashire's recent decline with *The People*, I told the committee that, although I would rather earn my money honestly by going to another club, I would have no option but to take up *The People* offer if they declined to let me do so. Fortunately, they changed their mind and I joined Leicestershire, although of course I left with a degree of resentment. I hated the way in which I went and didn't go to Old Trafford for three years after I finished, but the people responsible died, new men came onto the committee, and I failed to see the sense of bearing umbrage against people I didn't know. Now I have nothing but a great sense of gratitude at having been asked to play for Lancashire. I have loved the game and Lancashire above anything.

'He was the dressing-room spokesman at Lancashire,' says Margaret, 'which didn't always go down well in the committee. He was opinionated and the difference of opinion triggered his departure from Lancashire, as he wasn't one to sit back and say nothing. He wasn't a yes-man, which you had to be sometimes in those days and was extremely upset to leave Lancashire, as he had been very loyal to them. He found another county in Leicestershire without any difficulty which he enjoyed, although his love was always Lancashire.'

Wharton spent three years at Leicestershire in which time he hit a further 3,500 runs and six more centuries. His first season in 1961 saw him team up with Willie Watson in two outstanding partnerships which broke previous long-standing Leicestershire records. The pair put on 316 for the unbroken third wicket against Somerset at Taunton, Wharton scoring 120, but the partnership that gave him more pleasure was the 287 that they put on for the second wicket against Lancashire at Grace Road. Wharton's share was 135 and he said rather gleefully, 'I can remember being naughty as there were three Lancashire committee men on the balcony when I came off and I gave them a wave!'

After a mediocre 1963 season by his standards (scoring 833 runs), he decided that he ought to return full-time to teaching. 'Playing at Leicestershire put pressure on my family life as I was virtually away from home for five months, so when the option to renew my contract came up I decided to retire,' he said.

Wharton played two further years as a professional at Kendal in the Northern League and two more as an amateur for Colne, during which time he broke Colne's amateur batting record when scoring 721 runs. He was to become president of Colne Cricket Club for 14 years and eventually club president. He also played for a season with Cumberland in the Minor Counties Championship while with Kendal. At the end of the 1967 season, 22 years after his debut in the first-class game, he packed away his cricket gear for the last time and went back to teaching.

> There is no way I would have changed anything I did, but if I had been more tactful I might have got on better. Having said that, I don't think I made any enemies, but I made a lot of friends.

Alan had mixed feelings about teaching, as Margaret confirms, 'He became head of English, but did become disillusioned in the later years with the teaching methods and took early retirement when he was 58. He had also become a magistrate at 28 in 1952, one of the youngest in the country and was chairman of Pendle magistrates until he had to retire in 1993 on his seventieth birthday, as the longest serving J.P. in the country. He loved it, best of all the talking.'

Wharton was a man of ceaseless conversation. 'If I could have gone for any other career it would have been as an advocate,' he said. 'That is why I was a barrack room lawyer – I was a good talker and stood up for people's causes. I was willing to take up those causes and it was bound to bring me into conflict with authority.'

'During his cricketing years in the winter he played golf,' says Margaret, 'which I took up on the basis that if you can't beat them join them, a decision I have no regrets about, as I still play now. He was captain of Colne Golf Club in 1974–5 and became very much involved with the Club in later years and in 1993 had just become honorary secretary when he died. He went regularly to Old Trafford, was a vice-president at Lancashire which he appreciated and had also accepted the post of the first president of the Past Players' Association.'

Wharton was a man of many activities and as an all-round sportsman, played golf, rugby union, football, table tennis, tennis and badminton! 'We met at Colne tennis club,' continues Margaret, 'which he played as a hobby – he was above average at most sports. We used to play badminton together but more as a hobby than a sport, like tennis.'

Despite his sporting prowess, he hadn't always had good health as Margaret recalled, 'Alan had a duodenal ulcer for many years and was often in pain, it interfered with his cricket and he may have played more than once for England if he had been free from pain. He had an operation though at the end of the 1959 season just before my daughter was born and since then he never looked back. It was a pity he didn't have the operation earlier, as the ulcers started way back during the war through stress, erratic meals etc.

'The week before he went into hospital in 1993 he had been away twice playing golf in a seniors competition. He was really sun-tanned, but started having pains and within six weeks had died of cancer. It was mercifully quick but there was no inkling of the illness. He led a very full life, enjoyed every minute of it and said given a chance would do it all over again. We married when he was 30 in 1953 and Alan came to Kelbrook, albeit only as a temporary thing until he finished cricket. We never moved though and he loved the countryside. He was always out visiting people for a chat and there was nothing he liked more than to go to the local when, as a Lancastrian living over the border in Yorkshire, he would entertain the locals during the Roses match.'

Memorable Game

Wharton's most memorable innings was the 137 he scored for Lancashire in 1956 at Manchester against the Australians when he felt better equipped for Tests and quietly hoped for a recall, but it never came.

23, 24, 25 May 1956. Match drawn

The Australian fast bowling in 1956 was the strongest in the world with opening pair Ray Lindwall and Alan Davidson, supported by Keith Miller and Ron Archer. Wharton took it apart in the second innings and was the first player to score a century for Lancashire against the Aussies since Ernest Tyldesley in 1934.

Lancashire

A. Wharton c Maddocks b Davidson	6	b Archer	137
J. Dyson c Davidson b Archer	41	c Maddocks b Lindwall	6
G.A. Edrich c Rutherford b Davidson	0	c Lindwall b Archer	26
C. Washbrook c Maddocks b Lindwall	10	run out	1
K. Grieves c Maddocks b Lindwall	10	c Davidson b Miller	4
G. Pullar c Archer b Crawford	28	c Maddocks b Davidson	24
P. Marner c Archer b Crawford	4	not out	23
M.J. Hilton c Rutherford b Archer	0	not out	2
J. Jordan not out	3		
J.B. Statham b Crawford	1		
R. Tattersall c Rutherford b Crawford	1		
L-b 3, n-b 1	4	B 3, l-b 12	15
	108	(6 wkts dec)	238

1/7 2/9 3/26 4/49 5/97 6/97 7/101
8/101 9/104

1/9 2/88
3/110 4/115 5/182 6/231

Australia

C.C. McDonald hit wkt b Hilton	21	lbw b Hilton		42
J. Rutherford c Wharton b Statham	0	retired hurt		0
K. Mackay c Jordan b Statham	1	not out		47
I.D. Craig c and b Craig	32	not out		0
K.R. Miller lbw b Statham	10			
R.G. Archer c Pullar b Dyson	39			
L. Maddocks b Dyson	36			
R.R. Lindwall b Dyson	3			
A.K. Davidson lbw b Dyson	1			
P. Crawford b Statham	11			
J. Wilson not out	1			
B 4, l-b 1	5	L-b 1		1
	160	(1 wkt)		90

1/5 2/7 3/47 4/62 5/72 6/134 7/142
8/148 9/153

1/77

Australia Bowling

	O	M	R	W	O	M	R	W
Lindwall	10	4	23	2	19	6	41	1
Davidson	9	0	40	2	19	4	45	1
Archer	10	7	10	2	21	4	61	2
Crawford	9.1	2	31	4	13	1	46	0
Wilson					2	0	20	0
Miller					8	2	10	1

Lancashire Bowling

	O	M	R	W	O	M	R	W
Statham	15.4	2	34	4	5	4	1	0
Marner	6	2	14	0	2	0	10	0
Tattersall	16	7	44	0	12	5	24	0
Hilton	17	4	46	2	12	7	25	1
Dyson	4	0	17	4	11	4	29	0

Umpires: H. Elliott and A. Skelding

He also rated as memorable a battling 24 out of an innings total of 36 against the fast bowling of Derbyshire's Cliff Gladwin and Les Jackson in June 1954 at Buxton, before succumbing to Jackson: 'That was the most horrific time I ever had on a cricket field.'

Proudest Moment

Wharton's proudest moment in cricket was when he played his single match for England in 1949, the drawn first Test against New Zealand at Headingley, scoring 7 and 13. It was a dream come true for him, albeit a bit too soon in his career. 'I must say that in defence of myself I was sent in at five on both occasions to have a bang because we had scored so many runs that it was a matter of getting on with the game. To give the selectors due credit they knew this and I was picked for the second Test but injured myself when I put my foot on a ball trying to pull it back from the boundary against Warwickshire at Edgbaston. I hurt my knee as well as tearing hamstring tendons and was never picked again. I didn't believe I was good enough in 1949,' he said candidly.

A left-handed batsman who liked to attack and useful right-arm medium-pace bowler, Wharton scored 21,796 runs (32.24) including 31 centuries, 237 wickets (31.59) and 289 catches. In 1 Test match he scored 20 runs (10.00).

–31–

Leo Harrison (b. 1922)

Hampshire

During the 1959 season I won two sets of gold cuff-links from Brylcreem. They used to give them out for the best batter, bowler and wicket-keeper of the month and one set was given to me for 27 victims in August. Jimmy Hill made the presentations and 1959 was the last year they were awarded. It must have been a good season for me with 83 dismissals – still a record for Hants. Bobby Parks would have beaten it one year but for the last match in Bournemouth when he was one short and they didn't bowl a ball!

I had opportunities to coach abroad in Rhodesia a couple of times during the winter-time and also went to Buenos Aires in Argentina for six months in 1960–1. Desmond Eager, the Hampshire secretary offered me the position via MCC who used to approach the counties for coaches. I went by boat which took three weeks each way – that was a holiday in itself! They only had about six teams in Buenos Aires in a little league but had a Test match between Argentina and Brazil when I was over there. Most of the Brazilian team were English players who worked for Western Union and lived in Rio. When they arrived at the Hurlingham club in Buenos Aires to play they were one short and it happened to be the wicket-keeper! I suggested to the Argentine skipper Alf Roberts that I played for Brazil, and scored a hundred for them – they weren't too pleased with me after that!

My ambition was to help Hampshire win the County Championship and I was very lucky in doing so in my last year 1961. We had finished third under Desmond Eager in 1955, the highest Hampshire had ever been in its history, then in 1958 we were runners-up. During the run-in to the end of the 1961 season all the games became important and there are many memories, but the match at Bournemouth against Derbyshire when we won was probably the greatest. I used to say in some of those declaration games, 'It ain't half a bloody game,' although my language was a bit stronger than that sometimes! A lot of it was down to Derek Shackleton as Colin [Ingleby-Mackenzie] made some diabolical declarations. He shouldn't really have got away with it but he did – he was a born gambler!

I played two or three matches in 1962 but Brian Timms, who I coached, had taken over by then. I was 39 and the committee understandably wanted to bring in a youngster although I didn't plan to retire just because we had won the Championship. I also played one match in 1966 at Basingstoke against Surrey as all the wicket-keepers were injured. I thought I kept wicket quite well and also scored 20-odd runs – not bad for a 44-year-old! I was on the staff as coach at the time, taking over from Arthur Holt, so I kept myself fit and continued coaching until 1967, but the pay was dreadful.

I then decided I had to do something else with my life and my other interest was in the building trade which my father was in. I had put my house up myself from October to May in 1958, with the help of my father and my two kids loading the bricks up. I would give them tuppence or threepence so we could make a good start in the morning! I financed it from my benefit in 1957 which realised £3,200, the highest for a Hampshire player at that time. I was then taken on full-time by a very good building firm in Bournemouth, A Lambert & Son, where I finished up as director. I actually started with them during the winter of 1961 and stayed until I fully retired in 1987. I live quietly in Mudeford now and have a sister living in a house either side of me and a daughter living locally, whilst my son lives abroad.

I still occasionally support the county although have no direct involvement with them – it's very different now but I have no regrets. John Arlott was my greatest cricketing mate. I first met him at the County Ground in Southampton when I used to catch the train up from Christchurch. John was a policeman in Southampton and would deviate from his beat to watch us at the nets. He was very good to me and a very generous man – I would visit him in Alderney right through to when he died.

My hobby was and still is fishing. I had a 20-foot boat in the harbour with an inboard engine and used to go out to sea, which was lovely on a nice day.

It became difficult on my own though when the knee started to play me up so I sold it in 1996. Going out to sea as a 74-year-old used to worry the family – they thought I would fall overboard! My right arthritic knee was definitely a legacy of wicket-keeping and isn't very good at all. I get a bit of discomfort in the left knee as well which is no surprise as just a day in the field with say 120 overs up and down – that's over 700 times you do the knees bend exercise. Take that over 15 years and it has got to have an effect.

Memorable Game

It is not easy to highlight one particularly memorable game as there were so many. My first hundred against Worcester at Southampton in 1951 I remember well.

14, 16, 17 July 1951. Hampshire won by five wickets

Harrison batted with great skill for his maiden century which earned him his county cap. His century partnerships with McCorkell and Walker enabled Hampshire to establish a base for a fine victory shortly before close of play on the final day.

Hampshire

N. McCorkell st Yarnold b Howorth	64	c Perks b Howorth	22
N.H. Rogers b Flavell	1	c Yarnold b Howorth	3
L.Harrison b Howorth	122	lbw b Perks	13
E.D.R. Eager st Yarnold b Howorth	20	c Yarnold b Perks	11
C. Walker c Perks b Jenkins	62	c Outschoorn b Howorth	3
J.R. Gray c Wyatt b Howorth	25	not out	18
D. Shackleton b Howorth	35	not out	7
G. Hill not out	13		
A.F.H. Debnam not out	1		
C.J. Knott did not bat			
V.H.D. Cannings did not bat			
B 3, l-b 4, n-b 2	9	B 4, l-b 1	5
(7 wkts dec)	352	(5 wkts)	82

Worcestershire

E. Cooper b Cannings	0	c Rogers b Knott	31
D.J. Kenyon c Rogers b Shackleton	0	b Walker	38
L. Outschoorn c Rogers b Knott	10	c Knott b Hill	1
R.E.S. Wyatt c Harrison b Shackleton	31	b Gray	16
G. Dews b Shackleton	4	lbw b Shackleton	4
R. Broadbent lbw b Shackleton	8	c Walker b Hill	93
R.O. Jenkins c McCorkell b Cannings	4	c Gray b Shackleton	51
R. Howorth not out	17	not out	28

H. Yarnold b Cannings	2	b Shackleton	0
R.T.D. Perks b Shackleton	1	c Harrison b Cannings	46
J. Flavell c Hill b Gray	8	b Cannings	0
B 5, l-b 3, w 5, n-b 2	15	B 5, l-b 16, n-b 2	23
	100		331

Worcestershire Bowling

	O	M	R	W	O	M	R	W
Perks	40	17	96	0	6.1	0	30	2
Flavell	13	3	42	1				
Howorth	54	22	109	5	6	0	47	3
Wyatt	4	0	21	0				
Jenkins	23	5	75	1				

Hampshire Bowling

	O	M	R	W	O	M	R	W
Shackleton	27	14	30	5	27	6	88	3
Cannings	24	12	19	3	23.5	5	64	2
Gray	7.3	2	16	1	9	2	29	1
Knott	8	2	20	1	23	6	59	1
Hill					22	7	35	2
Walker					22	12	33	1

Umpires: F.W. Price and T. Spencer

Also memorable were a ton [101] I scored against Yorkshire at Scarborough in 1952 and my highest score [153] at Bournemouth the same year against Notts. Having lived here all my life it was more or less my home ground so knowing the wicket must have helped. It was no good 'quickies' trying to bounce you out as it was such a placid wicket, whereas Portsmouth was just the opposite with the ball flying all over the place.

Proudest Moment
This has to be the winning of the Championship in 1961, especially after having waited for such a long time. I started pre-war as a batter and played twice in 1939, my first game against Worcestershire as a 17-year-old when I scored 12. Then I played against a very useful Yorkshire team with Sutcliffe, Verity, etc., who had to beat us to win the Championship. So I had played for many years and the game against Derbyshire to win the Championship was certainly one I remember. Danny Livingstone caught a skier out in the deep to win the match – it went up miles! To be part of a Championship-winning side was a wonderful way to end my career.

A technically very sound wicket-keeper and middle-order right-hand batsman, Harrison scored 8,854 runs (17.49) with 682 dismissals (579 ct, 103 st).

–32–

Jim Parks (b. 1931)

Sussex, Somerset and England

At the end of the 1959 season I thought I would go on tour as second keeper to the West Indies, but they picked Roy Swetman and Keith Andrew so I went to Trinidad coaching. Towards the end of the tour P.B.H. May was ill and Ken Barrington was injured in Guyana. I got the MCC call-up at 12 o'clock on the Saturday and was on the midnight flight after getting permission from Trinidad to go, as I was working for them. I arrived in Guyana in the early hours of Sunday and was taken for a long net that morning against Brian Statham, Fred Trueman and Alan Moss, as I hadn't played at all that winter. They were bowling bouncers at me as that was the sort of thing you got over there. At the last minute Kenny Barrington decided he was fit so I was 12th man and stayed with the team to play in the last Test at Port-of-Spain. I kept wicket against South Africa in the 1960 home series and went to New Zealand in 1960-1 which was not a full tour, but an 'A' team trip. We did play against New Zealand but they were not classed as Test matches. I went with John Murray but was injured early on and could not keep wicket. I was hit in the box which was really painful – Tony McGibbon made one nip back and I felt so rough I couldn't stand at the bar! John had to keep all the time – I just played as a batsman and had to see a specialist when I came back.

John Murray kept wicket for England in 1961 and 1962 and I expected to go to Australia in the winter of 1962–3 but he and Alan Smith went instead. John was injured so Alan kept for England, which was a remarkable thing.

For the 1963 season against West Indies the selectors started with Keith Andrew who was the best keeper of the lot and played in the first Test. England were annihilated at Old Trafford though, and it was decided to bring me in to bolster the batting. I played in the drawn second Test at Lord's and then had a run of about 30 consecutive Tests. I think that Lord's match was the best Test ever in as much as you not only had a great finish, but the game fluctuated throughout. On the last ball you could have had every result and it was a marvellous game. I also remember Brian Close took a battering from Hall and Griffith.

Jimmy Binks went to India with me in 1963–4 and John Murray to South Africa and Australia [1964–5 and 1965–6]. When I was eventually left out in the last Test against the West Indies in 1966, John came back in.

My sole Test bowling victim was Dilip Sardesai at Kanpur, India in the last Test match in 1964. We previously had four draws and at the end of the first day we were about 270–2. We had a party that night and chatted up 'Tiger' Pataudi, the Indian captain. We agreed to declare that night if he would declare the following night, so we each had one day and could then make a game from the last three days. 'Tiger' agreed but unfortunately the Indian Board wouldn't so we batted on and scored 559. I was batting at number seven and scored 51 not out when we declared. We put them in for about an hour and they were 20–2 overnight. We had four spinners in our side [Titmus, Mortimore, Wilson and Parfitt] and opened with Fred Titmus. We then had a rest day and on the third day bowled them out for 266 and made them follow on. It was impossible to bowl them out twice, though, and with the temperature at about 100 degrees for the first three days, by teatime of the last day Mike Smith said, 'You don't want to keep wicket any longer, do you?' I said, 'No I don't,' so had a bowl instead and Brian Bolus went behind the stumps. Sardesai was on 87 at the time and coasting to a century on a beautiful wicket. I bowled a little loosener first ball, then the second ball bowled a 'google' to him and, driving the leg-spinner, he got an inside edge and it was 'caught Edrich, bowled Parks'!

I went to the West Indies in 1967–8 as number two to Alan Knott at the age of 36 and also as a back-up batsman. Alan had a nightmare at the beginning of the tour and the night before the first Test in Trinidad the committee decided there was no way he was going to keep wicket, so I went into the nets the next morning and kept wicket in the first three Tests. I remember the wicket in Jamaica in the second Test cracked all over the place and Snowy bowled one that took off and went straight down to fine leg for four byes! We were fighting hard and Wes Hall on a length hit me on the Adam's apple. We made more of it than it was though as we were fighting against time! Then unfortunately I broke a finger in Barbados, Knotty came in for the fourth Test and I never played again for England.

With regards to my county cricket career with Sussex, 1959 was my first full season as a keeper. I took over at the end of 1958 and didn't know at the beginning of the '59 season if I would still be wicket-keeper. I didn't even practice as a keeper, just bowled my leg-spinners and batted. When the team went out for the first match, I was keeping wicket – it was typical of our skipper, Robin Marlar!

Sussex had a good season in 1959 and I scored the fastest hundred of the year at Old Trafford in 63 minutes in a funny match. Both sides were bowled out on the first day when it seamed around a bit and in fact we were batting overnight in the second innings. The next day Ted Dexter scored a magnificent century and was out just as the second new ball was being taken. I can remember crossing him going in to bat and saying, 'Fancy getting out now!' As fate would have it, they took the new ball straight away with Ken Higgs bowling. It was one of those days when everything came off and every shot seemed to go for four. I took 38 off Higgs's first two overs! Obviously you didn't slog Brian Statham down the other end but I was still managing to collect my runs off him. I scored 50-odd in half an hour and realised the hundred was on. They took Ken Higgs off and put Colin Hilton on. He was the quickest of the lot but bowled them all over the place. I only hit one six but got to 90-odd in 55 minutes and the lads on the pavilion were giving me the signal but I had plenty of time to get my hundred so there were no panic stations. I won two cups that year, one for the wicket-keeping award and one for the fastest century which Denis Compton presented to me. He was my hero so that was rather nice.

Sussex certainly worked out the one-day cricket quicker than anyone else and that was down to Ted Dexter who decided on how to play the game. The very first Gillette Cup match we played Kent at Tunbridge Wells in 1963 and scored over 300 runs in 65 overs when they were still playing the game properly with slips, gully etc. We defended from the start with one slip and everyone back as they do nowadays. We won quite easily and although Peter Richardson scored a century, they scored about 250 without getting anywhere near us. I remember our secretary received a letter from the chairman of Kent saying what a disgusting performance by Sussex – we hadn't played in the true spirit of the game! Our policy was to bat first and get enough runs to put pressure on the other side before everyone else worked the game out. For two years when we won the Gillette Cup in 1963 and '64 it worked perfectly.

I was captain of Sussex until mid-way through the 1968 season when the pressures got to me. I decided at the start of the season on my return from the West Indies we ought to have Mike Griffith keeping wicket and I would play as a fielder/batsman. We started badly and I went behind the stumps and tried to skipper from there but the pressure was too much and I gave it up. Funnily enough I relinquished the captaincy at the same time as Fred Titmus, and though we were good friends we hadn't talked about it, but the pressure was too much for him as well.

I continued playing for Sussex until 1972, leaving controversially at the end of that season. The then chairman of the club, Eddie Harrison and myself hadn't seen eye to eye for some time. I was working for Whitbread's at the time and asked my boss, who was keen on cricket, if I could play for one more year before retiring at the end of 1973, to which he agreed. I went to the county as I knew the committee was meeting to discuss players' contracts and asked the secretary Arthur Dumbrell for one more year. I had friends on the committee and found out from Walter Denman, John Denman's father, that they would only offer match money if I was fit, which I felt it to be the biggest insult for somebody who never broke down in 24 years. I only missed one match in 1972 in the Gillette Cup against Worcester which we lost. I was one of two players to score 1,000 runs with Geoff Greenidge that season and was fit as a fiddle. I nearly walked out of the ground in the middle of a match when I heard, but hung on until the end of the season when they formally told me. All I wanted was a contract for a year to start as wicket-keeper/batsman. We had Alan Mansell pushing for a place and my argument was that it would have been good to have me there when 'Snowy' and 'Greigy' were playing in the Test match. Mansell would have played for half of the season and it would have been a good way to bring him on but eventually I withdrew my registration with Sussex. The committee wanted to see me straight away, but I finally saw them in March 1973 and remember sitting at one end of the table with Eddie Harrison at the other. There were about a dozen on the sub-committee in those days and I looked around and thought there was no-one there who knew anything about cricket! After half an hour I got up and said, 'Sorry, I think you have lost two for the price of one,' as my son Bobby was coming along then. I told them exactly what they could do with their contract and walked out, rang Somerset the same night, drove down and signed the next day. Brian Close had been on to me all winter. The last thing I wanted to do was to leave Sussex, but in the end I had two very happy seasons with Somerset, playing with Brian and Tom Cartwright. Ian Botham and Viv Richards also came through in their first seasons.

I then went to work for Whitbread's full-time. I had started with them in 1968 so had six years with them in the winter and playing in the summer. I remember Eddie Harrison one winter asking me how I kept fit working in the beer trade. I replied, 'It's not easy – from 1 January I start running into the pubs instead of walking!' I had a complete break from the game until I came back in 1987. I was in senior management by then and was offered early retirement by Whitbread's in the autumn of 1986. I was coming up to 55 and, as the terms were favourable and they were shedding workers of my age I accepted. I cannot fault the company; they looked after me well and still do.

There was no intention of coming back to Sussex. In fact, as my wife is Welsh, we were looking for properties in Wales when Sussex phoned to ask me to look after the second XI for a couple of months after Stewart Storey had left as coach. I did so and then the marketing job came up at the county. I can't prove it but I think it was in the back of their minds all along. I remember ringing my wife and she agreed, as it was a job I very much liked to do. We sold the house and bought a car! I stayed with Sussex as marketing manager until my retirement in 1997.

It was marvellous to see so many friends and to have all the family there in the last match I played in at Haywards Heath in August 1997 [for an Old England XI]. In fact I will continue to manage the Old England XI until the year 2000. We have sponsorship until then from American Express.

In the '60s I turned to writing. The background to my book *Runs in the Sun*, which came out in 1961, was that I got to know John Graydon, who was editor of Provincial Newspapers as they were then known before they became United Newspapers. In fact he 'ghosted' that book – I didn't write it. I then worked for him for about three years in the winter, reporting football matches and learning to write. So when it came to my second book *Time to Hit Out*, in 1966 I wrote it myself. The four Commonwealth books of cricket came later when there was another editor, who got me involved with the publishers. I wrote most of them and edited them myself, with help from friends like Ted Dexter, Fred Titmus and David Allen, who wrote articles for me.

As for my hobby of photography, I don't really have the time for it now. I used to take cine films on tour and keep saying to myself that I must put them on to video tapes now.

Memorable Game

The most memorable game I played was in the fifth Test at Port-of-Spain, Trinidad in 1960 when I scored my maiden Test century. M.J.K. Smith and I added 197 for the seventh wicket in that Test, which is still a record against the West Indies. We added 60 overnight going into the fifth day and, as I had been coaching in Pointe-a-Pierre, a whole group came up to see me and we went out that night and I was well away. I returned to the hotel at about one o'clock in the morning, which you couldn't do nowadays. I remember arriving back and the Press, who were still in the bar, beckoned me over for a drink! They were our friends in those days; they weren't out to do you down.

The next day I went out and scored a hundred and enjoyed it! It was the first time I had played Sonny Ramadhin since I had faced him in 1950 as a young boy when they caught us on a wet wicket at Hove. I had a marvellous match then scoring nought and one [albeit trapped both times by Gerry

Gomez]. I hadn't seen Sonny since and playing against him on a beautiful wicket and in perfect sunlight I could actually watch the ball going round in the air so you could pick him. It was nice to gain revenge and score a hundred against him.

25, 26, 28, 29, 30, 31 March 1960. Match drawn
On a wicket which favoured the batsman, Parks and Smith successfully batted into the fifth day of the last Test. Their record partnership foiled any hope of a West Indies revival as England won the series 1–0.

England

G. Pullar c Sobers b Griffith	10	c and b Sobers	54
M.C. Cowdrey c Alexander b Sobers	119	c Worrell b Hall	0
E.R. Dexter c and b Sobers	76	run out	47
R. Subba Row c Hunte b Hall	22	lbw b Ramadhin	13
K.F. Barrington c Alex'der b Ramadhin	69	c McMorris b Sobers	6
M.J.K. Smith b Ramadhin	20	c Alexander b Hunte	96
J.M. Parks c and b Sobers	43	not out	101
R. Illingworth c Sobers b Ramadhin	0		
D.A. Allen c sub b Ramadhin	7	run out	25
F.S. Trueman not out	10	not out	2
A.E. Moss b Watson	1		
B 7, n-b 9	16	B 2, l-b 3, n-b 1	6
	393	(7 wkts dec)	350

1/19 2/210 3/215 4/268 5/317
6/350 7/350 8/374 9/388

1/3 2/69 3/102 4/136
5/145 6/148 7/345

West Indies

C. Hunte not out	72	st Parks b Illingworth	36
E. McMorris run out	13	lbw b Moss	2
F.C.M. Alexander b Allen	26	not out	4
G. Sobers b Moss	92	not out	49
C.L. Walcott st Parks b Allen	53	c Parks b Barrington	22
F.M. Worrell b Trueman	15	c Trueman b Pullar	61
R. Kanhai b Moss	6	c Trueman b Illingworth	34
S. Ramadhin c Cowdrey b Dexter	13		
W. Hall b Trueman	29		
C. Griffith not out	5		
C. Watson did not bat			
B 6, l-b 4, n-b 4	14	L-b 1	1
	(8 wkts dec) 338	(5 wkts)	209

1/26 2/103 3/190 4/216
5/227 6/230 7/263 8/328

1/11 2/72 3/75
4/107 5/194

West Indies Bowling

	O	M	R	W	O	M	R	W
Hall	24	3	83	1	4	0	16	1
Griffith	15	2	62	1	9	1	40	0
Watson	18.2	3	52	1	14	1	52	0
Ramadhin	34	13	73	4	34	9	67	1
Worrell	8	1	29	0	22	5	44	0
Sobers	20	1	75	3	29	6	84	2
Walcott	4	2	3	0	7	2	24	0
Hunte					5	1	17	1

England Bowling

	O	M	R	W	O	M	R	W
Trueman	37.3	6	103	2	5	1	22	0
Moss	34	3	94	2	4	0	16	1
Allen	24	1	61	2	15	2	57	0
Illingworth	12	4	25	0	16	3	53	2
Dexter	4	1	20	1				
Barrington	8	0	21	0	8	2	27	1
Subba Row					1	0	2	0
Smith					1	0	15	0
Pullar					1	0	1	1
Cowdrey					1	0	15	0

Umpires: C. Jordan and C. Kippins

Proudest Moment
The proudest moment in cricket for me was receiving my first England cap when I made my debut against Pakistan in 1954 at Old Trafford.

A brilliant right-handed stroke-player and wicket-keeper, Parks scored 36,662 runs (34.81) including 51 centuries, took 51 wickets (43.82) and 1,181 dismissals (1,088 ct, 93 st). In 46 Test matches, he scored 1,962 runs (32.16) including 2 centuries, took 1–43 and 114 dismissals (103 ct, 11 st).

–33–

George Tribe (b. 1920)

Victoria, Northants and Australia

1959 was my last season in county cricket with Northamptonshire. The main reason we returned to Australia was that we hadn't been over for about eight years and, whilst I had lost both my parents, my wife's parents hadn't seen their grandchildren Janet and David during that time. So while I was fairly comfortable at the county, I also had to take into account the family side of things. I was 38 and we had to make a decision whether to go home then or carry on with the twins' education in England. I told Northampton I had decided to go home, and the feedback from the people connected with the club was so unexpected – I didn't realise the amount of their respect for what I had achieved with the county. In 1958 I didn't have a very good season with the bat and decided I had better concentrate a bit more and score a few more runs in 1959, so that we could get further up the Championship.

I remember my first and last matches at Lord's. In the first game in 1952 I took Syd Brown's wicket with my first ball and finished with figures of 1–90. I also thought I had Denis Compton plumb lbw from the Nursery end, it kept low and hit him in the ankle but Paddy Corrall, the old Leicestershire wicket-keeper, gave him not out. Denis never said anything, he just smiled then started to carve me up a bit and scored a century! Then the last time I played at Lord's at the end of the 1959 season, Middlesex scored 261 in their first innings. We were 230–9 when I was joined by Martin Dilley, the fast bowler. Fred Titmus was bowling and when we had levelled the score I said to him, 'Look at the Long Room, I am going to try and mark the window up there.' There was nothing in the result, as we were about fifth or sixth in the championship. If Fred pitched it up I was going to have a go anyway and hit it with a left-handed 'slog' like Rodney Marsh used to. It went over the top, landed about ten feet from the window and rolled back! We played Surrey in my last game at the Oval and I ended up with 1,001 runs for the season. So I did the 'double', but was so disappointed I didn't hit the window!

I didn't like to bowl against defensive batsmen like Trevor Bailey as you had less chance of getting a wicket, although I had admiration for him as he had great concentration. I enjoyed playing against Denis Compton as he would give you a chance – not that I got him out many times. I didn't mind bowling against Gary Sobers either, who gave you a chance, and I knocked down his stumps a couple of times in 1957. In 1961 he paid me the greatest compliment at a cocktail party in Melbourne when I said, 'Gary, I will come and bowl at you in the nets if you like.' He said, 'No, no man, you keep away from me, you will get me out of form!'

I think I only once went onto a pitch with an injury so I was a bit fortunate, though I had a few bruises along the way! Freddie Ridgway was the only player who really hurt me when he hit me in the thigh.

I had a lovely farewell dinner with over 400 people at the Tavistock Hotel in London attended by Jim Laker and Ben Barnett. Then Freddie Brown and a couple of other guys came to see me on the ship, the SS *Orion*, the next day and we started our 11,000-mile trip back to Australia.

We came back to Melbourne, where I had VIP treatment from the Victoria Cricket Association, who wanted me to play in first-grade cricket again. I could have got back into the Victoria side, but I had been away for eight seasons, living in a suitcase in the summertime and thought I ought to settle down and get a job. So I worked for British Timken, a Queensland printing company in Melbourne for about 15 years. They made envelopes and photographic wallets, I was on the road for them and also became manager for a while. At the same time I played second-grade competition with Yarraville, where I was born, which was the same club I played for when I was a boy. I was there for five seasons, captaining and coaching the team and giving the kids the opportunity I had when I was playing against men at the age of about 13. We won the Premiership one year and I was back on the honours board after 30 years.

After five years I decided to retire from competitive cricket. By that time Frank Tyson was involved in coaching Melbourne University and, with his ABC commentating commitments, asked me if I could assist him in the coaching one night a week. I took on the coaching and was there for the next nine years until about 1974. We coached both Jimmy Higgs and Paul Sheahan, who went on to play for Australia, but in the end I was finding it difficult to combine the cricket with my business work. I was getting up a five o'clock in the morning to keep fit and it became too much for me.

I had a break for one year, then was persuaded by Peter Williams, who I knew from Melbourne University, to go to Richmond Cricket Club. I was also interested because Jimmy Higgs had joined from university and Graham Yallop was also there with Bob Cowper's brother, Dave. At about the same time Frank became director of coaching for the Victoria Cricket Association and set up the association of coaching for coaches which I became involved with, going round the country areas. I stayed at Richmond for four years until 1980 – we had a good side and won the Championship one year. However my wife was ill and died of cancer so I gave it up for a while, as it took me some time to get over that.

I am not involved any more in coaching – my partner and I live in retirement at Rye, south of Melbourne about two miles from the ocean. We go away to Queensland in the winter and when I come back I do work around the house like painting and I have a fairly big garden to look after.

Memorable Game

The most memorable game I played was at Adelaide in November 1945 when I got Bradman out. He was stumped off the third ball I bowled to him in the second innings when he was on 119. We got 548 and after South Australia followed on, we had to score 79 in half an hour. Lindsay Hassett said we will bat to six and everybody was to pad up as we had to catch the train at 6.20 p.m. Coming back from Adelaide celebrating the victory, when we arrived on Murray Bridge, the station master came out to tell me the team for the first Test has been picked and I had been selected. About a week later I was on a plane for the first time flying to Brisbane for my Test debut – it all happened very quickly!

15, 16, 18, 19 November 1945. Victoria won by nine wickets

Tribe staked his claim for a place in the Test side with an impressive haul of 13 wickets in the match. Likewise, Miller played a superb innings and Victoria completed the victory with two minutes to spare.

South Australia

R.J. Craig b Tribe	36	c Hassett b Johnson	3
V.R. Gibson b Miller	5	b Tribe	1
P.L. Ridings lbw b Tribe	27	b Tribe	9
R.A. Hamence lbw b Tribe	2	c and b Freer	116
D.G. Bradman st Baker b Johnson	43	st Baker b Tribe	119

R. James b Miller	73	c Meuleman b Ring	34
K. Gogler lbw b Tribe	36	b Tribe	33
J.L. Mann c and b Tribe	20	lbw b Tribe	5
B. Dooland c and b Tribe	2	not out	16
G. Noblet b Tribe	9	lbw b Tribe	1
W. Englefield not out	4	b Ring	4
B 4, l-b 8, w 1	13	B 11, l-b 3, n-b 1	15
	270		356

Victoria

G.E. Tamblyn c and b Dooland	75		
K. Meuleman c Englefield b Dooland	87		
M. Harvey c Englefield b Gibson	9	not out	3
K.R. Miller run out	188	c Englefield b Mann	33
A.L. Hassett b Ridings	114	not out	36
I. Johnson c Dooland b Gibson	17		
F. Freer run out	15		
D. Ring b Ridings	5		
E.A. Baker st Englefield b Dooland	1		
G. Tribe b Dooland	7		
W. Johnston not out	5		
B 12, l-b 8, w 2, n-b 3	25	B 7	7
	548	(1 wkt)	79

Victoria Bowling

	O	M	R	W	O	M	R	W
Johnston	8	0	30	0	13	1	35	0
Freer	7	1	19	0	21	8	84	1
Miller	11	1	32	2	2	0	10	0
Johnson	20	4	55	1	14	3	43	1
Tribe	30.5	4	85	7	23	2	68	6
Ring	10	0	36	0	25	1	99	2
Hassett					1	0	2	0

South Australia Bowling

	O	M	R	W	O	M	R	W
Noblet	24	7	57	0	2	0	21	0
Gibson	36	11	96	2	2	0	25	0
Ridings	27	5	79	2	2	0	14	0
Dooland	54.3	2	229	4				
Mann	28	10	50	0	1.7	0	12	1
Gogler	4	0	12	0				

Umpires: J.D. Scott and L.A. Smith

Proudest Moment

One of the proudest moments for me in cricket, naturally, was being picked to play for my country for the first time at Brisbane in 1946 against England. However my proudest moment was getting back into the side for the fifth Test. I played in the first two Tests and was dropped for the Melbourne and Adelaide matches. Then when Victoria played MCC at Melbourne in February '46, I scored 60 runs batting at number nine though was actually late getting to the ground – the train was held up and I was lucky to bat all! I had just got into the dressing-room, changed and put my pads on when I was in. I took six wickets in the second innings, everything happened within about five hours and I was back in for the last Test at Sydney. Until I was dropped after the second Test at Sydney, I had never been left out of a team since I established a regular place in the Yarraville first XI at the age of 18. Then out of the blue I had this telegram when I was playing in the last Test recommending me to play in England. Don Bradman said to me, 'Don't forget to come back and try and get on the 1948 tour.' However I couldn't get a passage back, so I missed the tour and never played another first-class game in Australia!

A genuine all-rounder but best remembered as a back-of-the-hand left-arm spinner, Tribe scored 10,177 runs (27.35) including 7 centuries, took 1,378 wickets (20.55) and 239 catches. In 3 Test matches, he scored 35 runs (17.50) and took 2 wickets (165.00).

–34–

William (Gilbert) Parkhouse (b. 1925)

Glamorgan and England

In 1959 I scored my highest number of runs in a season [2,243 at an average of 48.76]. My special memory of that season was my highest Test score of 78 against India at Headingley [putting on 146 with Geoff Pullar for the first wicket and setting a new England record against India, when recalled to the Test arena after a gap of nine years – England won by an innings and 173 runs].

I retired from first-class cricket at the end of the 1964 season to take up coaching. I coached for the Quick Cricket Club in Hague, Holland in 1975, then was Worcester coach in 1966. In August 1966 I took a post at Melville College, Edinburgh, later to become Stuarts Melville, until retirement.

I was an international hockey umpire, travelling to Spain and Belgium and was also a Scottish selector for their senior cricket. In March 1977 I was invited to the centenary Test between Australia and England in Melbourne and in 1990 went to Jamaica for the fortieth anniversary of the West Indies first Test match played at Lord's.

My hobbies were golf and fishing and also the occasional shoot. I enjoyed these activities from 1966 until I retired in the mid '80s. Since retirement I have been unable to participate in any sport and do not venture out nowadays due to ill-health. However I still avidly follow sport through television coverage.

Memorable Game

The most memorable game I played in was when I made my Test debut at Lord's against the West Indies in June 1950. It was a great honour and the second innings was worth remembering. I also was introduced to King George VI before the start of the game.

24, 26, 27, 28, 29 June 1950. West Indies won by 326 runs

The West Indies were worthy winners of their historic first Test victory in England. Parkhouse was one of the few England batsmen to offer any resistance against the guile of Ramadhin and Valentine. He grew in confidence to display an array of strokes in an attractive partnership with Washbrook in the second innings.

West Indies

A.F. Rae c and b Jenkins	106	b Jenkins	24
J.B. Stollmeyer lbw b Wardle	20	b Jenkins	30
F.M. Worrell b Bedser	52	c Doggart b Jenkins	45
E. Weekes b Bedser	63	run out	63
C.L. Walcott st Evans b Jenkins	14	not out	168
G.E. Gomez st Evans b Jenkins	1	c Edrich b Bedser	70
R.J. Christiani b Bedser	33	not out	5
J.D. Goddard b Wardle	14	c Evans b Jenkins	11
P.E. Jones c Evans b Jenkins	0		
S. Ramadhin not out	1		
A.L. Valentine c Hutton b Jenkins	5		
B 10, l-b 5, w 1, n-b 1	17	L-b 8, n-b 1	9
	326	(6 wkts dec)	425

1/37 2/128 3/233 4/262 5/273
6/274 7/320 8/320 9/320

1/48 2/75 3/108 4/146
5/199 6/410

England

L. Hutton st Walcott b Valentine	35	b Valentine	10
C. Washbrook st Walcott b Ramadhin	36	b Ramadhin	114
W.J. Edrich c Walcott b Ramadhin	8	c Jones b Ramadhin	8
G.H.G. Doggart lbw b Ramadhin	0	b Ramadhin	25
W.G.A. Parkhouse b Valentine	0	c Goddard b Valentine	48
N.W.D. Yardley b Valentine	16	c Weekes b Valentine	19
T.G. Evans b Ramadhin	8	c Rae b Ramadhin	2
R.O. Jenkins c Walcott b Valentine	4	b Ramadhin	4
J.H. Wardle not out	33	lbw b Worrell	21

			A.V. Bedser b Ramadhin	5	b Ramadhin	0
R. Berry c Goddard b Jones	2	not out	0
B 2, l-b 1, w 1	4	B 16, l-b 7	23
	151		274

1/62 2/74 3/74 4/75 5/86 6/102
7/110 8/113 9/122

1/28 2/57 3/140 4/218 5/228
6/238 7/245 8/258 9/258

England Bowling

	O	M	R	W	O	M	R	W
Bedser	40	14	60	3	44	16	80	1
Edrich	16	4	30	0	13	2	37	0
Jenkins	35.2	6	116	5	59	13	174	4
Wardle	17	6	46	2	30	10	58	0
Berry	19	7	45	0	32	15	67	0
Yardley	4	1	12	0				

West Indies Bowling

	O	M	R	W	O	M	R	W
Jones	8.4	2	13	1	7	1	22	0
Worrell	10	4	20	0	22.3	9	39	1
Valentine	45	28	48	4	71	47	79	3
Ramadhin	43	27	66	5	72	43	86	6
Gomez					13	1	25	0
Goddard					6	6	0	0

Umpires: D. Davies and F.S. Lee

Proudest Moment

My proudest moment in cricket, barring meeting the King, was my double century [201] scored for Glamorgan against Kent at Swansea on 23 May 1956.

A sound right-handed opening batsman and brilliant slip fielder, Parkhouse scored 23,508 runs (31.68) including 32 centuries and 323 catches. In 7 Test matches, he scored 373 runs (28.69) and 3 catches.

Trevor Bailey

Wilf Wooller

Roy Tattersall

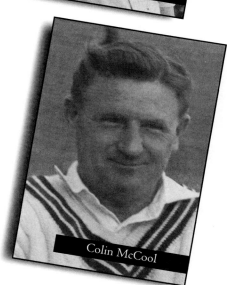

Colin McCool

Donald Carr

Les Jackson

Alan Moss

Robin Marlar

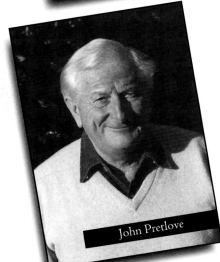
John Pretlove

Martin Horton

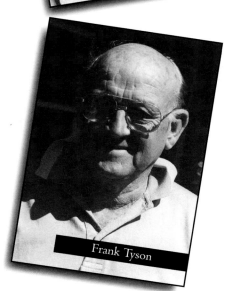
Frank Tyson

Reg Simpson

Godfrey Evans

Don Shepherd

Maurice Tremlett

Eric Bedser

Brian Boshier

Fred Titmus

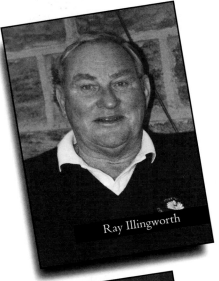

Ray Illingworth

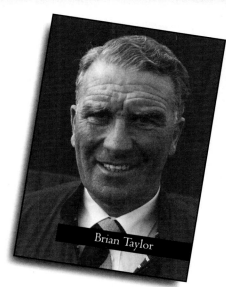

Brian Taylor

Derek Shackleton

Derek Richardson

Gamini Goonesena

Mike Smith

Keith Andrew

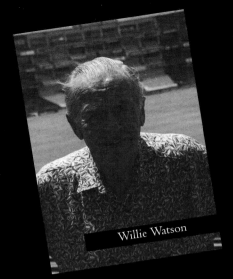

Willie Watson

Maurice Hallam

Cyril Washbrook

Alan Oakman

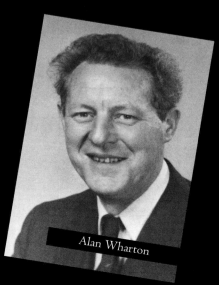

Alan Wharton

Leo Harrison

Jim Parks

George Tribe

William Parkhouse

Don Kenyon

Norman Horner

Fred Trueman

Doug Insole

Malcolm Hilton

Allan Watkins

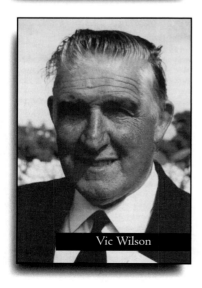

Vic Wilson

Jack Robertson

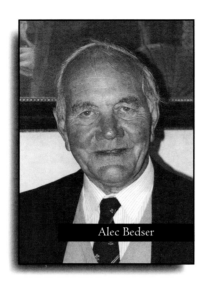

Alec Bedser

Don Smith

Colin Ingleby-Mackenzie

Roy Marshall

Brian Close

Raman Subba Row

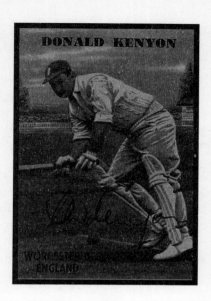

–35–

Don Kenyon (1924–1996)

Worcestershire and England

As told by Mrs Jean Kenyon

Don captained Worcester right through from 1959, when he was asked by the committee to be the first professional to captain the side just two weeks before the start of the season, until he retired. He was a shrewd man and had good judgement in making decisions needed as a captain. In 1967, his last season, Don scored just one century but it was an excellent one against Essex. Don hit 21 runs off the final six balls which helped win the match with a minute to spare.

I remember when Worcester won the County Championship in 1964, the wives were still not allowed into the pavilion so we stood outside with the crowd. In an interview Don recalled the last game of the season, 'I was lucky enough to score a hundred in the match against Gloucester at the end of the season and we scored almost 400. Once the total of almost 400 was there we knew we had a good chance of beating them. We eventually won by an innings and two runs. Having to wait for an hour to hear that Warwickshire had lost at Hampshire, immediately we knew we had won the Championship. We were a great side with at least seven England players and the finest two quick bowlers in the country at that time, so it was an easy one to skipper. I was very pleased because it gave me great pleasure to have been captain of a Championship-winning side for the first time.'

That winter they went on tour for four months round the world and also to Jamaica the following winter. The managing director of the steel company where Don worked had just bought a cine camera and Don borrowed it and took it on tour. They went to Kenya, India, Kuala Lumpur, Hong Kong, Singapore and Rhodesia and had a wonderful reception. He had a particularly warm welcome in Rhodesia, where Don had coached for two years during the winter of 1948–9 and 1949–50. I went out with him for the second year.

During the winter months, for the first two years as a pro Don delivered cars for one of the committee men who had a garage. He took a year off to clear the ground when our house in Worcester was built (we also built our Stourbridge home in 1961). He then became a salesman for a steel stock-holder called the Dudley Iron & Steel Co. from about 1949. He worked full-time for them when he retired from cricket until he took redundancy when he was about 58.

Don was a Test selector for seven years from 1965 to 1972 but was not awarded the MBE, contrary to press reports. He was on the Worcester committee for a number of years but gave it up when he felt he couldn't combine it with his work and do it properly. Don was Worcestershire president for four years from 1986 to 1989. He was also a vice-president, honorary life member of the county and president of Stourbridge cricket society. There was a Don Kenyon knock-out competition which has now become the Don Kenyon memorial cricket knock-out competition, of which I am the patron. He was very proud of being a Black Country man.

Since retirement from cricket, Don's time was occupied by golf, the garden and wine-making, together of course with his family (grandson in particular) – he was very much a family man. If he took any sport on, he had to play it properly and this was certainly the case with golf. He played at Enville Golf Club to a handicap of about seven. I originally made some wine and I think he thought he could do it better so he took over and became very knowledgeable about wines. He also loved going to France – we would go every year, twice a year. In particular he liked the sunshine in the south of France. He was always keen on gardening, particularly geraniums and roses.

He loved his cars, he was a good driver and he would never have anything other than a Rover. Initially it was because in the steel trade, they dealt with Rover and you couldn't go through the gate unless you were in a Rover!

Don was taken ill at a Worcestershire members' evening meeting at the County Ground at New Road in November 1996. He was preparing to show a film of Worcester's 1964 World tour when he collapsed in the Kenyon Room and died, at the age of 72. Strangely, both his father and brother also died at the same age.

One of the nicest tributes I saw came from Jack Bannister, I think because he knew him and knew he had a sense of humour. Jack recalled how Don resolved a difficult situation in a TCCB meeting in the 1970s. Surrey fast bowler Geoff Arnold was up on a charge of using foul and abusive language towards umpire Peter Wight in a Sunday match at Edgbaston. Wight would not reveal the actual words used and was asked to write them down. Don was becoming somewhat impatient with the proceedings and asked, 'Mr Chairman, did the player use any four letter words and if so, did they begin with two letters of the first six in the alphabet?' As soon as Wight nodded, back came Don with, 'Well what are we wasting our time for? He (pointing at Jack) called me that every time he missed the middle of my bat!'

Memorable Game
The most memorable game for Don I think was in 1956 when he made his highest first-class score against Yorkshire at Kidderminster.

11, 12, 13 July 1956. Worcestershire won by an innings and 94 runs
This was the highest individual innings by any batsman in the world since Tom Hayward scored 273 in 1899. His innings was full of attacking strokes in most directions, as Worcestershire convincingly secured their first victory at home over Yorkshire since 1939.

Worcestershire

D. Kenyon c Close b Taylor	259
L. Outschoorn lbw b Appleyard	10
R.G. Broadbent b Wardle	4
G. Dews c Binks b Wardle	57
D.W. Richardson lbw b Appleyard	27
M.J. Horton b Taylor	43
J. Lister not out	20
R.O. Jenkins did not bat	
R. Booth did not bat	
L. Coldwell did not bat	
R. Berry did not bat	
B 8, l-b 8, n-b 4	20
1/18 2/55 3/172 4/239 (6 wkts dec)	440
5/383 6/440	

Yorkshire

F.A. Lowson lbw b Coldwell	18	lbw b Horton	47
K. Taylor c Coldwell b Outschoorn	0	c Jenkins b Horton	28
J.V. Wilson c Booth b Berry	37	c Broadbent b Jenkins	13
D.E.V. Padgett c Horton b Jenkins	12	c and b Jenkins	9

W. Watson c Dews b Horton	45	c Broadbent b Jenkins	7
D.B. Close st Booth b Berry	4	c Lister b Horton	41
R. Illingworth not out	22	b Jenkins	8
J.H. Wardle c Dews b Berry	8	c Broadbent b Horton	17
J.G. Binks b Berry	0	c Richardson b Horton	5
P. Broughton b Berry	12	not out	5
R. Appleyard c Booth b Horton	3	absent hurt	0
W 2	2	B 1, l-b 1, w 1	3
	163		183

1/2 2/32 3/63 4/67 5/79 6/133
7/146 8/146 9/160

1/39 2/87 3/91 4/102 5/135
6/153 7/173 8/173 9/183

Yorkshire Bowling

	O	M	R	W
Broughton	23	1	93	0
Appleyard	34	9	79	2
Wardle	37	13	78	2
Taylor	18.4	5	44	2
Illingworth	18	2	71	0
Close	20	10	55	0

Worcestershire Bowling

	O	M	R	W	O	M	R	W
Coldwell	15	4	35	1	9	2	31	0
Outschoorn	4	0	14	1	5	1	11	0
Berry	26	9	49	5	14	8	13	0
Jenkins	7	0	32	1	22	4	61	4
Horton	10	3	31	2	25	11	64	5

Umpires: H. Elliott and W.T. Jones

Proudest Moment

I think the proudest moment for Don would have been when he played for England against Australia in 1953, Coronation year. Don felt that playing for your country at Lord's was the ultimate for an English cricketer.

A prolific right-handed opening batsman, Kenyon scored 37,002 runs (33.63) including 74 centuries and 327 catches. In 8 Test matches, he scored 192 runs (12.80) and 5 catches.

196

–36–

Norman Horner (b. 1926)

Yorkshire and Warwickshire

Looking back from 1959, I remember the 1960 season in particular as it was my most successful. I was older and playing in a more controlled way than in the '50s. Billy Ibadulla and I had an unbroken first wicket stand of 377 against Surrey at the Oval that year, which broke all Warwickshire partnership records. I hit my highest score of 203 not out on a very good wicket. It was 12 o'clock though before I scored my first run, but one of the few times that I managed to keep my concentration all day! My problem was that I had too many shots and used them too often – it was the only way I could play. I kept my head down this time though and was very tired at the finish when we declared at about ten to six on that first day. Alec Bedser was the opening bowler with David Sydenham. I remember there was also a tall boy called Allom who came from Charterhouse and took 0–53 in the game. He was in the bar afterwards and told us, 'That's it, I'm not playing this game, it's ridiculous!' It was the only game he ever played for Surrey. They batted that night, all next day and it rained all day Friday, so we never got a point out of it!

I remember playing in the Players v Gentlemen game at the end of the 1962 season, which was part of the Scarborough festival [scoring 30 and 49 not out for the Players in helping secure a seven wicket victory]. It was very well attended and a social week where they looked after you – the cricket was almost incidental. The cricket suited me as I could play my shots and we also played against Pakistan the same week. I had my benefit that year as well which was a county record at that time.

I enjoyed playing in the Gillette Cup when the one-day game was introduced. In 1964 we had won all the previous rounds by batting first and so when Mike Smith won the toss in the final we naturally batted. What we hadn't taken into account was the fact that the match commenced at 10.30 a.m., it was also quite misty early morning and when I saw the first ball from Ian Thomson swing away and nearly end up a wide I knew we were in trouble and of course we were bowled out cheaply. Conditions eased as the day progressed and Sussex collected the runs they needed without much trouble. Since that match very few sides have risked batting first.

I intended to finish playing in 1964, but in 1965 the county had many injuries and I was recalled several times during that year. I remember one match towards the end of the season, fielding at mid-on when Tom Cartwright was bowling. The ball went up in the air and I didn't have to move. As it was coming down I started to shake, which was something I had never experienced before. I didn't get a touch and at the age of 38, I knew it was time to retire, especially as I had been a good fielder. I didn't quite make my ambitions to take a wicket or score 2,000 runs in a season, my highest being 1,902 runs in 1960.

During my playing days I worked on the ground during the winters. There was a very good groundsman's association, with lectures and courses which interested me. I took that up and it was always my intention to become a groundsman on retirement. I started my own firm and ended up contracted to look after about ten grounds in the area. Steve Rouse, the present head groundsman at Edgbaston started with me. I carried on with this until 1977, when unfortunately I became beset with ulcers. We took a pub in Hereford with some friends for two years but with the ulcers getting worse, it didn't work out. Luckily I had the chance to go to Warwick School as cricket coach and head groundsman from 1979 to retirement in 1989, which I enjoyed very much, although still had to retire early because of the ulcers.

We then moved back to Yorkshire and rented a property while house hunting, but I became concerned about my health and being a long way from the family. We had two daughters in the Midlands and a son in London, so we bought a house near Redditch. I visited a young consultant who mentioned that ulcers could be caused by bacteria. He recommended antibiotics and within two weeks I felt better after ten years of pain. We then moved back to Yorkshire where we have lived in retirement ever since.

Whilst gardening is a hobby of mine, I have never gone into it seriously, like turf culture etc., but I do now have a lot of lawn to take care of!

As a youngster my elder brother was a professional cricketer with the Bradford League. When I was 11 I used to go around on Saturday afternoon with the score-book. When E.A. Martindale signed for Bingley, I remember being there when he arrived for his first game. He was the first black man I had ever seen and his wife was also there dressed in a variety of colours with two or three children. When he started bowling, his run-up was such a smooth and easy action. I watched him for that full season and it stuck in my memory. That's how he became my favourite player.

Memorable Game

The most memorable games that I played in were two in the space of a week in 1953. We first played the Australians at Edgbaston when Fred Gardner and I put on 143 for the first wicket. It was the highest opening stand against them that season and against a full side – Lindwall, Miller, etc. I hit 61 and Fred went on to score a century. The ground was packed, there were 20,000 people there and I had never played in an arena like that before. We nearly beat them but the game ended in a draw.

> **5, 6, 7 August 1953. Match drawn**
>
> Warwickshire came closer than any other county that season to defeating the tourists after a sensational start from the opening pair. Gardner and Horner scored 43 off the first seven overs from Lindwall and Johnston and reached a century stand in less than a run a minute. The Australians defended resolutely though to avoid defeat on the last day.

Warwickshire

F.C. Gardner lbw b Lindwall	110	not out	33
N.F. Horner lbw b Miller	61	hit wkt b Miller	12
J.R. Thompson c and b Miller	0	run out	16
J.S. Ord b Johnston	15	not out	1
H.E. Dollery b Lindwall	18		
A. Townsend lbw b Lindwall	11		
R.T. Spooner not out	21		
A.V. Wolton b Lindwall	4		
T.L. Pritchard b Miller	2	b Miller	6
K.R. Dollery did not bat			
W.E. Hollies did not bat			
B 15, l-b 13	28	B 4, l-b 4	8
	(8 wkts dec) 270		(3 wkts dec) 76

1/143 2/143 3/176 4/217
5/232 6/255 7/259 8/270

1/20 2/61 3/71

Australia

A.L. Hassett c Hollies b Pritchard	60	not out		21
C.C. McDonald st Spooner b Hollies	46	c Townsend b Hollies		5
I.D. Craig c Gardner b Wolton	29	lbw b Wolton		0
G.B. Hole lbw b Hollies	12	c Townsend b Hollies		4
K.R. Miller st Spooner b Hollies	0	b K. Dollery		10
J.H. de Courcy lbw b Wolton	13	c and b Wolton		11
R.Benaud c Gardner b Hollies	7	not out		0
R.R. Lindwall b Wolton	1			
D.Ring c and b Pritchard	5			
W.A. Johnston not out	1			
D. Tallon c Gardner b Hollies	1			
B 4, l-b 1, n-b 1	6	L-b 2		2
	181		(5 wkts)	53

1/104 2/112 3/132 4/143 5/157 6/166
7/170 8/179 9/179

1/12 2/24 3/39 4/52
5/52

Australian Bowling

	O	M	R	W	O	M	R	W
Lindwall	18	3	47	4	9	2	13	0
Johnston	27	6	84	1	7	3	21	0
Ring	15	5	25	0				
Benaud	8	2	28	0				
Hole	8	3	10	0				
Miller	21.4	7	48	3	15	4	34	2

Warwickshire Bowling

Pritchard	32	11	60	2	12	6	9	0
K. Dollery	15	3	32	0	6	0	16	1
Hollies	33.3	15	45	5	22	16	14	2
Townsend	5	2	18	0	3	1	2	0
Wolton	12	2	20	3	15	8	10	2

Umpires: E. Cooke and A.E Boulton-Carter

We then went to Bradford the following weekend and I scored my first Championship century, 115 against Yorkshire, which gave me great pleasure for obvious reasons.

Proudest Moment

The proudest moment in cricket for me was in 1960 when Billy Ibadulla and I walked off the Oval after the opening partnership mentioned earlier. I also remember with pride being presented with my county cap at Edgbaston in 1953 at tea by Tom Dollery. In fact I wasn't picked in the side at the start of the '53 season. We were in a flat, I was on poor money, as second team players didn't get much in those days and was going to pack it in as I had had one or two offers as a pro/groundsman. I went to see if the chairman would release me from my contract, but he refused and told me to stay until September. I went away feeling dejected, sauntered through to the dressing-room when they were just bringing Jimmy Ord off the field with a broken finger. Tom Dollery said he had been looking for me and told me I was in for the next match at Worcester. I scored 50-odd and never looked back – it was a strange quirk of fate.

A sound right-hand opening batsman, Horner scored 18,533 runs (29.79) and took 130 catches.

–37–

Fred Trueman (b. 1931)

Yorkshire and England

In 1959 there were only about half of us with caps, the rest were youngsters coming into the side or trying to make their way. We still managed to stop the monopoly of Surrey, who were a magnificent side and had won the Championship seven years on the trot. We took it away from them under the captaincy of Ronnie Burnett, who came into the Yorkshire side to try and sort out the problems. It went on from there and we became a very feared side.

1960 was the most outstanding season of my career as I took 175 first-class wickets, including 25 in five Tests against South Africa. I only played about 21 games for Yorkshire. I had taken 153 wickets in a season, but to get 175 bowling at my pace was something unheard of and gave me tremendous satisfaction. It was round about this time, when I was 29–30, that I gave up trying to bowl flat out as I realised how many overs I was bowling in a day. I could be just as effective, if not more, cutting my pace down, getting my sideways action even more sideways, and getting my body action into it and bowling the ball around. I had learned to bowl the nip-backer, which I couldn't at one time. Also I was running off just over a third of my long run but could revert to my long run if I wanted to, as I still used to practise off my long run-up in the nets. It got more difficult as I got older but I got prolific swing off the short run-up. Sometimes I could bowl just as quickly as off the long run-up, especially when the balance, rhythm and co-ordination clicked, the ball went through at a very lively pace. I bowled the off-cutter later in my life and took a lot of wickets. On wet wickets they were soft and the spinners did the bowling, but if I could get in and bowl my off-cutters quicker, and pitch it to bite, I would take wickets. I also bowled it on dry turners, which gave me another string to my bow.

The period from 1959 to 1968 was to become a very wonderful part of my career, as Yorkshire won the County Championship seven times and in between we beat the all-powerful West Indies by ten wickets in 1963 at Middlesbrough, where I took ten wickets and scored 55 runs.

1964 was an excellent year for me when I broke the barrier and became the first player in history to take 300 Test wickets [fifth Test against the Australians]. When I came off the field of play, I went downstairs to find the umpires and got hold of Syd Buller, who was a lovely man and a very fine umpire. I had to ask him for the ball as he was hoping he could keep it. I paid for it to be mounted myself – there was nothing from MCC or Yorkshire in those days. Even when I was the first man in history to take 250 Test wickets [in March 1963 against New Zealand at Christchurch], it was ironic that the only cricket club that I did not get a telegram from congratulating me was Yorkshire.

The most amazing thing though, was that on 1 January 1965, my great friend Brian Statham was awarded with the CBE in the Honours List. He rang me up and couldn't believe it! Then 25 years later, my old pal hit hard times, nobody seemed to be doing anything and I took it on to help with a friend of mine, Mike Buckingham. We organised a big do for Brian, which was befitting one of our great players. Then somebody suggested me as I had never been honoured, so they gave me an OBE for helping Brian, but I never received anything for cricket!

I have watched people take 300 Test wickets since I was the first to do it, with the crowd standing up and the music playing to absolutely wonderful scenes. At the time they said it would never be done again, but of course we didn't realise that cricket was going to be turned into a travelling circus, which it is now. Practically every month of the year there is a match being played somewhere and the great spectacle of Test match cricket, as far as I am concerned, has been broken. We don't get the crowds we used to because of the influx of overseas players into the domestic game. There's no sense of excitement about international players, as you have already seen them. It has also been the downfall of the standard of Test cricket that our team is now playing, which I say with sadness.

I remember my highest score of 104 against Northants in 1963 and I also scored a century against Middlesex [101 in 1965 at Scarborough] and 100 not out for England against Young England [at Scarborough in 1963]. I always thought I was quite capable of making more runs, but I used to go in anywhere between 8 and 11. If it was a good wicket, I didn't get in and if it was a bad wicket, I would put my head down trying to fight it out.

In 1968 we beat the Australians by an innings at Sheffield, which holds terrific memories for me. I had the great privilege and satisfaction of being captain at that game, although I know it upset some of the hierarchy at Yorkshire as they had never achieved that [Yorkshire's first victory over an Australian side since 1902]. What made it worse was that I was captain – they didn't like that either! One of the old committee men, who I have known for years and is still on the county committee, told me he could never believe some of the goings-on in that committee room, where on different occasions they talked of sacking me. When asked why, they said I was too successful and popular with the Yorkshire crowd and getting too many wickets! How true that is I don't know, but as the years have gone by I am quite willing to believe the committee man, who said he was appalled. Being the God-fearing man that I am, I sometimes wonder why the Lord above chose the county of Yorkshire for me to be born in.

I always enjoyed playing cricket and believe I could have carried on for another three seasons in 1968 when I left Yorkshire at the age of 37. I decided to ask for another benefit after all the years' hard work I had done. Although I never got a proper reply, it was implied that I hadn't done enough, so my newspaper *The Sunday People*, asked me if I fancied doing the job as a cricket correspondent, which was double the money I was being paid with Yorkshire. Journalism has always been my life's second best interest and I agreed. When I wrote out my official letter of resignation on the Saturday night, I went off to try and do the correct thing and saw the president of Yorkshire CCC (once again my ill-mannered ways!), Sir William Worsley, at his home at Hovingham, then I drove to see the chairman Brian Sellers at Bingley, and also John Nash, the secretary of the club at Pudsey. I gave them all my letter of resignation and none of them could understand why. In fact when I went to see Sir William Worsley he took me into his lounge and asked if I would change my mind. I said I had already announced my retirement and it would be in *The Sunday People* the next day. He asked if I could get the story stopped, as there was to be a meeting of the club in a couple of weeks' time and they were going to make me captain of Yorkshire – they didn't tell me that before. I still think it's the best decision I made and I have been with *The Sunday People* for 30 years since retirement and ten years before that. It's a great newspaper, I love working with them and, contrary to what people think, we have the best sports coverage in any newspaper in this country, because we use experts who know what they are talking about.

I did come back and play half a dozen Sunday League games for Derbyshire in 1972. The chairman asked me to play when they had a lot of injuries and I enjoyed it. After I retired from first-class cricket, I played in a number of charity cricket games and also for MCC against the Public Schools in an effort to help the kids and teach them what the game was all about. It was a waste of time, though, as you played in a one-day game and within two overs there was nobody round the bat. They had been watching this idiot one-day game on television we have unfortunately placed ourselves in. My last game of cricket was at the age of 58 one weekend in 1989 when I played for an Old England XI for charity at Hull. I said, 'I'll show you what fast bowling is about,' and by the following Wednesday I was still trying to get out of bed! It was also Tom Graveney's last game – he couldn't walk for a couple of days either.

I took more wickets than any fast bowler in the history of the game in a fairly short time – over 2,300 [2,304]. In 1949 I only played in 8 games, 14 in 1950, nearly a full season in 1951, but in 1952–3 I was in the air force, so out of the 20 years of first-class cricket I was in, you could take three years away when I didn't play, so basically got my wickets in 17 years, which I am very proud of, averaging about 140 wickets a year.

I had a wonderful international career but the only other thing I would liked to have achieved was to score those few runs to have done the Test match 'double', but I was 19 short of 1,000 runs. You think about the wonderful players that we had like Hutton, Compton, Washbrook, May, Cowdrey, Barrington, Graveney and Dexter, I never batted.

In a very competitive era we were always the best or second best side in the world and now we are sixth. We played against the likes of Worrell, Weekes, Walcott, Kanhai, Sobers, Neil Harvey, Bert Sutcliffe, Mankad, Hanif Mohammed, etc. – they could play! Each wicket cost me 21.5 and Brian 23 against about 30 now. The standard of the game today has definitely declined and doesn't bear comparison – I can't watch the county game nowadays. There were also some very fine cricketers I was in the company of who played in county cricket, but never thought they were good enough to play for their country – they would have walked into the Test side now. I would say without fear of contradiction that Les Jackson, who waited 12 years between his two Tests, was the best six day a week bowler, day in day out, that I ever played against. He was 26 before he played the first-class game and took over 1,700 first-class wickets. I always took pride in getting into the England side, as I had competition from Bedser, Bailey, Statham, Tyson, Jackson, Gladwin, Loader, Moss and Flavell, yet still managed to play 67 Tests. Likewise the spin bowling department with Wardle, Appleyard, Laker, Lock, Hilton, Tattersall and Don Shepherd, with 2,000 first-class wickets and never played in an MCC game! Then later Illy, Titmus, Allen and Mortimore all played very few Test matches because of the competition.

I took up insurance as a part-time job outside my duties with *The Sunday*

People. I was with Hambros for quite a while which I enjoyed, taking my exams and qualifying which was good experience. I have written seven or eight books and am also very much in demand for after-dinner speaking and personal appearances. I have no contact with Yorkshire CCC nowadays. The Yorkshire county members got rid of me, Ray Illingworth and Brian Close. If you can find better cricket brains than those three, I would be very surprised – I do not know what the members really want. I am a life honorary member but just go to the Test matches at Headingley as a member of the *Test Match Special* radio commentary team, which I enjoy.

I have helped raise millions for charity, mainly with the Variety Club of Great Britain, for under-privileged children and raise funds to buy the Sunshine coaches. I play golf with and meet great guys from showbusiness and sport. My own charity is called Stepping Stones and helps the paraplegic hospital in Wakefield. I decided to raise money for them after seeing an old miner, which is part of my background, who was determined to walk up the aisle to give his daughter away in marriage. He threw the sticks down and made it up the aisle and you could see the effort. It was obvious the man was in pain but he did it, and it inspired me to want to do something to help. I also started my own golf day, and we gave the first lot of money we raised to some kids in the local village whose parents were killed in a terrible road crash. I worked for the local hospital and also raised money for the local policeman who was shot and killed.

Ray Lindwall was always my idol, right up to when he died. He was without doubt the greatest fast bowler I have ever seen – a fast bowler with a medium-pace bowler's control. People used to say to me, 'You're the king of the fast bowlers,' and I would say, 'No, not while Ray Lindwall is alive.' I might have assumed the mantle when he passed away. He was a lovely man and I used to talk to him about fast bowlers and he was never too big to talk to anyone.

I used to read a bit and was a fine snooker player. I played a lot when I was a youngster and used to win a few quid, it was my spending money! My highest break was about 105, it was the only time I ever had a century break – I got into the seventies and eighties quite a few times. I used to love playing – if my eyes were all right I would still play – but nowadays I love watching and playing golf. I have been very fortunate to play with some of the biggest names in golf on the best courses in the world, including Valderrama, the Ryder Cup course in Spain. I play at Ilkley, a lovely course and was down to a handicap of about 9 at one time, although play off 14 now, as I don't play enough. I don't get the exercise I would like as all those years playing cricket have taken their toll and my doctor wonders how I walk about with my back. I also had a new knee fitted in the last two years from the days of dragging my right foot when bowling.

I am also a very big Western buff and love all Westerns. I was in

Hollywood once and saw Gene Autrey in a restaurant. I never spoke to him but sat a couple of tables away. I always wanted to meet Winston Churchill, saw him a few times but never got to shake hands with him.

One of my biggest interests today is birds – I was brought up watching birds as a kid in the '30s. I used to know all sorts of birds – if I saw one fly I would know what it was. From my house I can see woodpeckers, tree-creepers, nut-hatches, finches, wagtails, wrens, spotted fly-catchers, robins and tits. I have even got a sparrow-hawk which I don't want! We have lived for about 30 years in the Yorkshire Dales, which we love and, within a mile radius of here there are a known 137 different species of bird.

Memorable Game

It is impossible to highlight just one game – there were so many wonderful games over the years. My 300th Test wicket in the fifth Test against the Australians at the Oval in 1964 was certainly a highlight.

13, 14, 15, 17, 18 August 1964. Match drawn

Trueman, who had been recalled to the side, became the first bowler in Test history to take 300 wickets when capturing the wicket of Neil Hawke on the third afternoon. Rain on the last day prevented any chance of a positive result.

England

G. Boycott b Hawke	30	c Redpath b Simpson	113
R.W. Barber b Hawke	24	lbw b McKenzie	29
E.R. Dexter c Booth b Hawke	23	c Simpson b McKenzie	25
M.C. Cowdrey c Grout b McKenzie	20	not out	93
K.F. Barrington c Simpson b Hawke	47	not out	54
P.H. Parfitt b McKenzie	3		
J.M. Parks c Simpson b Corling	10		
F.J. Titmus c Grout b Hawke	8	b McKenzie	56
F.S. Trueman c Redpath b Hawke	14		
T.W. Cartwright c Grout b McKenzie	0		
J.E.S. Price not out	0		
L-b 3	3	B 6, l-b 4, n-b 1	11
	182	(4 wkts) 381	

1/44 2/61 3/82 4/111 5/117 6/141
7/160 8/173 9/174

1/80 2/120 3/200 4/255

Australia

W.M. Lawry c Trueman b Dexter	94
R.B. Simpson c Dexter b Cartwright	24
N.C. O'Neill c Parfitt b Cartwright	11
P.J. Burge lbw b Titmus	25

B.C. Booth c Trueman b Price   74
I.R. Redpath b Trueman   45
A.T.W. Grout b Cartwright   20
T.R. Veivers not out   67
G.D. McKenzie c Cowdrey b Trueman   0
N.J.N. Hawke c Cowdrey b Trueman   14
G.E. Corling c Parfitt b Trueman   0
B 4, l-b 1   5
                                    379

1/45 2/57 3/96 4/202 5/245 6/279
7/343 8/343 9/367

Australia Bowling

	O	M	R	W	O	M	R	W
McKenzie	26	6	87	3	38	5	112	3
Corling	14	2	32	1	25	4	65	0
Hawke	25.4	8	47	6	39	8	89	0
Veivers	6	1	13	0	47	15	90	0
Simpson					14	7	14	1

England Bowling

	O	M	R	W
Trueman	33.3	6	87	4
Price	21	2	67	1
Cartwright	62	23	110	3
Titmus	42	20	51	1
Barber	6	1	23	0
Dexter	13	1	36	1

Umpires: C.S. Elliott and J.F. Crapp

Other highlights were taking my 2,000th wicket, the Bramall Lane game in 1968 when we beat the Australians and also when we beat West Indies in 1963. In years to come, people will look back and say that Yorkshire side must have been some team.

Proudest Moment

The proudest moment for me is easy – every time I put on an England or Yorkshire sweater gave me immense pride. People don't realise when there are only 11 people walking out there and you are one representing the country out of 40 million, it's a magnificent feeling.

One of the greatest fast bowlers of all time Trueman scored 9,231 runs (15.56) including 3 centuries, took 2,304 wickets (18.29) and 438 catches. In 67 Test matches, he scored 981 runs (13.81), took 307 wickets (21.57) and 64 catches.

–38–

Doug Insole (b. 1926)

Cambridge University, Essex and England

I was captain of Essex from 1950 to 1960. I remember 1960 as a pretty good season for us as we finished sixth. We had some good young players making their way, Barry Knight being the obvious example. The innings I remember well in that year was scoring 100 against South Africa at Ilford. I had a bit of a 'to-do' with 'Toey' Tayfield out in South Africa in 1956–7, he wasn't my favourite and I had made up my mind on that tour not to get out to him. I actually succumbed in the last innings of the series because I had a swing and got caught on the square-leg boundary. He was a very abrasive man and possibly the most unpopular cricketer universally – mind you he was a terrific bowler. I made up my mind to take him on at Ilford and was eventually given out lbw, which I didn't enjoy as I was on the front foot smearing again! I enjoyed the innings very much, though.

After 1960 I played just a few games for Essex until 1963. I was told by my company I was needed in the office so the time was right to retire and I had enjoyed a good run. When I left Cambridge I didn't even know I was going to play regularly. It was only when in 1949 I was captaining Cambridge and went along to Essex and scored quite a few runs that George Wimpey, my employers, asked me if I would like to play for Essex for a year or two, and that eventually became 11 years. I was employed for the whole time by them, not by Essex, so at any time they could have called me in, but I think that happened only once. I was employed on the marketing/PR side while I was playing cricket as I couldn't give them continuity. The minute I stopped playing I moved onto the commercial side where I stayed until 1969, becoming general manager of their private housing division. In 1969 I moved on to the Board of Town & City Properties, a major property development company. They became vulnerable because of the property crisis and in 1974 were taken over by Sterling Guarantee Trust. Jeffrey Sterling had a clear-out and I left without any animosity. I then joined Trafalgar House on the construction side where I became marketing director of the construction holding company and found that very enjoyable. Trafalgar House were then taken over by a Norwegian company who now pay my pension. I gave up full-time employment in 1991 when I was 65 and worked for two days a week until 1993.

People don't believe this, but I had no ambition to become involved in cricket behind the scenes. I didn't ask to be involved at all when Surrey proposed me as a Test selector. I thought that was because I used to score runs against them and it would get me out of the way for a while! Gubby Allen put me up for membership of the MCC committee when I was 29, which in MCC terms was very young. I think I was also the first non-public schoolboy ever to go on the committee. Gubby felt I was a young man not frightened to speak my mind. I was a Test selector from 1959 and had four years as chairman from 1965 to 1968, with the idea that the job ran between Australian tours. People call me a political animal and I was intensely interested and still enjoy the involvement, but never said to myself I am going to do this and that. In fact I never felt I would be allowed to do so, as when you are in business these things are very time-consuming. When I asked Victor Matthews, the MD of Trafalgar House if I might be allowed to become chairman of the TCCB, he agreed readily on the assumption that it would take no more than one day a week of the firm's time, but it was not that easy. The Packer crisis, for example took me away from the office for four or five weeks – I was in the witness box for the best part of a week!

The D'Oliveira affair [when, as a 'coloured' all-rounder from Cape Town, his selection for the MCC tour to South Africa was not deemed acceptable to the South African government, leading to their expulsion from the international game] was awful. In 1968 the TCCB was formed, but prior to that it was MCC who ran the game and as chairman of selectors it was to MCC that I was responsible. I had a very good selection committee but MCC were still involved in the selection process for overseas tours. I defended a situation that was brought about by an absolutely genuine selection process [in not originally picking D'Oliveira for the tour] but nevertheless it was a difficult time because of the political implications. I received a telegram from someone saying, 'I agree absolutely with your decision – Adolf Hitler'. A few years after, I could read it out with some equanimity, but at the time it wasn't very pleasant.

Of the jobs I have had in cricket administration, the chairman of selectors role was the most enjoyable until the South African tour situation cropped up, then that rather spoiled it. My most prized cricketing possession is a salver which was presented to me and is signed by all the cricketers picked for England while I was chairman, 50 to 60 in total. I think it was organised by Colin Cowdrey and came out of the blue. I remember writing a thank you to all of the players which started, 'I don't know how far your arm was twisted but...' I had one reply only from Geoff Boycott who, with massive protestations wrote that he would never send his money to a cause he could not support and that his arm was not twisted! I still have the letter. The chairman role was also the most challenging and I had a much closer relationship with the players than was the case previously or subsequently.

The 1963 Lord's Test match against the West Indies was one of the most exciting I can recall and I have one memory in particular as it was the match that Colin Cowdrey broke his arm. I drove him down in thick traffic to Bill Tucker's surgery at Park Street to have the arm X-rayed and set so that he could come back and bat if necessary. I remember parking my car and sticking a sheet of paper on the windscreen saying, 'Do not tow away – Colin Cowdrey inside.' I drove him back to the ground and of course he had to go in. It was the first really obvious and overt example of an over rate being slowed down in Test cricket to about 12 an hour when we were winning the game. In the end I was quite relieved to come out with the draw. I remember Brian Close being battered all over the place in the match.

I have enjoyed my Essex involvement right the way through. I was made vice-chairman in 1964 and from then until 1993 I was either chairman or vice-chairman. I worked with terrific people and we had a great spirit with very few black spots. It was very hard work in the early days and particularly difficult to tell people when having to cutback that you couldn't keep them, even though they were your friends and you had worked with them for years. We all had to turn our hands to any job that needed doing – selling scorecards, running the car park, manning the gate and so on. My father used to collect trading stamps and collected cash instead of goods to raise money. For some years it was a hand-to-mouth existence but everyone pulled together.

There were just 12 players on our staff at one time. Five of them were under 20, amongst them John Lever, Robin Hobbs and Ray East. With Brian Taylor at the helm and the advent of one-day cricket though they became very successful. I picked the overseas players for years and we never paid them more than our own players. Lee Irvine was our first, a left-hander from South Africa, who had come over the previous year on a tour and looked very good. Then he got picked for the '70s side to come over here and asked for more money when we didn't have any. Then Bruce Francis was introduced to us by Derek Ufton and played for three years. Ken McEwan came along after playing against our second XI for Sussex and had many successful seasons.

I have been president now [1998] for five or six years and so far the club has always felt the role provides an element of continuity. It is up to Essex how long I am president for but I am happy to continue as long as the club feels I can be of use.

In footballing terms I have been on the FA council for 18 years representing Cambridge University. It has been very interesting and I have served on a number of sub-committees including instructional, on whose behalf I have done a lot of work recently on pushing through mini-sided legislation for junior football.

The book I wrote in 1960, *Cricket from the Middle*, came about as a result of a chat with John Arlott, who suggested it was time to set my thoughts down while I was still in the game and he introduced me to a publisher. He read the proofs and assured me the contents were vaguely interesting! There was a change almost immediately in cricket when I was writing it as we were thinking about a knock-out competition, but one that was based on three-day cricket. It was deemed to be impractical for many reasons. By looking for ways of broadening the game we came up with one-day competition and the Gillette Cup was born in 1963. I remember arguments on the MCC committee with Gubby Allen about limited overs cricket. He was saying you should play the one-day game as it was played in club cricket but I disagreed as so many clubs declared late, leaving no time for the opposition to score the runs and creating ill feeling. It had to be on equal participation at the wicket and we must have decided on the format in about 1961. It was a notable first for cricket in that the Gillette Cup was unique at the time as a sponsored competition in a major sport.

Another major change was playing on Sundays a few years on when nobody else played sport on that day. There were initially enormous battles with religious bodies and Essex were the first county to play a Championship match on a Sunday. We had buckets at the turnstiles then refined it minimally by making people one-day members. Progressively, of course, opposition wilted until every major sport began using Sunday as a main competition day.

The big technique change has been brought about by covering wickets in England which also altered the nature of the game. If people wanted to kill the three-day game on covered wickets it was easy to do so. I don't know anyone of my generation who wouldn't say that the techniques of batting and bowling would be improved enormously by going back to uncovered wickets. There are all sorts of reasons, though, for that not happening, partly commercial and partly that no-one seems prepared to discover how uncovered wickets would behave now.

Peter May was my favourite player during my career for reasons ranging from esteem to regard for his technical ability and prowess. Since then I have enjoyed watching Ian Botham in terms of excitement, Graham Gooch as a colossal performer but the best cricketer I have seen, and a personality I like, is Gary Sobers. I actually played against him in his first Test match in England in 1957, along with Kanhai and Collie Smith, a tremendous bunch.

I have also had a long connection with Sir Don Bradman. I was first involved with him officially in meetings held in 1959–60 to do with the throwing controversies at the time. He came over here and I was a young observer. He has been a very good friend since. The most satisfying involvement in cricket has been making so many friends along the way.

Memorable Game

The most memorable game I played in was the Varsity match in 1949, which had a pretty high profile in those days. Oxford were the only team to beat New Zealand that summer, had also defeated Middlesex and Yorkshire and were a very fine side. As captain of Cambridge I was very involved in sifting through the freshmen and organising the trials. Approximately 40,000 people paid at the gate to watch the match at Lord's and there was a lot of interest. We won it with a quarter of an hour to spare on the third day and it gave us a terrific lift. The best aspect was that we talked about their players and how we were going to get them out, and the first four were out in exactly the way we planned.

2, 4, 5 July 1949. Cambridge won by 7 wickets

This was a tremendous team performance as Cambridge completed a surprise but well-deserved victory. Contributions from the main strike batsmen in the first innings laid the foundations for victory and in the field the side excelled under the shrewd captaincy of Insole.

Cambridge University

J.G. Dewes c Carr b Kardar	48	c Campbell c Carr	45
R.J. Morris b Wrigley	46	st Campbell b V'Ryn'veld	25
M.H. Stevenson c Boobbyer b Wrigley	70	c Hofmeyr b V'Ryn'veld	37
G.H.G. Doggart b Whitcombe	60	not out	6
A.G.J. Rimell c Kardar b Chesterton	57	not out	8
D.J. Insole c Van Ryneveld b Kardar	5		
A.C. Burnett b Kardar	0		
P.J. Hall c and b Van Ryneveld	12		
O. Popplewell st Campbell b V'Ryn'veld	17		
J.J. Warr not out	15		
O.J. Wait c and b Van Ryneveld	2		

| B 10, l-b 17 | 27 | B 5, l-b 5, w 2 | 12 |
| | 359 | (3 wkts) 133 |

Oxford University

M.B. Hofmeyr not out	64	c Doggart b Rimell	54
B. Boobbyer b Wait	10	c Burnett b Doggart	17
C.E. Winn c Doggart b Wait	2	b Warr	30
C.B. Van Ryneveld run out	12	c Popplewell b Warr	47
D.B. Carr c Burnett b Hall	13	run out	35
A.H. Kardar lbw b Doggart	25	c Doggart b Wait	11
I.P. Campbell c Popplewell b Doggart	0	b Doggart	16
C.R.D. Rudd b Hall	5	b Warr	0
P.A. Whitcombe c Popplewell b Warr	14	lbw b Doggart	47
G.H. Chesterton b Warr	9	not out	39
M.H. Wrigley b Warr	0	c Burnett b Warr	11
B 10, l-b 3, w 1, n-b 1	15	B 3, l-b 7, w 2, n-b 3	15
	169		322

Oxford University Bowling

	O	M	R	W	O	M	R	W
Whitcombe	21	4	48	1	1	0	5	0
Wrigley	18	3	67	2	5	0	22	0
Chesterton	18	4	40	1	4	0	20	0
Kardar	49	21	79	3	7.5	0	41	0
Van Ryneveld	38.1	8	98	3	8	1	28	2
Carr					1	0	5	1

Cambridge University Bowling

	O	M	R	W	O	M	R	W
Warr	21.3	7	43	3	33.2	6	91	4
Wait	18	6	31	2	20	5	66	1
Hall	17	3	46	2	19	4	64	0
Rimell	12	9	7	0	10	3	29	1
Doggart	8	3	10	2	21	7	57	3
Stevenson	4	0	17	0				

Umpires: F. Chester and E. Cooke

My most memorable Essex game was the one at Clacton in 1957 against Surrey who were on top of the world. We trailed by 133 in the first innings but managed to beat them in the end by two wickets with a very young side. I remember the hats flying up in the air!

Proudest Moment
My proudest moment is difficult to define. Certainly I was very pleased to get my Test hundred in South Africa [110 not out at Durban in January

1957], but I was so tied up in saving the match that it didn't really register at the time. Another proud moment is when I was selected for England for the first time [in the third Test against West Indies at Trent Bridge, Nottingham in July 1950].

A powerfully built right-handed batsman with plenty of courage and resolution, Insole scored 25,237 runs (37.61) including 54 centuries, took 138 wickets (33.95), 363 catches and 6 stumpings. In 9 Test matches, he scored 408 runs (27.20) including 1 century and 8 catches.

–39–

Malcolm Hilton (1928–1990)

Lancashire and England

As told by Mrs Vera Berry

Malcolm had a joint benefit with Roy Tattersall when Lancashire played Yorkshire in the Roses match on August bank holiday in 1960. I remember the weather being beautiful and a big crowd supporting the benefit, but sadly Malcolm was playing for the second XI at Scarborough.

Malcolm was young when he finished playing for Lancashire in 1961 at the age of 33, but it was his decision to move on, he had just had enough of playing county cricket. He played league cricket for eight years, firstly as professional at Burnley Cricket Club and then went to Radcliffe, where he was for two years. He then went into the Huddersfield League for Marsden, had two years with Oldham and ended at Werneth, the club he started with as a boy. He was very well thought of, particularly at Burnley where they gave him a stainless steel cigarette box when he was there. That nicely complemented a silver cigarette box presented to Malcolm by Lancashire on sharing the County Championship with Surrey in 1950. He played amateur cricket for a few years after his professional days until about the age of 46 when he fully retired.

When he left Lancashire Malcolm took a job with H.R. Howard & Co., a textile firm in Ashton. Major Rupert Howard, who was the secretary at Old Trafford and his two sons managed the firm. He worked there for 20 years as despatch manager until he was 56. During that time it was taken over at least twice and the Howards relinquished interest in the company. He was made redundant as Howards decided to send their knitting to a firm in Leicester and Malcolm's job just disappeared. It was a worrying time and Malcolm was out of work for quite long periods but managed to get jobs on a short term basis. When he was 60 he started to become ill, I nursed him at home and he was 61 when he died of cancer in July 1990. We were living on the coppice at Oldham at that time. Malcolm and I had a son and daughter who live in the Oldham area.

Malcolm didn't have a lot of hobbies outside cricket – he worked very hard at Howards, starting early and working long hours. He didn't go to Old Trafford very often once he left Lancashire. He used to watch Werneth and a lot of cricket on television. He was extremely keen on crosswords though, was an avid book reader and a very good crib player which he picked up on the rainy days at Old Trafford. He also particularly enjoyed all the wildlife programmes on TV, especially the David Attenborough films.

He was a modest, unassuming person though who would play things down – he would always quote Harry Makepeace, the coach at Old Trafford who would say, 'On the bad days, think of the good, on the good days, think of the bad.' He never got swollen headed. He was also a humorous man. I remember some confusion at Old Trafford in one game when Malcolm fielded the ball, and collided with another player in the process. Cyril Washbrook came up to him after and said in his beautifully cultured voice, 'By the way Hilton, do you know any other daft tricks?'

I recently came across a letter Malcolm received in 1965 from the Chief Constable of Oldham police, expressing his appreciation when Malcolm assisted one of his officers in arresting a youth for trying to steal a car. Such was the true nature of the man I was married to for almost 40 years.

Memorable Game

I think Malcolm's most memorable game would be the match against Australia in 1948 when he shot to fame. I remember the excitement when he took the wicket of Don Bradman in both innings at Old Trafford. I don't know, in hindsight, if it was a good thing – there was a lot of publicity in the papers and there was an awful lot of fuss about it. I remember the Press being outside his home and lots of photographs being taken and it was a lot to live up to.

26, 27, 28 May 1948. Match drawn
In addition to his success in the first innings, 19-year-old Hilton, in his third match for the county, beat Bradman with three successive balls in the second

before being stumped. Loss of the first day through rain always made a draw the most likely result.

Australia

S.G. Barnes c Cranston b Hilton	31	c Roberts b Cranston	31
A.R. Morris c E. Edrich b Pollard	22	c G. Edrich b Pollard	5
D.G. Bradman b Hilton	11	st E. Edrich b Hilton	43
I.W. Johnson lbw b Hilton	5		
S.J. Loxton b Roberts	39	run out	52
R.N. Harvey b Roberts	36	not out	76
R.A. Hamence b Pollard	2	not out	49
R.A. Saggers not out	22		
R.R. Lindwall c Lawton b Hilton	0		
W.A. Johnston b Pollard	24		
E.R.H. Toshack b Roberts	4		
B 6, l-b 2	8	B 1, l-b 2	3
	204	(4 wkts)	259

Lancashire

C. Washbrook lbw b Toshack	33
W. Place c Lindwall b Toshack	24
G.A. Edrich b Johnston	55
J.T. Ikin lbw b Lindwall	7
K. Cranston b Lindwall	14
E.H. Edrich b Johnston	5
A. Wharton c Johnston b Lindwall	24
R. Pollard c Hamence b Johnston	4
W.B. Roberts st Saggers b Johnston	1
W. Lawton b Johnston	0
M. Hilton not out	0
B 11, l-b 4	15
	182

Lancashire Bowling

	O	M	R	W	O	M	R	W
Pollard	20	8	37	3	12	2	48	1
Lawton	9	4	21	0	8	1	43	0
Hilton	19	4	81	4	13	0	54	1
Roberts	21.4	4	57	3	14	3	35	0
Cranston					9	1	40	1
Wharton					7	1	20	0
Ikin					4	0	16	0

Australian Bowling

Lindwall	19	6	44	3
Johnston	29	14	49	5
Toshack	28	8	40	2
Johnson	8	2	16	0
Loxton	8	1	18	0

Umpires: H. Elliott and C.N. Woolley

He was not a great batsman but in 1955 scored his only century, 100 not out against Northants, and that would certainly be high on his list of memorable matches. There was also a match at Old Trafford in July 1950 when Malcolm took 11 wickets in one day against Sussex. He opened the bowling and the ball was turning at right angles.

Proudest Moment

I think Malcolm's proudest moment in cricket would be when his club Werneth presented him with a mounted cricket ball with which he took the wicket of Don Bradman in 1948. When he played his first Test match against the West Indies at the Oval in 1950, it was also a very proud time for not only himself but also his parents, who watched him with myself. Walking into the Great Western Royal at Paddington and shaking hands with Len Hutton and meeting the other players was wonderful. On occasions he was also 12th man for England on the strength of his agility and fielding. Socially it was a very nice life, we met lots of wonderful people, like Denis and Leslie Compton and Tom Graveney – cricket is full of nice people.

A devastating slow left-arm spinner on a turning wicket and excellent fielder, Hilton scored 3,416 runs (12.11) including 1 century, took 1,006 wickets (19.41) and 204 catches. In 4 Test matches he scored 37 runs (7.40), took 14 wickets (33.64) and 1 catch.

–40–
Allan Watkins (b. 1922)

Glamorgan and England

I recall when we were playing Leicestershire at Swansea in 1960 I scored a hundred but had terrible pains in my chest. I gave my wicket away, came in and sat in the dressing-room. I could hear Glamorgan skipper Wilf Wooller coming down the stone steps. He came through the door and started, 'What the . . .' and stopped there. I had gone white and they rushed me off to hospital where the specialist diagnosed it as nervous asthma. I was scheduled to take over from Wilf as skipper but had to retire from cricket early at the age of 39 in 1961.

We bought a delicatessen in Usk but I didn't like it. I was then approached by the commissioners of the open borstal in Usk to join the service as a temp to take the boys for sport and I enjoyed it for 18 months. Eight of us made a beautiful cricket square, we drained the soccer pitch, levelled the rugger pitch and it was great fun. I was also playing cricket for the commissioners, but one prison officer in particular was envious of the role I played and eventually I resigned. I went back into the shop and in 1965 rang Donald Carr at Lord's, who offered me a coaching job at Framlingham where I stayed for six years, although I did have a season at Christ's in Brecon. Then the College job at Oundle cropped up and I stayed ever since, although latterly I didn't coach the Seniors any more, just the

Colts. 1997 was my last year, as 60 years in cricket is a long time.

I don't play badminton any more, but I do play golf. I did have a handicap of 9 but it went up to 13. I did have some trouble with my 'waterworks' and eventually went for a scan at Peterborough Hospital and found I had cancer of the kidney. After the kidney was taken out I found I couldn't swing the club so easily so they gave me a handicap of 18. I play three times a week even though my knees and legs are going – I have only got one cartilage left.

Memorable Game

The most memorable match I played in was the fourth Test in 1949 against South Africa when I scored my first Test hundred at Ellis Park, Johannesburg. We weren't doing very well as Cyril Washbrook and Denis Compton were both out when I came into bat. I was on 94 when Jack Young came in last. He said, 'Don't worry, I'll be there, I nearly became a Glamorgan player,' as at that time we were trying to bring in players from other counties. The first ball he cracked for four and luckily for me I scored 100, which was a great feeling as it was in front of a huge crowd. My house is named Ellis Park, which was the rugby pitch, and there were between 60,000 and 70,000 people watching the game.

13, 14, 15, 16 February 1949. Match drawn

Watkins drove, hooked and pulled to excellent effect as he top-scored in the first innings. South Africa declined a reasonable target set by skipper Mann and the match petered out as a draw.

England

L. Hutton b Tuckett	2	b A. Rowan	123
C. Washbrook c E. Rowan b McCarthy	97	lbw b A. Rowan	31
J.F. Crapp b A. Rowan	51	hit wkt b McCarthy	5
D.C.S. Compton c A. Rowan b Tuckett	24	b Markham	25
A. Watkins hit wkt b McCarthy	111	b A. Rowan	10
F.G. Mann c Wade b McCarthy	17	lbw b A. Rowan	16
R.O. Jenkins lbw b Mitchell	25		
A.V. Bedser lbw b Tuckett	1	b McCarthy	19
C. Gladwin b McCarthy	19	not out	7
S.C. Griffith c Mitchell b McCarthy	8		
J.A. Young not out	10		
B 2, l-b 12	14	B 5, l-b 11, n-b 1	17
	379	(7 wkts dec)	253

1/3 2/123 3/172 4/180 5/213 6/282
7/287 8/316 9/346

1/77 2/151 3/186
4/204 5/222 6/237 7/253

South Africa

B. Mitchell c Griffith b Bedser	2	c Compton b Gladwin	6
E. Rowan run out	6	not out	86
K. Viljoen run out	0	b Watkins	63
A.D. Nourse not out	129	b Watkins	1
W. Wade lbw b Young	54	lbw b Bedser	27
T. Harris b Bedser	6	not out	1
A. Rowan b Gladwin	12		
L. Tuckett b Young	0		
L. Markham c Griffith b Jenkins	20		
N. Mann c Griffith b Gladwin	14		
C. McCarthy not out	0		
B 4, l-b 10	14	B 7, l-b 1, n-b 2	10
	(9 wkts dec) 257		(4 wkts) 194

1/4 2/4 3/19 4/125 5/137   1/23 2/136 3/140 4/182
6/156 7/161 8/192 9/236

South Africa Bowling

	O	M	R	W	O	M	R	W
McCarthy	35.7	3	114	5	12.2	2	50	2
Tuckett	29	2	109	3	10	0	43	0
A. Rowan	23	1	70	1	34	10	69	4
Markham	5	1	38	0	8	0	34	1
Mann	10	3	26	0	7	0	20	0
Mitchell	3	0	8	1	7	1	20	0

England Bowling

	O	M	R	W	O	M	R	W
Bedser	24	3	81	2	17	0	54	1
Gladwin	24	7	43	2	16	6	39	1
Jenkins	8	1	39	1	9	2	26	0
Young	23	6	52	2	11	6	14	0
Watkins	2	0	9	0	3	0	16	2
Compton	4	0	19	0	9	2	35	0

Umpires: J.V. Hart-Davis and R.G.A. Ashman

It was a very memorable tour for me. We spent three weeks on the boat to South Africa and in a statement skipper George Mann said, 'I am not interested in names, I am interested in form and ability.' I was frightened, amazed and nervous to be in the first Test at Durban, the only reason was because of my reputation for close to the wicket fielding. I remember going in for the second innings when Denis Compton was at the wicket and he looked after me like a baby. They were eight ball overs and for three overs I never touched the ball. He got a run off the last ball of each over, came up to me and said, 'Which end do you want?' He really looked after me until I got over my nerves. We won the Test on the last ball of the match with a leg bye.

From Ellis Park over Christmas we went down to Cape Town. In the second innings of the Cape Town Test, when I went out, George Mann told me to get on with it so that we could declare. I mentioned this to Denis when I joined him at the wicket and he said, 'I never know when you are telling me your bloody Welsh lies!' When we declared I was 64 not out and Denis was on 51. It was thrilling for me to go past the great Denis Compton's score as we put on a century partnership.

We went to Port Elizabeth for the last Test. Jack Young was bowling with George Mann at mid-on and Denis Compton at short leg – they all played for Middlesex. This was my specialist position and Denis was therefore asked to field at fine leg but he wouldn't go, so there we were side by side. Denis told me to go down there for a change but I said I wasn't going as I couldn't throw a ball anyway! Jack looked at the two of us, stopped his run and said to George, 'I know I'm a great bowler and very accurate but I'm buggered if I want two short legs!' Denis had to go to fine leg.

I think our fee for the tour in South Africa was £450. We were fined if we dropped a catch or swore. At one of the weekly meetings our manager Brigadier Green told us that the South Africans were so pleased with the tour they gave us each a hundred pounds extra, which was a lot of money in those days.

Proudest Moment

My proudest and most nervous moment was when we were playing at Weston-Super-Mare in 1948 and the Test side was picked on the Sunday. We were listening to the wireless when the team was announced. I looked at my wife Molly and said, 'Did you hear what I heard? I'm in the team!' When I walked on the field for the last Test at the Oval for my England debut against Australia I was terribly nervous. I had never played in a representative game and went to Test cricket straight from Glamorgan. In the first innings Ray Lindwall bounced me and, typical of me, I hooked it. It hit me badly on the shoulder and Neil Harvey caught it down at third man. I battled on only to be given out by umpire Dai Davies lbw for a duck to a ball from Bill Johnston. The Press didn't realise what happened but when I took my clothes off my shoulder was blue with the bruise. They called in Bill Tucker who had a surgery at Grosvenor Square. He put six injections in my shoulder and strapped me across the top of the shoulder. Norman Yardley, who was the captain, made me open the bowling. I bowled no more than four overs and made a mess of it obviously, then walked off. I didn't play again for a fortnight – my shoulder was cracked. That was my baptism at Test cricket!

A sound, enterprising left-handed batsman, penetrating medium-pace bowler and dynamic fielder, Watkins scored 20,362 runs (30.57) including 32 centuries, 833 wickets (24.48) and 461 catches. In 15 Test matches, he scored 810 runs (40.50) including 2 centuries, took 11 wickets (50.36) and 17 catches.

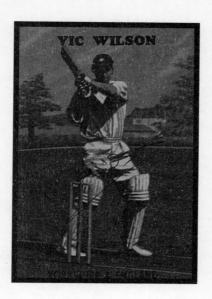

–41–

Vic Wilson (b. 1921)

Yorkshire

Looking back to 1959, that was the season I lost form and was actually in and out of the team during the year [although top-scoring with 105 for Yorkshire in the end of season game v Rest of England]. I was appointed captain in 1960 which was obviously a much more successful year for me, as it was my best season and also the team's because we won the County Championship. I did not get off to a good start, though, as I do remember the first game at Hove when we lost against Sussex. I made a mistake in declaring when Yorkshire were 281 for no wicket in the first innings. I thought Ted Dexter would set us a good target but he didn't. We had an impossible task. However, it did get better from there.

In 1961 we were pipped to the post by Hampshire which was like a 20/1 outsider winning against the odds. I think I was too complacent as captain – nonetheless it was still a good year to finish as runners-up.

As captain in 1962 we again won the Championship in my final season. I remember in particular the last day at Harrogate when we beat Glamorgan on a wet wicket, as at one time [when the second day was completely washed out] I didn't feel we would actually secure a result. I had made up my mind earlier in the season to retire from Yorkshire cricket because of my farming activities and it was marvellous to go out on a high. I felt I had also learnt lessons from 1961 which helped me captain the team successfully to the Championship.

I played for MCC a few times in 1963 and then, whilst playing for Wakefield, Johnny Lawrence, who was also there, introduced me to Lincoln-shire, where I played for three years from 1964 to 1966.

I have always been involved in farming and now help my son in running the farm. I also owned a horse at one time which won eight races but still lost me money! I am not as active as I used to be, which is frustrating for me having played so much sport, including football, in my life.

Memorable Game

The most memorable match I played in was the fourth Test at Adelaide in 1955 where I was 12th man and spent a lot of the time fielding. It was our first Ashes win in Australia since the 'Bodyline Tour' of 1932–3 and was marvellous to be involved on such an occasion. I think I was selected to tour because of my fielding ability and my team attitude more than anything else. I actually spent almost all of the first Test at Brisbane on the field as Denis Compton wasn't fit.

28, 29, 31 January, 1, 2 February 1955. England won by five wickets

Under captain Len Hutton, this victory secured the series for England. It was again fast bowlers Frank Tyson and Brian Statham who were instrumental in the success, well supported by Bailey and Appleyard.

Australia

C.C. McDonald c May b Appleyard	48	b Statham	29
A.R. Morris c Evans b Tyson	25	c and b Appleyard	16
J. Burke c May b Tyson	18	b Appleyard	5
R.N. Harvey c Edrich b Bailey	25	b Appleyard	7
K.R. Miller c Bailey b Appleyard	44	b Statham	14
R. Benaud c May b Appleyard	15	lbw b Tyson	1
L. Maddocks run out	69	lbw b Statham	2
R.G. Archer c May b Tyson	21	c Evans b Tyson	3
A.K. Davidson c Evans b Bailey	5	lbw b Wardle	23
I.W. Johnson c Statham b Bailey	41	not out	3
W.A. Johnston not out	0	c Appleyard b Tyson	3
B 3, l-b 7, n-b 2	12	B 4, l-b 1	5
	323		111

1/59 2/86 3/115 4/129 5/175 6/182
7/212 8/229 9/321

1/24 2/40 3/54 4/69 5/76
6/77 7/79 8/83 9/101

England

L. Hutton c Davidson b Johnston	80	c Davidson b Miller	5

W.J. Edrich b Johnson	21		b Miller		0
P.B.H. May c Archer b Benaud	1		c Miller b Johnston		26
M.C. Cowdrey c Maddocks b Davidson	79		c Archer b Miller		4
D.C.S. Compton lbw b Miller	44		not out		34
T.E. Bailey c Davidson b Johnston	38		lbw b Johnston		15
T.G. Evans c Maddocks b Benaud	37		not out		6
J.H. Wardle c and b Johnson	23				
F.H. Tyson b Burke b Benaud	1				
R. Appleyard not out	10				
J.B. Statham c Maddocks b Benaud	0				
B 1, l-b 2, n-b 4	7		B 3, l-b 4		7
	341		(5 wkts)		97

1/60 2/63 3/162 4/232 5/232 6/283
7/321 8/323 9/336

1/3 2/10 3/18 4/49 5/90

England Bowling

	O	M	R	W	O	M	R	W
Tyson	26.1	4	85	3	15	2	47	3
Statham	19	4	70	0	12	1	38	3
Bailey	12	3	39	3				
Appleyard	23	7	58	3	12	7	13	3
Wardle	19	5	59	0	4.2	1	8	1

Australia Bowling

	O	M	R	W	O	M	R	W
Miller	11	4	34	1	10.4	2	40	3
Archer	3	0	12	0	4	0	13	0
Johnson	36	17	46	2				
Davidson	25	8	55	1	2	0	7	0
Johnston	27	11	60	2	8	2	20	2
Benaud	36.6	6	120	4	6	2	10	0
Burke	2	0	7	0				

Umpires: M.J. McInnes and R. Wright

Proudest Moment

The proudest moment for me was being appointed captain of Yorkshire in 1960. I remember Brian Sellers ringing me at Christmas, it was a great surprise to me and thrill to be the first professional captain of the county.

I am also very pleased to have achieved my ambition mentioned on the card of scoring over 20,000 runs for Yorkshire in my career.

A middle-order left-hand batsman and excellent fielder, Wilson scored 21,650 runs (31.33), took 9 wickets (48.33) and 548 catches.

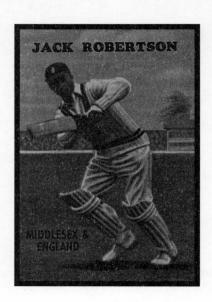

–42–

Jack Robertson (1917–1996)

Middlesex and England

As told by Mrs Joyce Robertson

Jack had suffered a few injuries in 1959 and at the end of the summer he was called to Lord's to be offered the Middlesex coaching job. We had already bought a hotel in 1959 at Perranporth in Cornwall to run when he retired from cricket, so we had to sell it. He certainly achieved his ambition of playing for as long as possible. Jack coached at the cricket school in Finchley with Jim Alldis, who was in charge, in the winter months, even when he was playing. Apart from coaching the Middlesex side, he also started coaching in schools and continued every day in the London area, even when Don Bennett took over as Middlesex coach in 1968. He was a modest man and had great patience with young children, coaching Mike Gatting and Mark Ramprakash from the age of 11. He also coached and managed the Young England team. The only cricket he played after retirement was for the Lord's Taverners, until he was taken ill.

In the Easter holidays of 1982 at the age of 65, Jack was coaching with Maurice Hallam at Uppingham and stayed with him in Leicester. They had been out for a meal the night before and Jack woke up in the night feeling so ill he got Maurice up. Maurice called the doctor who got him to hospital straight away as he was suffering from food poisoning. The next day, Jack had an 18-hour operation and there were four five-inch splits (caused by the continuous violent sickness) in the oesophagus and it had to be taken out. The surgeon had been in America for three years studying the operation as it hadn't been performed in England and was the only person in the country who could have undertaken it. He happened to be working at Leicester at the time, otherwise Jack would not have survived, together with the fact that he was a strong and fit man. He couldn't take anything by mouth for four months – it had to fed by tube in the stomach as there was nothing there. Then he had a second operation to transplant the colon from the bottom of the stomach to make a false oesophagus. Surgeons from all over Europe came over to watch the operation and study the technique. He was the first person in this country to survive the two operations and was in Leicester for nearly six months. He was subsequently very limited in what he could eat and couldn't do a lot after that, he was a complete invalid.

We moved from Bushey, where we had lived for 36 years, to Suffolk a few years ago, to be near to our son and family. We have two grandchildren Caroline, 15 and David, 11. The last time Jack went out was in the summer of 1996 when Middlesex were playing at Fenners. Joe Hardstaff the county secretary, who we had known since he was a little boy, asked Jack if he would like to go to Cambridge. Jack had a wonderful time sitting in the pavilion with the players.

Bill Edrich was the only player from Jack's days who kept in touch with him regularly when he became ill. He wouldn't let me get the doctor but he wasn't eating at all. Jack was in hospital for exactly a month and was under eight stone in the end. When Jack died in October 1996 Jim Swanton was the first to phone me. Jack joined the groundstaff at Lord's the same year as Laurie D'Arcy, who played for Middlesex seconds. They kept in touch with each other though and became good friends. Strangely I had a call to say that Laurie died on the same day as Jack, an extraordinary coincidence. In 56 years of married life, not once did we have a row. We didn't always agree but we agreed to disagree. Jack never raised his voice to me, nor to anyone come to that. He was a very quiet and dignified person who didn't talk much about his playing days and never had a nasty word to say about anyone.

Jack's main hobby was photography – we have boxes of slides and albums, mainly holidays, but also cricket tours. We travelled all over Europe and loved our holidays – we latterly went to Spain and Portugal but no further. In the last two and a half years of his life, Jack took up oil painting although he had never had a lesson in his life, he'd never touched any sort of painting. He starting sketching and his first painting was from a chocolate box cover. The paintings are mostly taken from our holiday slides, although the last one was of Kersey in Suffolk nearby.

Memorable Game
Probably the most memorable game for Jack was his hundred at Lord's in the second Test match against New Zealand in 1949, but the big disappointment for him was that he was dropped for the next Test and never played for his country in England again. He was unfortunate to be around at the same time as Washbrook and Hutton.

25, 27, 28 June 1949. Match drawn
In a high-scoring match Robertson, deputising for the injured Washbrook, crafted a fine century in the second innings. With Hutton, he averted any danger of defeat on the last day with a record opening stand against New Zealand of 143.

England

J.D. Robertson c Mooney b Cowie	26	c Cave b Rabone	121
L. Hutton b Burtt	23	c Cave b Rabone	66
W.J. Edrich c Donnelly b Cowie	9	c Hadlee b Burtt	31
D.C.S. Compton c Sutcliffe b Burtt	116	b Burtt	6
A. Watkins c Wallace b Burtt	6	not out	49
F.G. Mann b Cave	18	c Donnelly b Rabone	17
T.E. Bailey c Sutcliffe b Rabone	93	not out	6
T.G. Evans b Burtt	5		
C. Gladwin run out	5		
J.A. Young not out	1		
W.E. Hollies did not bat			
B 9, l-b 2	11	B 9, l-b 1	10
(9 wkts dec)	313	(5 wkts)	306

1/48 2/59 3/72 4/83
5/112 6/301 7/307 8/307 9/313

1/143 2/216
3/226 4/226 5/252

New Zealand

B. Sutcliffe c Compton b Gladwin	57
V.J. Scott c Edrich b Compton	42
W.A. Hadlee c Robertson b Hollies	43
W.M. Wallace c Evans b Hollies	2
M.P. Donnelly c Hutton b Young	206
F.B. Smith b Hollies	23
G.O. Rabone b Hollies	25
F.L.H. Mooney c Watkins b Young	33
T.B. Burtt c Edrich b Hollies	23
H.B. Cave c and b Young	6
J. Cowie not out	1
B 16, l-b 3, w 3, n-b 1	23
	484

1/89 2/124 3/137 4/160 5/197 6/273
7/351 8/436 9/464

New Zealand Bowling

	O	M	R	W	O	M	R	W
Cowie	26.1	5	64	2	14	3	39	0
Cave	27	2	79	1	7	1	23	0
Rabone	14	5	56	1	28	6	116	3
Burtt	35	7	102	4	37	12	58	2
Sutcliffe	1	0	1	0	16	1	55	0
Wallace					1	0	5	0

England Bowling

Bailey	33	3	136	0
Gladwin	28	5	67	1
Edrich	4	0	16	0
Hollies	58	18	133	5
Compton	7	0	33	1
Young	26.4	4	65	3
Watkins	3	1	11	0

Umpires: W.H. Ashdown and F. Chester

Proudest Moment

His proudest moment was possibly when he was awarded his county cap in 1938 or his first England cap in 1947 against South Africa, or maybe the 331 not out at Worcester in July 1949 when he batted all day, a record unbeaten for Middlesex [the highest individual score for Middlesex and only exceeded in English cricket three times, with well-timed drives and wristy cuts as Middlesex won by an innings and 54 runs]. They gave Jack a little trophy to commemorate it.

A correct right-handed batsman of high class and a fine fielder, Robertson scored 31,914 runs (37.50) including 67 centuries, took 73 wickets (34.74) and 351 catches. In 11 Test matches, he scored 881 runs (46.36) including 2 centuries, took 2 wickets (29.00) and 6 catches.

–43–

Alec Bedser (b. 1918)

Surrey and England

My last season in first-class cricket was 1960, when I was also captain of Surrey, as Peter May was ill when he came back from the West Indies. I had also captained the county from 1957 to 1959 when Peter played for England. In fact over the two years when we won the County Championship in 1957 and '58, I was captain for 50 per cent of the time.

I was involved with England and MCC for many years after retiring from playing and enjoyed all my roles as manager, selector (from 1962) and chairman of the selection committee (from 1969 to 1982). It was a great experience to go with the Duke of Norfolk as his assistant on the MCC tour to Australia in 1962–3, although I had to do all the work as the Duke wasn't familiar with cricket tours at all. In those days the manager had to do everything – the accounts, all the admin and booking the hotels etc., unlike today. Now there are about six people involved which to my mind is ridiculous! I was a selector until about 1986, by which time I felt I was getting too old! You were only elected yearly on the selection committee and I did it on a voluntary unpaid basis, again unlike today. I believe in loyalty and principles in people. My other involvement in cricket was as president of Surrey in 1987.

I still play golf in our home town of Woking. Eric and I do charity work and are trustees for a hospital charity at home. We've always had something to keep us busy including our garden to look after.

I always used to enjoy touring Australia when I was playing, where we have so many friends. We go there every winter – it is now our way of life. We have kept in touch with the same friends in Sydney since 1953 and stay with the grandchildren now. I have been a great friend of Sir Donald Bradman ever since we played, and see him every year.

Memorable Game

It is difficult to pick out one most memorable match that I played in as there are so many. The matches where you did well you remember better, like the first Test against Australia at Trent Bridge in 1953 when I took 14 wickets, that was a great thrill.

11, 12, 13, 15, 16 June 1953. Match drawn

Bedser's match analysis of 14–99 was the best by an England bowler since 1934. His performance was a magnificent exhibition of controlled swing and accuracy. Rain foiled any chance of an England win with the game evenly poised.

Australia

G.B. Hole b Bedser	0	b Bedser	5
A.R. Morris lbw b Bedser	67	b Tattersall	60
A.L. Hassett b Bedser	115	c Hutton b Bedser	5
R.N. Harvey c Compton b Bedser	0	c Graveney b Bedser	2
K.R. Miller c Bailey b Wardle	55	c Kenyon b Bedser	5
R. Benaud c Evans b Bailey	3	b Bedser	0
A.K. Davidson b Bedser	4	c Graveney b Tattersall	6
D. Tallon b Bedser	0	c Simpson b Tattersall	15
R.R. Lindwall c Evans b Bailey	0	c Tattersall b Bedser	12
J.C. Hill b Bedser	0	c Tattersall b Bedser	4
W.A. Johnston not out	0	not out	4
B 2, l-b 2, n-b 1	5	L-b 5	5
	249		123

1/2 2/124 3/128 4/237 5/244
6/244 7/246 8/247 9/248

1/28 2/44 3/50 4/64 5/68
6/81 7/92 8/106 9/115

England

L. Hutton c Benaud b Davidson	43	not out	60
D.J. Kenyon c Hill b Lindwall	8	c Hassett b Hill	16
R.T. Simpson lbw b Lindwall	0	not out	28
D.C.S. Compton c Morris b Lindwall	0		
T.W. Graveney c Benaud b Hill	22		

P.B.H. May c Tallon b Hill   9
T.E. Bailey lbw b Hill   13
T.G. Evans c Tallon b Davidson   8
J.H. Wardle not out   29
A.V. Bedser lbw b Lindwall   2
R. Tattersall b Lindwall   2
B 5, l-b 3   8   B 8, l-b 4, w 2, n-b 2   16
     144   (1 wkt) 120

1/17 2/17 3/17 4/76 5/82 6/92   1/26
7/107 8/121 9/136

England Bowling

	O	M	R	W	O	M	R	W
Bedser	38.3	16	55	7	17.2	7	44	7
Bailey	44	14	75	2	5	1	28	0
Wardle	35	16	55	1	12	3	24	0
Tattersall	23	5	59	0	5	0	22	3

Australia Bowling

	O	M	R	W	O	M	R	W
Lindwall	20.4	2	57	5	16	4	37	0
Johnston	18	7	22	0	18	9	14	0
Hill	19	8	35	3	12	3	26	1
Davidson	15	7	22	2	5	1	7	0
Benaud					5	0	15	0
Morris					2	0	5	0

Umpires: D. Davies and H. Elliott.

I also remember the century I scored at Taunton [126 v Somerset, 1947 – highest score], which is a nice memory – I was 99 not out overnight. I felt I could bat a bit although used to go in lower down the order.

Proudest Moment

My proudest moment in cricket would be receiving a knighthood at the end of 1996, although there have been so many. Probably the best way to put it is: proud to be there and very grateful to have had such a career.

A truly great medium-fast bowler with a model action, Bedser scored 5,735 runs (14.51) including 1 century, 1,924 wickets (20.41) and 290 catches. In 51 Test matches, he scored 714 runs (12.75), took 236 wickets (24.89) and 26 catches.

–44–

Don Smith (b. 1923)

Sussex and England

Since 1959 I played on for Sussex until retirement in 1962, after which I coached part-time at Lancing College. I also busied myself with my rose business before selling out to my partner in 1964. I was then fortunate to be offered a full-time post at Lancing as coach and supervised the grounds, gardens and estates. I did come out of retirement for one extraordinary match in 1964 in that I had not batted at all after having retired from cricket two seasons earlier. An invitation to play for Colonel Stevens XI against Cambridge University at Eastbourne came out of the blue but happened to coincide with a slack time in the business. I was never a keen net player and so arranged for one of the college boys to throw about 24 balls at me on an old pitch the day before the match. I borrowed a bat from one of the boys and off I went. None of the bowlers seemed to make the ball do anything and every ball hit the middle of the bat, going exactly where intended and I scored 140. An amusing memory for me of the innings was meeting Colonel Stevens at lunch midway through my knock. He greeted me with the usual pleasantries then asked, 'Have you batted yet?' I like to think I answered him civilly and to the effect that I was enjoying myself!

I coached at Lancing for 22 years and thoroughly enjoyed my life. The school allowed me to pursue my coaching outside the college when the national coaching organisation asked me, which happened fairly often and was something I loved doing. I also coached in Denmark during the school holidays at Easter and in the summer which was also most rewarding, because for part of each day one was dealing with boys and girls who had quite often never seen a game of cricket!

Then in 1984 I was invited to coach Sri Lanka on their tour of England. We had a very good time and the best of a drawn Test at Lord's. The success of that tour induced the Sri Lankan Board to invite me in July 1985 to prepare and work with the team during India's tour there. That was highly successful and Sri Lanka won their first ever Test. From that came an invitation to return for two years starting at the beginning of 1986. In between the Sri Lankan jobs I went to Australia with a touring team from Lancing and met a lady I had known 20 years before in England. One thing led to another and I came back to Australia to marry her and am now a naturalised Australian. On finishing the Sri Lankan stint I returned to Australia to semi-retirement and coached St Peter's College and their Old Collegians for five years. St Peter's is a private school like Eastbourne or Lancing College. I am now fully retired and live in Linden Park, South Australia.

I still enjoy gardening, though not more than is needed to keep a fairly large garden in order. I stopped playing golf in about 1982 having developed osteoarthritis in both knees. I have, however, become a very keen lawn bowler which, thanks to the weather, is played all year round outdoors in Australia.

Memorable Game

It is difficult to scale the most memorable matches I have played in. My first match at Lord's in 1942 for the Sussex Home Guard was memorable, as to play there is surely the Mecca to all cricketers. It was in fact my first visit to Lord's, but the game was called off shortly after lunch when Andrew Ducat, the Surrey and England player, died. My second visit to Lord's was to be checked for the correct fit of my RAF uniform, great-coat and all, on a day of very high temperature – two not-to-be-forgotten days.

23 July 1942. Match abandoned

The match was called off in tragic circumstances when Andrew Ducat died at the wicket. Eaton was about to bowl when the facing Ducat suddenly collapsed.

Surrey Home Guard

Pte H. Moss b Eaton	32
Pte H.E. Wood b Bartlett	8
Pte P. Cowan c and b Eaton	26
Lt D.A.M. Rome lbw b Eaton	30
Pte A. Ducat not out	29
Lt R.H. Attwell not out	1

Pte J.C. Johnston did not bat
Pte R.A. Levermore did not bat
Pte R.A. Eede did not bat
Pte A. Jeffery did not bat
Lt-Col T.C.D. Hassall did not bat
B 4, l-b 2   6
                                               (4 wkts) 132

Sussex Home Guard
Pte H.S. Mather
Pte J.V. Eaton
Pte V.C. Humphrey
Pte C. Steele
Lt N.C. Fuente
Pte T. Bartlett
Pte D.V. Smith
Lt A.C. Somerset
Lt-Col W.E. Grace
Pte H.R. Sexton
Major E.H. Firth

Sussex Home Guard Bowling

	O	M	R	W
Eaton	18.2	7	34	3
Smith	12	2	35	0
Bartlett	8	0	47	1
Fuente	5	1	10	0

Umpires: T.W. Natcham and Pte. J. Moyer

Also I remember my first match on the County Ground, Hove, playing for my father's club side at the age of 14. I scored 50 not out and he took all 10 wickets!

Proudest Moment
My proudest moment in cricket was my first Test match for England at Lord's in 1957 against the West Indies. I think I remember more detail of that match than most and, of course, I had hoped for as long as I could remember that one day I would play for England. I'd have paid to play, unlike some present-day players, whose main concern seems to be money.

A powerful left-handed opening batsman and useful left-arm medium pace bowler, Smith scored 16,960 runs (30.34) including 19 centuries, took 340 wickets (28.44) and 232 catches. In 3 Test matches, he scored 25 runs (8.33) and took 1–97.

237

–45–

Colin Ingleby-Mackenzie (b. 1933)

Hampshire

Apart from 1959, which was my most successful as a batsman [1,613 runs], the 1961 Championship-winning season was the most memorable. As skipper of Hampshire, we started very poorly then had a great run winning a lot of very tight declaration matches in the last ten minutes or so. My sense of adventure was something inbred. One played naturally but my nature is that the game should be played for fun and I think you play better for it. It encapsulates your desire to play amusing and fun cricket, which makes a side more successful and entertains the public, a two-pronged benefit. There were some very nail-biting performances and 'Butch' White was lethal in getting rid of the opposition. The penultimate match against Derbyshire at Bournemouth was the crucial one and the highlight of the summer. We knew we had to beat them in the first of the two matches played there to end the season. That match was undoubtedly one of the most memorable in my career as we managed to defeat them, with Derek Shackleton doing the trick yet again. Yorkshire told everybody that if we didn't beat Derbyshire they'd thrash us in the second game, which they duly did! We were still somewhat over-celebrated by the time we played them in the final match, although Roy Marshall made a fine hundred. Whilst Roy was a tremendous player, if I had to pinpoint one particular person who was the jewel in the crown in those days, it had to be Derek Shackleton. He did everything. He bowled endlessly and though he bowled seamers was also so accurate. He would turn himself into an off-spinner late on in a game, as he had worn a patch on the wicket.

I carried on as captain for Hampshire until 1965, which was my last season. I retired, having played since 1951 when I made my debut against Sussex. I had been captain for eight years and as 1965 was not a great year I thought it was time for somebody else to have a go. I also felt I should start thinking about my future. My insurance business with Holmwoods had been running parallel with my cricket since 1959, although I was not a very active member in truth and I also worked at the same time for Slazengers. I am still chairman of Holmwoods, although we are owned by Hong Kong & Shanghai Bank. My involvement with Hampshire CCC is now merely on a supportive basis. I joined the MCC committee in 1980 for my first three year run after which I had a year fallow, and found my two-year role as president [1997–8] extremely interesting and exciting.

Whilst skiing and philately were hobbies in 1959, my main interests now are racing and golf. I was keen when I was younger on philately and Desmond Eager was a terrific philatelist. My interest in horses goes back to my Eton days and I own bits and pieces of a number of horses on the flat and over the jumps on a syndicated basis, which I find exciting and very stimulating. My ambition to be a millionaire was tongue in cheek and was more from the song than real life. When you knew you couldn't be, it was exciting to think that you might be.

Memorable Game

There are two memorable games in particular I recall, firstly when I scored the fastest century of the season in 1958 against Somerset at Bournemouth which I recalled in my autobiography, *Many a Slip*:

> When we arrived at Bournemouth for our match against Somerset (after a somewhat late night out) I told Maurice Tremlett, the opposition skipper, that it was most important that we won the toss. I wanted us to bat first and avoid a day in the field – I did not feel up to it. Maurice called wrongly so, greatly relieved, we batted first. I was glad to go into a deep and relaxed sleep in the dressing-room after telling the team to wake me up when I was next man in. I believe Wally Hammond always used to sleep before batting, although I am no Wally. On this occasion, however, the formula worked. When my turn came to bat, with the score already 255–4, I went in and lashed out at everything. I was amazed to connect repeatedly and instead of declaring and leaving them half an hour's batting, I went on in a dream until, at close of play, I had scored 113 not out from a total of 427–5. Furthermore, I easily beat my own fastest century of the season, reaching my 100 this time in 61

minutes, thus drawing my insurance money over the previous quickest effort (having paid a premium of £25 against the prize of £100) and also winning the prize at the end of the year!

18, 19, 20 June 1958. Match drawn

Ingleby-Mackenzie hit 17 fours in his entertaining innings as Hampshire sought an early declaration. Despite the best efforts of spinner Burden with 11 wickets, a combination of rain and defensive play from Somerset thwarted victory for the home side.

Hampshire

R.E. Marshall c Alley b Palmer	75
J.R. Gray c Stephenson b Biddulph	61
H. Horton c Langford b Alley	112
H.M. Barnard b Langford	16
R.W.C. Pitman c and b Biddulph	26
A.C.D. Ingleby-Mackenzie not out	113
P.J. Sainsbury not out	5
L. Harrison did not bat	
D. Shackleton did not bat	
M. Heath did not bat	
M.D. Burden did not bat	
B 4, l-b 12, n-b 1, w 2	19
(5 wkts dec)	427

1/114 2/166 3/196 4/255 5/416

Somerset

J.G. Lomax c Pitman b Shackleton	0	lbw b Sainsbury	13
P.B. Wight c Sainsbury b Burden	31	lbw b Burden	15
B. Roe c Sainsbury b Heath	0	lbw b Burden	0
C.L. McCool c Horton b Heath	25	c Marshall b Burden	87
M.F. Tremlett c Shackleton b Burden	8	c Shackleton b Burden	53
W.E. Alley b Burden	16	c I'Mackenzie b Marshall	13
K.E. Palmer c Marshall b Burden	3	lbw b Burden	4
H.W. Stephenson c Barnard b Sainsbury	12	c Sainsbury b Stephenson	0
C. Greetham c I'Mackenzie b Sainsbury	16	not out	4
B. Langford c Gray b Burden	17	not out	4
K.D. Biddulph not out	2		
L-b 1	1	L-b 4	4
	131	(8 wkts)	197

1/0 2/1 3/47 4/59 5/76 6/79 7/86
8/100 9/127

1/26 2/30 3/32 4/156
5/175 6/189 7/189 8/189

Somerset Bowling

	O	M	R	W
Lomax	14	5	43	0
Biddulph	30	8	82	2
Alley	17	2	63	1
McCool	26	6	87	0
Palmer	6	0	37	1
Langford	25	12	82	1
Greetham	3	0	12	0
Tremlett	1	0	2	0

Hampshire Bowling

	O	M	R	W				
Shackleton	15	5	30	1	10	1	35	0
Heath	14	6	37	2	7	2	25	0
Burden	19	11	25	5	28	14	84	6
Sainsbury	13.4	4	38	2	7	4	14	1
Gray					10	3	14	0
Marshall					13.5	9	21	1

Umpires: A. Skelding and T.W. Spencer

Proudest Moment

The other memorable game I played in and also my proudest moment in cricket was when we beat Derbyshire in 1961 at Bournemouth and I became captain of the first Hampshire side ever to win the County Championship which I also related in *Many a Slip*:

At the start of the 1961 season I decided to give up betting and stick to cricket. I was so broke that I could not afford to back the series of winners that I was given by my racing friends. I am proud to say that this is one of the few resolutions I have ever made that I have managed to keep for quite some while, and perhaps it was a contributory factor to our Championship victory that I made this decision. My hopes were high. Firstly it was Roy Marshall's benefit year, and I was sure this would give him just that little extra killer instinct. Secondly I felt in good nick myself after Jim Swanton's tour [to the West Indies].

The stage was set for the vital match with Derbyshire and we were helped by the absence of a key player from the opposition, Donald Carr, so often a thorn in Hampshire's flesh. We were therefore delighted to greet 'Wild Will' Richardson, a very popular performer, as leader of the opposition. We fielded our strongest side, Butch White's fitness having been decided the previous Sunday in a benefit match for Roy Marshall at Highclere against Lord Porchester's XI. We were lucky enough to bat first in the crucial match and scored the reasonable total of 306 to which several players made good contributions, particularly the openers. At one stage in their first innings, they were only 35 runs behind with six wickets in hand, so we were satisfied to dismiss them for a lead of only 12. The onus was still very much on us to make runs quickly in order to be able to set them a reasonable final-innings target, and once again the gallant Roy led the onslaught with a rapid 86. Peter Sainsbury and Mike Barnard also made sizeable contributions and I timed my declaration to give Derbyshire 192 minutes in which to score 252. The wicket was still perfect and I was far from confident that we would in fact do the trick, but Derek Shackleton did the trick. With no help from the wicket, he took six wickets for 39 and, having been held up for an agonising half-hour by Richard (Bob) Taylor, he finally holed out deep on the mid-wicket boundary. West Indian Danny Livingstone positioned himself to take the catch, and a fraction of a second later he was hugging the ball safely to his chest. Hampshire had won the county cricket Championship for the first time.

We received numerous telegrams which made wonderful reading, including one from our beaten rivals. I was also flattered and touched to receive one from Percy Chapman, once a great captain of England, who died a few weeks later. The rest of that day was filled with congratulations, speeches, pictures, champagne, television and radio interviews. I don't remember what time I went to bed that night, but I do remember, vaguely, coming-to next morning and staring through a throbbing haze at the papers.

A forcing middle-order left-hand batsman and extrovert character, Ingleby-Mackenzie scored 12,421 runs (24.35), took 1 stumping and made 205 catches.

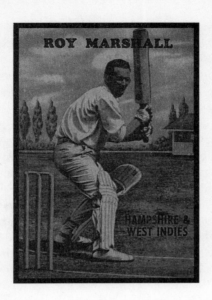

–46–

Roy Marshall (1930–1992)

Barbados, Hampshire and West Indies

As told by Mrs Shirley Marshall

The year 1961 was a happy one as Hampshire won the Championship, which was always Roy's ambition. It was a wonderful season even though Colin's [Ingleby-Mackenzie] declarations drove the players mad! He got on well with Colin and they quite often went out together. Roy had a wonderful memory and could remember every match and innings he played in. Roy recalled in his autobiography *Test Outcast*:

> 1961 was a happy season for me as it was also my benefit year and I scored 2,607 runs, my best aggregate in county cricket, culminating in being honoured as one of *Wisden*'s Cricketers of the Year. In addition one of the best performances in my career came when I scored the first double century of my career against Somerset at Bournemouth. I made an early error against the bowling of Ken Palmer, when he got an inside edge which shaved my leg-stump and went through for four. Apart from that, I could do nothing wrong in scoring 212, batting for 260 minutes and hitting 7 sixes and 21 fours.

[The double century was in 1962 eclipsed by Roy's highest score 228 not out against the Pakistan touring side, again at Bournemouth.]

Roy played for Hampshire until the end of the 1972 season, captaining the side for four seasons from 1966 to 1970. He was on the county committee for a while before we moved. He played and enjoyed ordinary club cricket for a couple of years for the Deanery in Southampton after he retired from county cricket. Their home ground was the County Ground, so he was quite happy with that.

Roy worked four or five winters for a travel firm connected with a shipping line. We left Southampton for Taunton in 1975 when Roy secured a coaching appointment at Kings College in Taunton. He wanted to do some coaching for a while and decided on this one as we always liked the West Country. He coached until about 1991 when he was too ill to carry on. He was also chairman of cricket at Somerset CCC until 1991 and was an adjudicator in one-day matches. We also ran a pub from 1978 for 13 years in Taunton. Roy was pretty fit until the later years and died in 1992 of skin cancer.

Roy played golf and squash and enjoyed swimming and fishing. He loved golf and played to a handicap of about 11 and would go fishing sometimes with Arthur Holt, the old Hampshire coach. His enjoyment of swimming dated back to the Caribbean when he was a good swimmer but he swam little in this country, more when we went abroad. He hated squash, though – it was just a way of keeping fit in the winter. He was also a good tennis player and a natural sportsman. He loved music, particularly jazz, swing, Frank Sinatra, Nat King Cole, etc., and enjoyed watching Southampton Football Club.

Memorable Game
It is difficult for me to highlight the most memorable game Roy played in, as he considered they were all important. His ambition was to see Hampshire win the County Championship, and he recalled the joy of achieving this ambition in *Test Outcast*:

Hampshire's penultimate match in the 1961 season when we beat Derbyshire at Bournemouth to clinch the County Championship for the first time in our 98-year history was the greatest moment of my cricketing life.

30, 31, August, 1 September 1961. Hampshire won by 140 runs
Marshall was in excellent form as he steered Hampshire to match-winning scores in both innings. Shackleton exhibited his usual control and accuracy in taking six wickets as Hampshire made certain of the title amidst jubilant scenes.

Hampshire

R.E. Marshall c Lee b Smith	76	c Lee b Morgan	86
J.R. Gray run out	78	b Rhodes	4

H.Horton c Taylor b Jackson	13	lbw b Rhodes	0
D.A. Livingstone c Lee b Smith	7	c Johnson b Smith	11
P.J. Sainsbury c Rhodes b Smith	1	c Lee b Smith	73
H.M. Barnard c Rhodes b Morgan	19	c Taylor b Smith	61
A.C.D. Ingleby-Mackenzie b Richardson	30	st Taylor b Smith	5
L. Harrison lbw b Morgan	35	b Jackson	0
A. Wassell c Taylor b Jackson	13		
D. Shackleton not out	27	not out	2
D.W. White b Morgan	0	not out	13
B 1, l-b 4, w 1, n-b 1	7	B 4, l-b 3, w 1	8
	306	(8 wkts dec)	263

1/120 2/145 3/160 4/166 5/182
6/229 7/230 8/256 9/304

1/8 2/16 3/40 4/141 5/240
6/247 7/248 8/250

Derbyshire

C. Lee run out	5	c Harrison b Shackleton	4
I. Gibson b Sainsbury	46	lbw b Shackleton	3
H.L. Johnson c Gray b Wassell	112	b Shackleton	14
W.F. Oates c Harrison b Shackleton	89	b Shackleton	2
D. Millner b Shackleton	14	c and b Wassell	17
D.C. Morgan b Wassell	13	c Gray b Wassell	3
E. Smith c Barnard b Shackleton	0	b Shackleton	9
G.W. Richardson c Horton b Wassell	6	b Shackleton	0
R.W. Taylor not out	12	c Livingstone b Sainsbury	48
H.J. Rhodes b Wassell	9	c and b Sainsbury	11
H. L. Jackson c I'Mackenzie b Wassell	4	not out	0
B 4, l-b 4	8		
	318		111

1/9 2/102 3/212 4/248 5/273 6/274
7/285 8/297 9/314

1/4 2/17 3/23 4/24 5/35
6/48 7/52 8/52 9/104

Derbyshire Bowling

	O	M	R	W	O	M	R	W
Jackson	24	9	44	2	14	5	25	1
Rhodes	22	4	48	0	18	8	19	2
Richardson	11	1	35	1	9	2	34	0
Lee	8	2	30	0				
Morgan	20.3	3	79	3	21	5	59	1
Smith	28	8	63	3	25	3	87	4
Oates					2	0	18	0
Gibson					2	0	13	0

Hampshire Bowling

Shackleton	39	15	70	3	24	10	39	6
White	10	3	22	0	3	1	5	0
Gray	7	2	19	0				
Wassell	42.1	13	142	5	24	10	62	2
Sainsbury	14	3	67	1	3.2	0	5	2

Umpires: H. Yarnold and A.E. Rhodes

Proudest Moment

His proudest moment would have been when he made his debut for West Indies in the first Test at Brisbane against Australia in 1951 which he described in his autobiography, *Test Outcast*:

> I batted at number 8 and on both occasions was out to bad shots. In the first innings, with the West Indies struggling against some fine fast bowling from Ray Lindwall, I attempted to lift Ian Johnson out of the ground after I had made 28. I hit right across the line of flight and was bowled. In the second innings when Keith Miller came on I was determined to show him I was boss. I wanted to show him he couldn't scare me. My effort ended in failure. When on 30 I swung, failed to middle it and skied a catch to mid-off. It was a long walk back and I was greeted by a silent dressing-room. Only one man had a good word for me, Sir Don Bradman [Marshall's favourite sportsman], who was watching the game from the dressing-room. He said, 'Nice innings, Roy.' 'Not too bad but a bloody awful shot,' I muttered. 'Never mind. Those runs will come in useful.'

Roy missed out on further Test cricket as he would have had to have qualified again for Hampshire if he played for the West Indies. In fact, Frank Worrell wrote to him in 1956 asking if he wished to play but by that time, with two children, he couldn't afford to be out of first-class cricket for another two years qualifying again. He couldn't play for England as he had already played for the West Indies and that is why his autobiography was called *Test Outcast*. By the time they changed the rules he was too old for Test cricket.

An attractive and forceful right-handed opening batsman with a variety of strokes, Marshall scored 35,725 runs (35.94) including 68 centuries, 176 wickets (28.93) and 293 catches. In 4 Test matches, he scored 143 runs (20.42), took 0–15 and 1 catch.

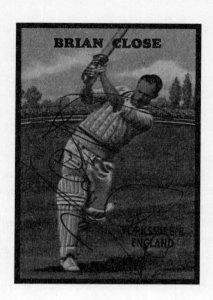

–47–

Brian Close (b. 1931)

Yorkshire, Somerset and England

For England, in 1959 I took four wickets against India [4–35 at Headingley – best bowling in a Test], held four catches, scored 27 runs and didn't play again for another two years! When I returned for the Australia Test at Old Trafford in 1961, in the first innings I was given out lbw by John Langridge off Graham McKenzie when I hit it. In the second innings, we needed 72 runs an hour and were in a possible position to win. Then Richie Benaud started to bowl round the wicket into the rough as a defensive ploy to stop us scoring with any degree of certainty and Raman Subba Row was playing carefully. I sat watching Ted Dexter and Subba Row on the balcony with Peter May, the captain and said to him, 'Don't get two left-handers in together, otherwise we could find ourselves in trouble, keep a right-hander and left-hander together.' Dexter was caught behind, Peter May was bowled round his legs and I finished up throwing my wicket away trying to win the game, which was a pity. If I had just got Richie away two or three times, he would have had to consider going back to bowling over the wicket and pitching on the good part, which was playable, or taking himself off. We owed it to ourselves to make an effort to win but, in the circumstances, after losing four or five wickets and not having a chance to win, then we should have 'shut up shop' and played for a draw, but the lower order were getting out to stupid shots. When Richie was bowling round the wicket into the rough, they didn't have to play the ball and six wickets fell cheaply after mine. All kinds of comments were made but instead of blaming the captain, they blamed me.

I went by the wayside again for two years then played all five Tests against the West Indies in 1963, as they had all the fast bowlers. I scored as many runs as most people, including 70 at Lord's [highest Test score], but was not selected again till the last Test at The Oval in 1966, when they also made me captain. There had been all the amateur captains over the years who had not made a good job of it. We had the best cricketers in the business, yet we were losing to teams we should have beaten. We had an awful series against the West Indies in 1966 again, then for some reason they made me captain. I think they wanted to prove I was no better than the others and would go the same way. When I went to the selectors' meeting, I made certain I had the best side. I knew the good performers who could all fight with their backs against the wall, and we beat them. Bob Barber played as an opening batsman but never bowled for Warwickshire and I had him on before lunch on the first day. Gary Sobers, to my mind, couldn't read wrist spinners and Bob got him out cheaply!

So they had to make me captain the next year. We went through India and Pakistan, then Crawford White phoned me. He advised me to watch my step as word was going round that the establishment wanted me out of the way and their own man in my place with any excuse to get rid of me. Then the Edgbaston affair cropped up [for allegedly using delaying tactics in a Championship match against Warwickshire]. This was stupid. We tried to win the game for Yorkshire, but were playing in a fine drizzle and actually broke an MCC rule to quicken the game up. There had been ball-tampering the previous season by certain sides. As a result the rule was that in the case of damp weather, you had to wipe the ball dry under the supervision of the umpire. Our bowlers Fred Trueman, Richard Hutton and Tony Nicholson took the cloths from the umpires and dried the ball walking back to their mark to bowl the next ball. If we had stuck strictly to the MCC rule the Yorkshire bowlers could have wasted time, but we didn't. They made a song and dance about it, brought me down to Lord's for a hearing and had no case at all to put against me, but found Yorkshire guilty of wasting time and held me responsible! England were touring the West Indies that winter and the selectors chose me to captain the side but MCC, under the presidency of Lord Home, over-ruled them and put their own captain in. A situation like that wouldn't and couldn't happen these days. I went out there for the Press and Colin Cowdrey, who took over, kept on ringing me to ask what he should do!

By 1976 I was in my dotage and all of a sudden got a call to play in the first three Tests against the West Indies and I didn't let them down! It was a very dry summer and my last Test was at Manchester. This was the worst Test wicket I have ever encountered. The faster you bowled, the more dangerous it was and the wicket went to pieces. Tony Greig was captain and called me up at Old Trafford after the practice and asked me to open the innings. I said, 'You must be joking, I haven't opened the innings since about 1955. What's Bob Woolmer in the side for, he's an opening batsman? I have pulled you out of the cart at Lord's and Trent Bridge, you need someone in the middle order responsible enough to pull things round if it doesn't go according to plan with the earlier batsmen.' He replied saying that the selectors thought Bob had a lot of Test cricket left in him and they didn't want him killed off! I opened with John Edrich. I had always loved a battle and we were the only ones to put on over 50 for England in the whole Test. Then they dropped both of us! The next Test was at Headingley and on a flat wicket, they put a lot of youngsters in and they were all bowled out for next to nothing in the second innings!

The harder it was, the more I enjoyed the battle. I would have given my life for the teams I played for, and nearly did several times. I was hit on the body scores of times batting on awkward wickets but never with a bouncer. I was hit on the head many times fielding close to the wicket, but I didn't worry about it – it was part of the game. The nastiest pair of bowlers I ever confronted were South Africa's opening pair Peter Heine and Neil Adcock in 1955. They were both over six foot, powerful and athletic, they're the real fast bowlers, not the lanky people. On that occasion I had just come back from my knee trouble and they brought me in to open with John Ikin in the last Test match at the Oval. We had won the first two Tests then lost the third and fourth, but we won the final one and the series 3–2. Wes Hall in 1963 was allegedly timed at 104 mph at Lord's, and they talk about 80–90 mph being fast these days. In those early days, they bowled off the back foot no-ball rule, the front foot of most fast bowlers was a yard to a yard and a half over the front line when they delivered the ball. Fred was timed in those days at between 90–100 mph – he was as fast as anyone when he wanted to be. Frank Tyson in the early-mid '50s had two years when he was like grease lightning.

I can remember games of county cricket and situations from the age of 11 and I certainly recall taking my best bowling figures [8–41 v Kent] at Headingley in 1959. There was an up and coming young fast bowler called David Pickles, who bowled very well in 1957 and '58. He looked as though he was going to turn into a real cracker, but in 1959 he lost everything and didn't play much after that. In the second innings of this match he was given a couple of overs, but couldn't get within a yard of the wicket. I said to Ronnie Burnett, 'You might as well let me bowl.' In those days I bowled a few seamers whenever it was necessary and the ball just started wobbling about, a few wickets went down and we won the game. I smashed my bad knee up in a car crash, so it was one of the few times I had bowled since 1956.

In 1959 Ronnie Burnett was captain. He was an amateur and a super lad, but he didn't know a lot about cricket, although he loved it. Vic Wilson was the senior professional, and as such would be expected to advise the captain and converse with him, but he was in terrible form and was dropped after about a month. I took over as senior pro and was influential in quite a few games. I said to Ronnie, 'If I come up to advise you, you had better do it.' Everything worked well for a few games and we got up to a challenging position, then for some unknown reason, he stopped taking my advice! We had a chance of winning the Championship after Surrey's reign of seven on the trot, so Ronnie and I had a few verbal scraps. I would keep nattering away at him until we sorted out the situation.

In the last Championship game at Sussex, by lunchtime on the last day, which was an early finish, we had seven of their side out in the second innings, but they were about 170–180 ahead already. As I followed Ronnie on to the field after lunch I said, 'What are your ideas, Ronnie?' He said all we could do was to put Fred on downhill and down wind. I replied, 'Fred's not bowled at all well this match, leave him out of it, let Illy have the wind and put Don Wilson on at the other end. If they can't do it, we are not going to make it.' I got my way and Illy got all three out. We were left to get 215 to win in 105 minutes. We got stuck into them, won the game and the Championship with minutes to spare. It was a very enjoyable occasion. We had a great little side with a few youngsters coming through and experience in Fred, Ray Illingworth and Jimmy Binks.

When I hit my highest first-class score [198 at the Oval in 1960 against Surrey], I hit Lockie twice on top of the Ladies Stand. At the end, when Peter Loader was bowling two or three foot wide of the off-stump into the rough, I hit him like a rocket knee-high. Ronnie Tindall dived and it stuck – it was the nearest I ever got to a double century. I remember the following year when I was batting with Brian Bolus again at the Oval, I hit one to deep third man off Lockie in the last over before lunch. I called for an easy two and, passing the wicket at the batting end, suddenly heard these footsteps accompanied by a 'run, run, run'. I found Brian at my end running for three so had to dash to the other end as Ron Tindall ran from deep third man to cover. He picked the ball up, chucked it at the bowlers end and hit the wicket – I had been run out for 132! As we walked up the stairs to the pavilion, I hit every single step shouting, 'That silly bugger, I'll kill him!' (Bolus, not Tindall.) We were playing for a draw and I had worked out that by the end of play, I would have scored about 350. They were not going to get me out on that wicket with nothing but a draw to play for!

In 1963, my first year as captain for Yorkshire, we were a good side. The youngsters that came in when we had Test calls were lads with talent but no experience. We taught them to think properly so that we could get the best out of them. A good captain helps to develop a player and I feel I made more youngsters into great players than anybody else. I don't see so much of that now. The amount of limited-over cricket which we play now leads to a negative mental attitude in this type of game. The game dictates to the player rather than the player dictating to the game, which leads to stereotype and negative thinking.

In 1964 we had lost the Championship by the end of June because of the weather, as we hadn't completed a game and Worcester and Warwick made a dash of it and got away. We weren't too bothered initially about the one-day cricket as we were busy winning championships, but we put our minds to it in 1965 and won the Gillette Cup. We weren't a good one-day side though, as totally different techniques were needed from the bowlers to bowl negatively in order to win these type of games. For six days a week I was encouraging my bowlers to attack and beat the bat, but that didn't win you limited over games as it gave too many runs away. By this time we realised you had to contain in the field to win these games, which went against our ideas of playing the game properly. We were out of the Championship though in 1965 and so set our stall to bowl negatively in the Gillette Cup, short of a length, straightish, at middle and off, so you could control it. We put our minds to it so well that we reached the final. We turned up at Lord's and, as the square was a bit on the damp side, Surrey having won the toss, put us in to bat and we murdered them! I was going in at that time at number five but, after about 12 overs, Ken Taylor and Geoff Boycott had only scored 15 runs against Geoff Arnold and David Sydenham, both pretty tight bowlers. Doug Padgett was due to go in at three, but was always a bit frightened of batting with Boycott, who ran him out too many times. He said to me, 'Skipper, don't you think you should go in?' I agreed and when Taylor was out I said to Geoff, 'If I call for a bloody run, you run.' In the next few overs we got three or four singles, so the field started coming in a bit to stop the single. I said to Boycs, 'Now then, they're coming in, we are not going to be able to get the singles, if anything is pitched up to you, belt it!' Geoff Arnold's first ball of the next over was a fairly full half-volley and he hit it through extra cover like lightning. Then they put Pat Pocock on at the Pavilion end and Boycs was frightened of slow bowlers. He thought that if you put force into the shot, you would have more chance of getting out, which was right. So I said to him, 'Listen Boycs, they know bloody well you can't hit an off-spinner off the square. He will pitch it up to you, hit him anywhere from long on to square leg, and if you don't I'll wrap this bat round your flaming neck!' On comes Pocock and bowls a perfect full-length ball and Geoff hit it straight over long on for four runs. It sent them into complete disarray and Boycs played a magnificent innings. We eventually broke the record for the number of runs scored in a 65 overs game, 317–4 wickets and won the game so easily I could have put anyone on to bowl. It was great fun, as we showed that we could play the one-day stuff as well.

We were back on the Championship trail in 1966 and were a hell of a good side. While we had our specialist bowlers, we actually had eight or nine in the side who could bowl, so we had plenty of variety. The art of cricket is to get the other side out and, while there are 1,001 ways of getting out, it's the bowling side that asks the questions and the batting side that has to find the answers. If I put a bowler on, I would go up to Jimmy Binks and ask if he looked like beating the bat. If a bowler had gone three or four overs and hadn't taken a wicket, I wasn't going to expend his energy. I might need him later on, so would find someone else who could get a wicket, so everybody bowled regularly. Our strength was our all-round ability – we had Freddie Trueman, still quick, although he had put in a lot of hard work as previous captains had overbowled him. I think I kept him in the game a bit longer as I looked after him and wouldn't let him bowl a lot. If he felt he could take wickets, he was very good. If he didn't, he would bowl within himself, as he had developed an attitude that he would be expected to bowl by previous captains at all times, irrespective of the circumstances. Nobody had ever collared him. I would say if he looked as if he were bowling within himself, 'Come on Fred, put your sweater on.' He still had the ability to bowl fast and take wickets though and was a great bowler if things were going his way. Then we had Tony Nicholson, Richard Hutton, Don Wilson's left-arm and Illy and myself as off-spinners. I also bowled a few swingers as did Illy and Ken Taylor, so there were plenty of options to create change and make people think. The more you make batsmen think, the better chance you have of getting them out. My attitude was if you don't try anything you are never going to succeed, so we were always ready to try something.

I got into trouble with the Yorkshire committee in 1968 when I had an injury to my calf and missed a few games. I was at home when I got a call from Crawford White, the *Daily Express* cricket writer. He said that he heard I was in a spot of bother with the committee – I didn't know anything about it. He went on to say that Tony Lock was at the end of his career at Leicestershire and Crawford had spoken to Mike Turner, the Leicester secretary, who said if it came to the worst, they would be happy for me to join them as captain. They would also pay twice as much as I was getting at Yorkshire. Funnily enough though John Nash, the Yorkshire secretary had rung and asked me to go in and see the chairman the next day. I was confronted by the 12-strong cricket committee plus the chairman Brian Sellers over a couple of points. I sorted it out with the committee and the players. Leicestershire had failed to get me and I didn't want to move anyway as, after 20 years with Yorkshire, it would have felt odd and the money situation never bothered me. I played this game for the love of it, not for money. Then we played Glamorgan at Sheffield, Yorkshire had a terrible time and lost. I was going to play but at the last minute decided not to. I wasn't confident enough with my leg injury. I came back the game after though and we went on to beat Surrey at the end of August to win the Championship again.

We never had contracts in those days – I didn't have one until I went to Somerset and that was only for registration purposes. Illy, who was a wonderful performer both with the bat and ball, wanted a contract, though. Geoff Cope was an up and coming youngster and one or two of the committee wanted him to play. Illy knew that as long as I was captain his place in the team was safe. We were at Bradford Park Avenue at the time when he put in a letter asking for a contract, which should have been put to the committee. The secretary passed it to Brian Sellers the chairman who, being a very autocratic person, made it available to all the Press. It all came out and there was no retraction on either side, so Leicester approached Ray and offered him the same conditions as they had offered me and he went. Fred retired at the end of 1968 as well. At his best he had a superb action, an outswinger, and he was a great character. Then Jimmy Binks left the year after, so over a couple of years the side changed and we lost a lot of experience.

We won the Gillette Cup again in 1969, although as a reorganised side we were not good enough to win the Championship. Our bowling wasn't strong enough. At the beginning of 1970, my last season with Yorkshire, we played Glamorgan in the first Sunday match of the season at Bradford, where there is a slight slope on the ground. I joined John Hampshire at the wicket and we attempted a quick two. The fielder at deep fine leg threw it in like grease lightning and I was running downhill and had to dive to get in the crease. I was not out but from the resultant dive, when I picked myself up, I couldn't move my right arm. I had badly damaged my shoulder and my arm was hanging loose. I couldn't move it and despite cortisone injections was off for several weeks. At the beginning of the season the committee had appointed Phil Sharpe as vice-captain, which was all right as long as I was there. He was a nice lad, a good player and the best first slip in the world, but had no experience as a captain.

We had a terrible time and it was about the middle of June before I could move my arm – I can still feel it now from time to time. We were languishing at the bottom of the Championship and the committee were all at sea. I remember watching us play in a Sunday League match against Notts when we made a big score [235] and I said from the dressing-room, 'If we don't win this game I'll eat my hat.' Our bowlers got knocked all over the place and we lost in the last over! Although I wasn't fit I came back, literally to run the side and we started to pick up. We won the next four Sunday League games in a row, picked up in the Championship and, with a fortnight to go, we were favourites to win it.

1970 was the season South Africa should have come here, but because of the D'Oliveira situation, the tour was cancelled and instead England played a Rest of the World side. We were becoming a good side with Don Wilson and Chris Old, who I looked after, performing well for us. For the last Test at the Oval [and the fourth] Chris and Don were picked for England, which left me with no bowlers! I couldn't bowl because of my shoulder injury, batting was difficult enough. I literally hung my top hand on the top of my bat and hoped it would stay there. I think we would have won the Championship were it not for losing those two, as we didn't win the last couple of matches, but finished in fourth place.

I'd had several arguments with the committee over the years and after one, had argued with Brian Sellers towards the end of the season, 'I'm putting the game and the team first, not you. You're trying to disrupt it.' The last Sunday League game in 1970 was at Old Trafford against Lancashire, who were a great one-day side but had no idea how to play first-class cricket. In the '40s and '50s when I first started, there were four top championship teams in the country, Lancashire, Yorkshire, Middlesex and Surrey. By the end of the '50s, Lancashire had lost the ability to bowl people out but became a very good one-day side. We played well and should have won the game but Lancashire snatched it out of the bag in the last few overs. I was disappointed as we had had a good run since my return after the injury and it would have been nice to end up with victory at Old Trafford. Cricket is a very emotional game and as captain, when things go wrong, it takes a while to get back your equilibrium. When I came off the field, I remember being a bit annoyed when a gentleman came into the captain's dressing-room. I did not know him, but it transpired it was the president of Lancashire, W.H.L. Lister, who was thrilled to bits that his team had been successful and won the Sunday League. I turned round and said, 'They were bloody lucky!' He obviously went back into the committee room and told Brian Sellers. I was taking my bag over to my car in the car park when I heard Sellers running towards me shouting at the top of his voice, 'Close, Close.' I said, 'Yes, chairman?' 'You've insulted the president of Lancashire' and I didn't know what he was talking about! That night I wrote their president an apology explaining I had no idea who he was and that he had caught me when I was feeling somewhat emotional and annoyed having lost the game. I sent a copy to John Nash, but that incident probably didn't do me any good! From that moment on, Sellers had it in his mind that I was going, and the Lancashire people were very annoyed that he had used that incident as an excuse to manufacture a scene to get rid of me.

In some respects I was looking forward to the next summer in view of the results, and we had a few of the youngsters developing and coming on. We had made a fantastic recovery in 1970 and it looked as if we had the nucleus of better things for 1971. I was at home in the November when I had a call from John Nash asking me to see the chairman the following day. I thought it was to discuss the team. They all knew that I didn't like the one-day cricket because of its stereotype nature. That didn't mean that I didn't take it seriously – after all we had won two Gillette Cup finals. At the meeting the first words Sellers said were, 'Well Brian, you've had a good innings. When you leave this place, you will either be sacked or resign.' I realised in a moment that there were going to be awful repercussions about this. He went on, 'I have two statements here – when you leave this office, one of them will be given to the Press at two o'clock (this was at 11 a.m.). I realised there was going to be one hell of a blow-up in the media and press and didn't want the upheaval. I'd had enough of that in my life so I replied that I would resign. I left the office and drove home and felt as sick as a pig. Twenty-two years of my life had gone into Yorkshire cricket and I had never ever put myself first. They had also used the situation of me not liking the one-day game to sack me! The real reason was to a large extent that I had beaten Brian Sellers in arguments.

When my wife Vivienne came back from collecting the children at school, I was in the kitchen and she asked me what the matter was – she said I looked like death warmed up. I told her I had just been given the sack but explained I had resigned. She said I ought to ring Jack Mewis and Roy Parsons and speak to them, which I did. They pointed out that I had been silly to resign and let them off the hook. So I rang John Nash – it took me about 20 minutes to get through – and said to him, 'I'm sorry about this but I have changed my mind, I am not resigning, you can sack me.' He stuttered and stammered for several minutes and, despite saying they were not giving the news out until 2 p.m., they obviously had done so as soon as I had left. Before the melee started, I had a message from Reg Hayter, a great cricket friend, who said I was going to be totally immersed with the Press at home. He suggested I put a pair of pyjamas and a toothbrush in a bag, come down to London and meet him at Wembley. That night I went with him to watch England play Austria and did an interview with David Coleman on *Sportsnight*.

Several counties rang me in the next few days. I turned it over in my mind. I was not at the point of wanting to retire from the game and I thought I might take my career somewhere and just be a player again. Being captain you come last – the game comes first, then the team, then yourself. If you are going to do the job properly, it didn't matter if I didn't score runs or take wickets. So literally I hadn't been a player for quite a few years. A few backed out as they thought, being a strong personality I might upset their captain. I thought afterwards I might have made them a better captain! In the end I went to Somerset and thought I would enjoy playing for two or three years. I played under Brian Langford and said, 'Don't worry Brian, if there is anything I can suggest, I will help you,' and I did. We got on like a house on fire. I fielded at forward short leg and silly mid off to him and made a few catches. When he resigned as captain, I tried to persuade him not to as I didn't want the job, I was enjoying being a player again. I became captain the following year and the year after we got Ian Botham then Viv Richards, two young lads. We became a very good one-day team although we were not quite good enough as a bowling side to win a championship. We might have done had Tom Cartwright, who was a great bowler, managed to stay fit and been able to play every game. I needed one top star bowler to take centre stage. Tom would have been that but regrettably his injury situation meant he wasn't always there and when he wasn't we were caught short. In the end, I still lived in Yorkshire and was spending my summers down there and realised Vivienne was having the kids in the summer and I was never seeing them. It got to the end of 1977 and although I was still enjoying the game, I retired. It was a thrill to look after the youngsters at Somerset and make them work on their game.

I had taken part in several tours in the winter months. The South African trips, including the International Wanderers and the two Derrick Robins tours I skippered in the '70s were great fun, with nice people and weather and good cricket in a lovely country. It was a pleasure to joust with them and try and outwit them.

I raised teams in my name during the '80s for the Scarborough festival and played my last first-class game against the New Zealanders at Scarborough in 1986. When I needed just six runs to score 35,000 in total, a New Zealand 'quickie' [Willie Watson] bowled one down the leg-side. It lifted a little and actually brushed my glove. I turned round and saw the wicket-keeper take it. They didn't know I had touched it but I did, so I walked off as that was the way I played the game. The New Zealand lads asked why I didn't tell them I only needed that number of runs. I said it was immaterial. If I knew I was out, I would walk under any circumstances. It was an honourable game and I was brought up that way. Blokes you would play against would be enemies on the field but mates off it. It disappoints me to see the game as it is now. Figures never worried me or meant anything to me, I was brought up to just enjoy playing and whatever game it was, play to win. If we were batting, our job was to get runs quickly enough to give our bowlers time to get the other side out.

I still play the odd charity game for a decent cause and enjoy batting, although the fielding's a bit of a struggle! I enjoy mostly golf now and play at Bradford off a handicap of nine. I used to be a bit lower down, but when I was at Somerset hardly played at all, as with the Sunday cricket it was seven days a week. I used to do a bit of shooting and fishing with friends but I no longer have the time.

I was on Yorkshire and England committees over the years and have always put the game first. When I eventually retired from cricket I went into insurance. I still work part-time in insurance as I can't live on an old-age pension. I used to work for Bell Fruit, but they got a new managing director while I was playing for Somerset. I had a benefit in 1976 and owed Somerset one more season. The managing director wanted me to give up first-class cricket but I said no, so left the company.

Memorable Game
The most memorable game for me was when I captained England for the first time in the fifth Test against the West Indies at The Oval in 1966 when we beat them.

18, 19, 20, 22 August 1966. England won by an innings and 34 runs
Close shrewdly led his team to victory shortly after lunch on the fourth day. In addition to fine hundreds from Graveney and Murray, Higgs and Snow both scored their maiden half-centuries in first-class cricket. Their partnership was only two runs short of the England record for the last wicket.

West Indies

C.C. Hunte b Higgs	1	c Murray b Snow	7
E.D. McMorris b Snow	14	c Murray b Snow	1
R.B. Kanhai c Graveney b Illingworth	104	b D'Oliveira	15
B.F. Butcher c Illingworth b Close	12	c Barber b Illingworth	60
S.M. Nurse c Graveney b D'Oliveira	0	c Edrich b Barber	70
G.S. Sobers c Graveney b Barber	81	c Close b Snow	0
D.A. Holford c D'Oliveira b Illingworth	5	run out	7
J.L. Hendriks b Barber	0	b Higgs	0
C.C. Griffith c Higgs b Barber	4	not out	29
W.W. Hall not out	30	c D'Oliveira b Illingworth	17
L.R. Gibbs c Murray b Snow	12	c and b Barber	3
B 1, l-b 3, n-b 1	5	B 1, l-b 14, n-b 1	16
	268		225

1/1 2/56 3/73 4/74 5/196 6/218
7/218 8/223 9/223

1/5 2/12 3/50 4/107 5/137
6/137 7/142 8/168 9/204

England

G. Boycott b Hall	4
R.W. Barber c Nurse b Sobers	36
J.H. Edrich c Hendriks b Sobers	35
T.W. Graveney run out	165
D.L. Amiss lbw b Hall	17
B.L. D'Oliveira b Hall	4

D.B. Close run out	4
R. Illingworth c Hendriks b Griffith	3
J.T. Murray lbw b Sobers	112
K. Higgs c and b Holford	63
J.A. Snow not out	59
B 8, l-b 14, n-b 3	25
	527

1/6 2/72 3/85 4/126 5/130 6/150 7/166 8/383 9/399

England Bowling

	O	M	R	W	O	M	R	W
Snow	20.5	1	66	2	13	5	40	3
Higgs	17	4	52	1	15	6	18	1
D'Oliveira	21	7	35	1	17	4	44	1
Close	9	2	21	1	3	1	7	0
Barber	15	3	49	3	22.1	2	78	2
Illingworth	15	7	40	2	15	9	22	2

West Indies Bowling

Hall	31	8	85	3
Griffith	32	7	78	1
Sobers	54	23	104	3
Holford	22.5	1	79	1
Gibbs	44	16	115	0
Hunte	13	2	41	0

Umpires: J.S. Buller and C.S. Elliott

Proudest Moment

The proudest moment for me was when I went to Buckingham Palace in 1975 to receive the CBE for my services to cricket. I have given my all. There were so many wonderful and enjoyable moments you could share being in a cricket team.

A courageous, gifted left-hand bat, versatile right-arm bowler and fearless close fielder, Close scored 34,994 runs (33.29) including 52 centuries, 1,166 wickets (26.41), 808 catches and 1 stumping. In 22 Test matches, he scored 887 runs (25.34), took 18 wickets (29.55) and 24 catches.

–48–

Raman Subba Row (b. 1932)

Surrey, Northants and England

I had four particularly good years in cricket from 1958 when I was captain of Northamptonshire. I especially enjoyed my last year in 1961 when I played in the Tests against the Australians, even though we didn't win the series. We certainly should have won at Manchester in the fourth Test when Richie Benaud bowled us out as we were 150–1 at one time chasing 256. I announced my retirement after the fourth Test match and played at the Oval in the final Test with the decision already taken. Scoring a century [137 in the second innings, his highest Test score] to go with my hundred at Edgbaston in the first Test [112 also in the second innings] was the greatest time [scoring 468 runs in the series, Subba Row headed the batting averages].

My last two first-class matches were played at Hastings during the festival week in September. I captained A.E.R. Gilligan's XI in the first game against the Australians [which the tourists won by three wickets], scored nought and one, and it was the closest I ever was to getting a pair. In the second innings Richie Benaud gave me one before I was caught by Wally Grout at the wicket!

Then I skippered an England XI versus a Commonwealth XI in my last game [Subba Row, applauded all the way to the crease, fluently hit 60 in an hour and 20 minutes, then was clapped and cheered to the dressing-room].

These were of course the old days of amateurs and professionals, and you had to decide whether to become a professional or not. I had a tremendous amount of fun out of the game both at county and international level and was lucky to play the volume of cricket that I did. I thought I had better go and do some work though and I don't regret that decision. Friendships that one made in cricket continue to this day and it is a great joy to meet up regularly.

I was a great advocate of starting local league club cricket. Surrey club cricket was gradually going downhill in the '60s, with people turning up late and not taking the game seriously. Norman Parks from Beddington and I sat down in 1966 and decided to do something about it. We had various meetings and set up the framework for a league to start in 1968. It has been going since then, although it would have happened anyway. There was a vast amount of administration work but the clubs backed it and in due course the league structure was extended to other counties.

Also in 1968 I was involved in the planning of the start of the Test & County Cricket Board to take over the running of first-class cricket in the UK from MCC, and I became the first chairman of the marketing committee. Already on the Surrey County Cricket Club committee, I was invited to become chairman in 1974 and served in that capacity until 1979. After managing the England side touring India and Sri Lanka in 1981–2, I was elected chairman of the TCCB in 1985. It was during that five-year tenure that I chaired the reorganisation committee of the old International Cricket Conference to create the new International Cricket Council – again to take over from MCC the responsibility for administering world cricket which the Club had nobly carried out for 80 years.

Outside of cricket I was employed by an advertising agency from 1962 to 1969, then set up my own public relations company, Management Public Relations Ltd, which I continued until 1994. It was a small business which I enjoyed – PR teaches one how to talk to and understand people. I am now retired, although remain involved in cricket as a match referee in Test matches.

Sir Frank Worrell was my favourite sportsman and motoring my hobby. Frank was a marvellous chap, a super player, such a gentleman and epitomised everything that is good about cricket, so gracious that you couldn't really believe it. I remember arriving in Jamaica with MCC in 1959–60 and finding a brand new car for my fiancée and myself to drive around in for three weeks. It was absolutely unasked for and courtesy of Frank, whom I went with on the Commonwealth tour to India in 1953–4.

Memorable Game

The most memorable game I played in was when scoring my first hundred in Test cricket at Georgetown, British Guiana [now Guyana] in 1960. When

I reached 96, Frank Worrell told me, 'I think it's time you had a full toss down the leg side.' I couldn't believe my ears but Frank was not the sort of chap who would con me, and there it was – bang! The game was dead by then, but he made sure I scored 100. Then I was out next ball, lbw Worrell!

9, 10, 11, 12, 14, 15 March 1960. Match drawn

Subba Row came into the side for the fourth Test and, whilst he chipped a knuckle in the first innings, shared in a stand of 148 for the third wicket with Ted Dexter in the second as England made certain of not losing the series.

England

G. Pullar c Alexander b Hall	33	lbw b Worrell	47
M.C. Cowdrey c Alexander b Hall	65	st Alexander b Singh	27
R. Subba Row c Alexander b Sobers	27	lbw b Worrell	100
K.F. Barrington c Walcott b Sobers	27	c Walcott b Worrell	0
E.R. Dexter c Hunte b Hall	39	c Worrell b Walcott	110
M.J.K. Smith b Hall	0	c Scarlett b Sobers	23
R. Illingworth b Sobers	4	c Kanhai b Worrell	9
R. Swetman lbw b Watson	4	c Hall b Singh	3
D.A. Allen c Alexander b Hall	55	not out	1
F.S. Trueman b Hall	6		
J.B. Statham not out	20		
B 5, l-b 2, w 2, n-b 6	15	B 6, l-b 4, n-b 4	14
	295	(8 wkts) 334	

1/73 2/121 3/152 4/161 5/169
6/175 7/219 8/258 9/268

1/40 2/110 3/358 4/320
5/322 6/322 7/331 8/334

West Indies

C. Hunte c Trueman b Allen	39
E. McMorris c Swetman b Statham	35
R. Kanhai c Dexter b Trueman	55
G. Sobers st Swetman b Allen	145
C.L. Walcott b Trueman	9
F.M. Worrell b Allen	38
F.C.M. Alexander run out	33
R. Scarlett not out	29
C. Singh b Trueman	0
W. Hall not out	1
C. Watson did not bat	
B 4, l-b 12, n-b 2	18
(8 wkts dec) 402	

1/67 2/77 3/192 4/212
5/333 6/338 7/393 8/398

West Indies Bowling

	O	M	R	W	O	M	R	W
Hall	30.2	8	90	6	18	1	79	0
Watson	20	2	56	1				
Worrell	16	9	22	0	31	12	49	4
Scarlett	22	11	24	0	38	13	63	0
Singh	12	4	29	0	41.2	22	49	2
Sobers	19	1	59	3	12	1	37	1
Walcott					9	0	43	1

England Bowling

	O	M	R	W
Trueman	40	6	116	3
Statham	36	8	79	1
Illingworth	43	11	72	0
Barrington	6	2	22	0
Allen	42	11	75	3
Dexter	5	0	20	0

Umpires: E. Lee Kow and C. Kippins

Proudest Moment

My proudest moment in cricket was listening on the radio, as one did in those days, to hear I had been picked for the first time for England to play against New Zealand in 1958. England had beaten New Zealand 3–0 in a five-match series, and because of that it was decided that it would be a good opportunity to bring in some new players – Messrs Dexter, Illingworth and Subba Row at Manchester. I was playing in a club match on the Sunday before, at New Malden, and suddenly heard that I was going to play for England – I couldn't believe it!

A sound left-hand batsman, slow leg-break or googly bowler and excellent slip fielder, Subba Row scored 14,075 runs (41.64) including 30 centuries, 87 wickets (38.47) and 172 catches. In 13 Test matches he scored 984 runs (46.85) including 3 centuries, 0–2 and 5 catches.

Acknowledgements

Topps U.K. Ltd incorporating A&BC
John Wisden and Co. Ltd
The Cricketer
Many a Slip (Colin Ingleby-Mackenzie) – Oldbourne Book Co. Ltd
Rev. Malcolm Lorimer, official Historian of Lancashire CCC
Brian Bearshaw and the *Manchester Evening News*
Test Outcast (Roy Marshall) - Pelham Books
Mr G.A. Stedall, Secretary of Somerset Cricket Museum Ltd
Island Cricketers (Clyde Walcott) – Hodder & Stoughton
The White Rose – Yorkshire CCC magazine
Who's Who of Cricketers – Philip Bailey, Philip Thorn, Peter Wynn-Thomas
Noel Wild
Gerry Wolstenholme

Appendix

TREVOR EDWARD (Barnacle) BAILEY
ENGLAND & ESSEX

Height: 5 ft. 10 in. Weight: 12 st. 10 lb.

Overs	Maidens	Runs	Wickets	Average
786	209	1,718	106	61.20

Was born in Westcliff-on-Sea. He first joined the Essex County Cricket Club in 1938 and was award-ed his county cap in 1948. He has played in 56 test matches and has been with the M.C.C on tours of Australia (three times), to the West Indies and to South Africa. A very talented all-rounder, who has always been at his best when the odds are stacked against him and his team. Has five times taken 100 wickets in a season with his fast medium swing bowling. His best bowling performance ever was 10 for 90 v. Lancs. in 1949. As a batsman has scored 18 hundreds, one in a Test match and has 10 times scored more than 1,000 runs in a season. His highest score ever is 205 v. Sussex in 1947.

©  PRINTED IN ENGLAND

WILFRED WOOLLER
GLAMORGAN

Height: 6 ft. 2½ in. Weight: 15 st.

Matches	Innings	Not out	Runs	Highest score	Average
21	29	8	268	38 n.o.	12.76

Was born at Ross-on-Sea, North Wales. He has been connected with Glamorgan since 1938 and was awarded his county cap in 1946. An outstanding all-round cricketer, he bowls medium fast and has twice taken more than 100 wickets in a season. His best performance ever was v. Warwickshire, 1953, when he took 7 for 21. With the bat his highest score is 128 v. Warwickshire, 1955, and he has made five hundreds to date. He has aso scored more than a thousand runs in five seasons. A Welsh international rugger player, his hobbies are Fishing, Gardening and Golf. His favourite sports-man is Peter May and his ambition for the future is to see Welsh cricket at the top.

© PRINTED IN ENGLAND

ROY (Tatt) TATTERSALL
ENGLAND & LANCASHIRE

Height: 6 ft. 2 in. Weight: 13 st. 7 lb.

Overs	Maidens	Runs	Wickets	Average
893.2	353	1,646	91	18.08

Born in Bolton, he joined Lancashire in 1948 and was awarded his county cap in 1950. A right-arm off-spin bowler, his best performance is 9 for 40 v. Notts in 1953. He has taken 100 wickets in a sea-son eight times, his highest total in a season being 193. His highest score is 58 v. Leicester in 1958. He has played in 16 Test matches and has toured Australia and New Zealand in 1950–51, and India, Pakistan and Ceylon with the M.C.C in 1952. His hobbies are Football and Motoring, and his favourite sportsman, Stirling Moss.

© PRINTED IN ENGLAND

COLIN LESLIE McCOOL
AUSTRALIA & SOMERSET

Height: 5 ft. 7 in. **4** Weight: 12½ st.

Matches	Innings	Not out	Runs	Highest score	Average
29	53	1	1,490	169	28.65

Born in Sydney, Australia, he joined Somerset in 1956 and was awarded his county cap in the same year. An attractive right-hand bat, he has scored 1,000 runs in a season three times and 12 centuries. His highest score is 172 for Queensland v. S. Australia. A more than useful leg-break bowler, his best performance was 8 for 74 v. Notts last year. He has played in 14 Test matches for Australia, five against England. Against England in 1946 he scored 104 not out, his only Test century. He has also toured England, New Zealand and South Africa with the Australian touring team. His hobby is Gardening and his favourite sportsman is fellow countryman and county colleague Bill Alley.

 © A&BC

DONALD BRYCE CARR
ENGLAND & DERBYSHIRE

Height: 5 ft. 9 in. **5** Weight: 10 st. 8 lb.

Matches	Innings	Not out	Runs	Highest score	Average
30	51	7	1,058	71	22.51

Born Wiesbaden, Germany. Made his debut for Derbyshire in 1946 and awarded his county cap in 1951. Played in two Test matches and has toured India, Pakistan and Ceylon in 1951–52 and Pakistan 1955–56 with M.C.C. A right-hand bat, he has 10 centuries to his credit and has scored 1,000 runs or more in a season four times, highest score is 170 v. Leicester in 1949. A useful slow left-arm bowler, best performance is 7 for 53 v. Lancs A. Cricket and soccer blue at Oxford, he won F.A. Amateur Cup winners medals with Pegasus in 1951 and 1953. Hobbies are Golf, Photography and Football, and his ambition is to lead Derbyshire to a championship victory.

 © A&BC

HERBERT LESLIE JACKSON
ENGLAND & DERBYSHIRE

Height: 6 ft. 1 in. **6** Weight: 13 st. 7 lb.

Overs	Maidens	Runs	Wickets	Average
753.2	285	1,363	135	10.09

Born in Whitwell, Derbyshire, he joined the county in 1948 and was awarded his county cap in 1949. A right-hand fast medium bowler, his best performance is 9 for 60 against Lancashire in 1952. He has taken 100 wickets or more in a season eight times. The most wickets he has taken in a season is 138. In 1949 he played for England v. New Zealand at Manchester and in 1950–51 he toured India with the Commonwealth team. Last season he headed his county's bowling averages, and did the 'hat trick' against Worcester. His favourite sportsman is John Charles and his ambition is to tour with the M.C.C.

 © A&BC

ALAN EDWARD MOSS
ENGLAND & MIDDLESEX

Height: 6 ft. 3 in. **7** Weight: 14 st.

Overs	Maidens	Runs	Wickets	Average
727.5	209	1,816	107	16.97

Born in Tottenham, London, he made his debut for Middlesex in 1950 and was awarded his county cap in 1952. A right-arm fast bowler, his best performance is 7 for 24 v. Kent in 1957. He has made two Test match appearances, one v. West Indies while on tour with the M.C.C in 1953–54 and one v. Australia in 1956. He was also a member of the M.C.C party which toured Pakistan in 1955–56. Also in 1956 he did the 'hat trick' v. Gloucester at Lords. His hobby is Photography, and his ambition is to tour the world.

©

ROBIN GEOFFREY MARLAR
SUSSEX

Height: 5 ft. 10 in. **8** Weight: 12½ st.

Overs	Maidens	Runs	Wickets	Average
640	175	1,644	83	19.80

Was born in Eastbourne, Sussex. He has been connected with the Sussex County Cricket Club since he was a schoolboy and received his county cap in 1952. An off-spinner bowler, he has four times taken 100 wickets in a season, his best ever being 139. His best individual bowling performance was v. Lancashire in 1955, when he took 9 for 46. His highest score, of which he is very proud, because it was made against the Australian touring team, is 64. His hobbies are Reading and Travelling, and his favourite sportsman is Sir Jack Hobbs. His future ambition is to be able to live abroad during the winter.

©

JOHN (Pretters) PRETLOVE
KENT

Height: 5 ft. 8 in. **9** Weight: 10 st. 7 lb.

Matches	Innings	Not out	Runs	Highest score	Average
27	42	1	830	112	20.24

Joined his present county, Kent in 1955. He was awarded his county cap in 1957. An all-rounder, his best bowling performance was v. Middlesex in 1955, when he took 5 for 55. This ex-Cambridge University player has scored eight centuries in his career, his highest score being 137 v. Essex in 1954. His hobbies are Reading and Music, and his ambition is to reach the top in everything he attempts. He certainly did this at his university, where he was a Double Blue at cricket and soccer.

©

MARTIN JOHN HORTON

WORCESTERSHIRE

 Height: 5 ft. 9 in. **10** Weight: 13 st. 8 lb.

Matches	Innings	Not out	Runs	Highest score	Average
29	53	5	1,540	133	32.08

Born in Worcester, he joined the county in 1949 and was awarded his county cap in 1955. A competent all-rounder, his highest score is 133 v. Hants in 1958. He has topped 1,000 runs in a season four times, and has scored three centuries. An off-spin bowler, his best performance was against the South Africans in 1955 when he took 9 for 56 and in the same season he took 103 wickets. He did the 'hat trick' against Somerset in the following season. His hobbies are Skittles and Reading, and his favourite sportsman is Denis Crompton. His aim is to improve his cricket.

©

FRANK HOLMES (Typhoon) TYSON

ENGLAND & NORTHAMPTONSHIRE

 Height: 6 ft. **11** Weight: 13 st. 8 lb.

Overs	Maidens	Runs	Wickets	Average
562.1	132	1,427	78	18.29

Born in Bolton, he joined Northants in 1952 and was awarded his county cap in 1954. His sheer pace, and ability to move the ball either way, makes him one of the best fast bowlers in present day cricket. His best performance is 8 for 60 v. Surrey in 1957 and his greatest number of wickets in a season 101. Although not a noted batsman, he can at times be difficult to dislodge. His highest score is 72 v. Hants in 1955. He has played in 13 Test matches and has toured the West Indies in 1955–56, South Africa in 1956–57 and Australia and New Zealand in 1954–55 and 1958–59 with the M.C.C. A Bachelor of Arts, his hobby is reading.

©

REGINALD THOMAS SIMPSON

ENGLAND & NOTTINGHAMSHIRE

 Height: 5 ft. 11½ in. **12** Weight: 13 st. 6 lb.

Matches	Innings	Not out	Runs	Highest score	Average
27	50	1	1,300	84	26.53

Born in Nottingham, he joined the county in 1946 and was awarded his county cap the same year. A fluent stroke maker and prolific run scorer, he has scored 56 centuries, four in Tests, 1,000 runs in a season 10 times, and 2,000 runs in a season four times. His highest score is 259 for M.C.C v. New South Wales, 1950–51. He has played in 27 Test matches and has toured South Africa, Australia and New Zealand twice with the M.C.C and also India with the Commonwealth team. His hobbies are Flying and Gardening, and his ambition is to score 300 runs in an innings.

©

THOMAS GODFREY EVANS
ENGLAND & KENT

Height: 5 ft. 9 in. **13** Weight: 13 st.

Matches	Innings	Not out	Runs	Highest score	Average
17	27	1	545	55	20.96

Born in Finchley, Middx., he joined Kent in 1939 and was awarded his county cap in 1946. Recognised as the greatest wicket keeper in the world. He made his début for England in 1946 and has played in 86 Test matches – a record. He has made over 200 dismissals in Test cricket. His highest number of victims in one match is nine for Kent v. New Zealanders in 1949. He has been on eight tours with the M.C.C., four of them in Australia and New Zealand. A capable and entertaining batsman, his highest county score is 144 v. Somerset, 1952 and for England 104 v. West Indies, 1950, and 104 v. India, 1952. He has scored 1,000 runs in a season four times.

©

DONALD JOHN (Shep) SHEPHERD
GLAMORGAN

Height: 6 ft. **14** Weight: 13 st. 8lb.

Overs	Maidens	Runs	Wickets	Average
960.2	291	2,129	88	24.19

Was born in Porteynon, near Swansea. He was taken on the staff of Glamorgan in 1948 and in 1952 was awarded his county cap. A right-arm medium pace off-spin bowler, he can turn his hand to seam bowling if the occasion demands it. He has three times taken 100 wickets in a season and in his best season he took 177 wickets. His best bowling performance was 9 for 47 v. Northants in 1954. His hobbies are Badminton and Breeding Poodles. His favourite sportsman is John Charles, and his ambition is to play for England.

©

MAURICE FLETCHER TREMLETT
ENGLAND & SOMERSET

Height: 6 ft. 2 in. **15** Weight: 14 st.

Matches	Innings	Not out	Runs	Highest score	Average
29	52	5	870	118	18.51

Born in Stockport, Lancs, he joined Somerset in 1938 and received his county cap in 1947. Although originally an all-rounder, he is probably better known as a batsman. A right-hand bat, he has scored 1,000 runs in a season nine times, and 2,000 runs in a season once. He has scored 14 centuries and his highest score is 185 v. Northants in 1951. A right-arm, fast medium bowler, his best performance was against Glamorgan when he took 8 for 31. In 1947–48 he played in three Test matches against West Indies while touring with the M.C.C., and has also toured South Africa. His hobbies are Golf and Fishing, and his favourite sportsman Peter Thompson.

©

ERIC ARTHUR BEDSER
SURREY

Height: 6 ft. 3 in. **16** Weight: 15½ st.

Matches	Innings	Not out	Runs	Highest score	Average
29	36	5	426	56	13.74

Born in Reading, he has been connected with Surrey since 1938 and was awarded his full cap in 1947. A most consistent all-round cricketer, he has six times scored 1,000 runs in a season and has scored 14 centuries during his career, with a highest score of 163 v. Notts, 1949. An off-break bowler, his opportunities for performing in this department have been limited at Surrey because of the abundance of top-class bowlers on their playing staff. In one season he took 92 wickets and his best bowling performance was against Leicester in 1955, when he took seven wickets for 33 runs. He has played for the M.C.C. on their tour of Tasmania. His hobbies are Golf and Gardening.

©

BRIAN STANLEY BOSHIER
LEICESTERSHIRE

Height: 6 ft. 5½ in. **17** Weight: 16 st.

Overs	Maidens	Runs	Wickets	Average
852.2	240	2,028	108	18.77

Was born in Leicester. He has been connected with that county since 1952 and received his county cap in 1958. A medium pace, right-arm bowler, his best bowling performance was 8 for 45 v. Essex in 1957, and in his best season to date he took 108 wickets. His hobby is Angling.

©

FREDERICK JOHN TITMUS
ENGLAND & MIDDLESEX

Height: 5 ft. 9 in. **18** Weight: 11 st. 7 lb.

Overs	Maidens	Runs	Wickets	Average
759.3	277	1,667	82	20.32

Born in London, he joined Middlesex in 1949 and was awarded his county cap in 1953. An all-rounder, he has scored 1,000 runs in a season three times, his highest score being 104 v. Hants in 1954. A right-arm off-spin bowler, his best performance is 8 for 43 for the M.C.C v. South Africans in 1955: another notable achievement was against Somerset when he took 8 for 44. He has taken 100 wickets in a season five times, and once took 191. In 1955 he played in two Test matches v. South Africa and toured Pakistan with M.C.C in 1955–56. His hobbies are Photography and Dogs, and his ambition is to reach the top in cricket.

©

RAYMOND ILLINGWORTH
ENGLAND & YORKSHIRE

Height: 5 ft. 11 in. **19** Weight: 12 st. 6 lb.

Overs	Maidens	Runs	Wickets	Average
626.2	197	1,390	81	17.16

Born in Pudsey, he joined Yorks in 1950 and was awarded his county cap in 1955. An all-rounder, he has made three centuries and scored 1,000 runs in a season twice. His highest score is 146 not out v. Essex in 1953. An off-spin bowler, his best performance is 9 for 42 v. Worcester, and he has taken 100 wickets in a season twice. His hobby is Golf and his favourite sportsman is Tom Finney. Ray's ambition is to score 10,000 runs and take 1,000 wickets. He made his Test match début v. New Zealand last year.

BRIAN TAYLOR
ESSEX

Height: 5 ft. 10 in. **20** Weight: 12½ st.

Matches	Innings	Not out	Runs	Highest score	Average
30	42	5	569	39	15.37

Was born in Westham. He joined Essex in 1948 and was awarded his county cap in 1956. In 1956–57 he was chosen to go on the M.C.C tour of South Africa. A batsman/ wicket-keeper, he has twice scored more than 1,000 runs in a season and has two centuries also to his credit. His highest score ever is 127 v. Glamorgan in 1956. Behind the wicket he has taken as many as 82 victims in one season and eight in one match. His hobbies are record playing and football. His favourite sportsman is Willie Watson and his ambition is to do the wicket-keeper's double. He also had a promising career before him as a professional footballer before he decided to concentrate on cricket.

DEREK (Shack) SHACKLETON
ENGLAND & HAMPSHIRE

Height: 5 ft. 11 in. **21** Weight: 11 st. 8 lb.

Overs	Maidens	Runs	Wickets	Average
1,292	498	2,496	163	15.31

Born in Todmorden, Lancs, he joined Hampshire in 1948 and was awarded his county cap the following season. A right-arm fast medium bowler, his best performance is 9 for 59 v. Gloucester 1958. He has taken 100 wickets in a season 10 times. His highest total of wickets in a season is 165. With the bat his best is 87 not out v. Essex, 1949. In 1950 he made his Test début v. West Indies and has also played in one Test v. South Africa, 1951, and one v. India 1951–52 while on tour with the M.C.C. His hobbies are Gardening and Interior Decorating, and his ambition is to own a small business.

DEREK WALTER (Dick) RICHARDSON
ENGLAND & WORCESTERSHIRE

Height: 5 ft. 11½ in. **22** Weight: 11 st. 2 lb.

Matches	Innings	Not out	Runs	Highest score	Average
28	48	5	861	60	20.02

The younger brother of Peter Richardson, Derek was born in Hereford. He joined Worcester in 1949 and was awarded his county cap in 1956. So far he has played in one Test match v. West Indies in 1957. A left-hand bat he has scored six centuries and reached 1,000 runs in a season three times. His highest score is 169 v. Derbyshire in 1957. A good field, he held 27 catches last season, a number exceeded only by wicket keeper Dawkes. His hobbies are collecting modern jazz records, and Golf. His ambition is to be invited to tour with the M.C.C.

©

GAMINI (Gami) GOONESENA
CEYLON & NOTTINGHAMSHIRE

Height: 5 ft. 7 in. **23** Weight: 10 st.

Matches	Innings	Not out	Runs	Highest score	Average
23	41	3	592	75	15.57

Born in Colombo, Ceylon, he made his début for Nottinghamshire in 1952 and was awarded his county cap in 1955. An all-rounder, he played for Ceylon before coming to England. A right-hand batsman, he has scored three centuries and 1,000 runs in a season twice. His hightest score is 211 v. Oxford University in 1957. A right-arm leg break bowler, he has taken 100 wickets in a season twice; the most wickets he has taken in a season is 146. His best bowling performance is 7 for 60 v. Leicestershire. His hobby is Motoring and his favourite sportsman Peter May. His ambition is to take all 10 wickets in an innings in a first-class match.

©

MICHAEL JOHN KNIGHT (Mike) SMITH
ENGLAND & WARWICKSHIRE

Height: 6 ft. 1 in. **24** Weight: 12 st. 4 lb.

Matches	Innings	Not out	Runs	Highest score	Average
23	38	3	1,631	131	46.60

Born in Leicester, he joined Warwickshire from Leicestershire in 1956, and was awarded his county cap in 1957. A stylish right-hand bat, strong on the on side, he has scored 1,000 runs in a season five times, 2,000 runs in a season once, and 12 centuries. His highest score is 201 not out v. Cambridge University in 1959. In 1958 he played in three Test matches v. New Zealand and his highest score was 47. He is interested in all forms of sport, and his favourite sportsman is Sir Jack Hobbs. His ambition is to lead his country to a championship victory.

©

KEITH VINCENT (Gloves) ANDREW
ENGLAND & NORTHAMPTONSHIRE

Height: 5 ft. 9 in. **25** Weight: 11 st. 4 lb.

Matches	Innings	Not out	Runs	Highest score	Average
28	33	11	188	31	8.54

Born in Oldham, Lancs, he joined Northants in 1952 and was awarded his county cap in 1954. An agile mover behind the wicket, he stumped 25 batsmen in 1958, 12 more than any other wicket keeper. He also held 46 catches. The total of 71 victims is his best ever in one season. His highest score with the bat is 76 v. Yorks in 1957. In the winter of 1945–55 he toured Australia and New Zealand with the M.C.C. and played in one Test match v. Australia at Brisbane. His hobbies are Golf, Squash and Gardening, and favourite sportsman Ben Hogan. His ambition is to play in a Test match in England.

© PRINTED IN ENGLAND

WILLIE WATSON
ENGLAND & LEICESTERSHIRE

Height: 5 ft. 11 in. **26** Weight: 12 st.

Matches	Innings	Not out	Runs	Highest score	Average
22	40	8	1,521	141	47.53

Was born at Bolton-on-Dearn, near Earnsley. He as taken on the staff of the Yorkshire County Cricket Club in 1939 and was awarded his county cap in 1947. In 1957, rather surprisingly, he left Yorkshire to join Leicestershire and was awarded his cap for this county in 1958. He has played in 19 Test matches and accompanied the M.C.C. on their tour of the West Indies in 1953–54 and to Australia in 1958–59. He has scored 35 hundreds in his career, two of them in Test matches; his highest score ever being 257 for M.C.C. v. British Guiana at Georgetown in 1953–54. Ten times he has scored more than 1,000 runs in one season. His hobbies are Music and Bridge.

© PRINTED IN ENGLAND

MAURICE RAYMOND HALLAM
LEICESTERSHIRE

Height: 6 ft. **27** Weight: 10 st. 12 lb.

Matches	Innings	Not out	Runs	Highest score	Average
29	51	1	1,247	134	24.94

Was born in Leicester. He has been connected with this county since 1949, and received his county cap in 1954. He has scored eight hundreds in his career, five times topping 1,000 runs in the season and once over 2,000. His highest score was 176 v. Kent in 1957. His hobby is Woodwork and his favourite sportsmen are Stan Matthews and Tom Graveney. His ambition is to play for England.

© PRINTED IN ENGLAND

CYRIL WASHBROOK
ENGLAND & LANCASHIRE

Height: 5 ft. 8½ in. **28** Weight: 11 st. 6 lb.

Matches	Innings	Not out	Runs	Highest score	Average
27	43	9	1,040	97	30.58

Has played for Lancashire since 1933. He was awarded his county cap in 1935. He has also played in 37 Test matches and has accompanied the M.C.C. on tours of Australia and South Africa. A most attractive and stylish batsman, he has 19 times scored more than 1,000 runs in a season and twice topped the 2,000 mark. He has also made 75 hundreds, six of them in Test matches and his highest score was 251 v. Surrey in 1947.

©

ALAN (Oakie) OAKMAN
ENGLAND & SUSSEX

Height: 6 ft. 4 in. **29** Weight: 14 st.

Matches	Innings	Not out	Runs	Highest score	Average
30	52	0	1,473	109	28.32

Born in Hastings. Has played for Sussex since 1948 and awarded his county cap in 1951. Has played in two Test matches and was chosen for the last M.C.C. tour of South Africa. Has had considerable success with both bat and ball, having scored nine hundreds already in county cricket and four times scored more than 1,000 runs in one season. His highest score was 178 v. Glamorgan in 1956. Bowls off spinners and in 1954 failed by one wicket to get 100 wickets in a season. Best individual bowling performance was against Glamorgan in 1954, when he took 7 for 39. His hobbies are Chess, Snooker, Table Tennis and Swimming, and his favourite sportsman is Harry Gregg of Manchester Un.

©

ALAN (Wharton Face) WHARTON
ENGLAND & LANCASHIRE

Height: 5 ft. 11 in. **30** Weight: 13 st.

Matches	Innings	Not out	Runs	Highest score	Average
26	40	2	1,039	85	27.34

Was born in Hayward, Lancs. He first joined that club in 1945 and was awarded his county cap in 1946. A stylish left-hand bat, he has played in one Test match and seven times has achieved over 1,000 runs in a season. He has also scored 20 centuries in his career and his highest score ever was 164 v. M.C.C. in 1957. A more than useful change bowler, bowling right-hand medium pace, he took 49 wickets in his best season and his best bowling performance was against Sussex in 1951 when he took 7 for 33. His hobbies are Badminton and Music.

©

LEO HARRISON

HAMPSHIRE

Height: 5 ft. 9 in. **31** Weight: 10 st. 7 lb.

Matches	Innings	Not out	Runs	Highest score	Average
26	32	7	333	42	13.32

Born in Christchurch, he joined Hampshire in 1937 and was awarded his cvounty cap in 1951. A wicket-keeper batsman, his highest score is 153 v. Notts in 1952. He has twice scored 1,000 runs in a season and seven centuries. His best season behind the stumps was in 1958, when he claimed 61 victims, 57 of them caught. His highest total of victims in one match is eight. One of the few pre-war players still playing in county cricket, his ambition is to help Hampshire win the County championship before retiring. His hobby is Fishing.

©

PRINTED IN ENGLAND

JAMES MICHAEL PARKS

ENGLAND & SUSSEX

Height: 5 ft. 11 in. **32** Weight: 12 st.

Matches	Innings	Not out	Runs	Highest score	Average
27	45	3	1,353	127	32.21

Born in Haywards Heath. Has played for Sussex since 1948 and received his county cap in 1951. Has played in one Test match and has been on the M.C.C. "A" team tour of Pakistan, 1955–56, and the M.C.C. tour of South Africa, 1956–57, when he had to return home due to illness. A batsman/wicket-keeper, his highest score is 205 not out v. Somerset, 1955. Has scored 22 hundreds, four times scoring 1,000 runs in a season and twice topped the 2,000 mark. As a wicket-keeper he once took six victims in one county match, and also claims a best bowling performance of 3 for 57 against no less a county than Surrey. His hobby is Photography and his favourite sportsman is Denis Compton.

©

PRINTED IN ENGLAND

GEORGE EDWARD TRIBE

AUSTRALIA & NORTHAMPTONSHIRE

Height: 5 ft. 6½ in. **33** Weight: 11 st.

Overs	Maidens	Runs	Wickets	Average
707	202	1,838	110	16.70

Born in Melbourne, Australia, he joined Northants in 1951 and was awarded his county cap the following season. A fine all-rounder. An unorthodox slow left-arm bowler, his best performance is 9 for 43 v. Worcester, 1958. He has taken 100 wickets in a season seven times and in the 1955 season he set a new county record by taking 175 wickets. A consistent middle order left-hand bat, his highest score is 136 not out v. Cambridge University in 1954. He has scored five centuries and 1,000 runs in a season six times. In 1946–47 he played in three Test matches for Australia v. England and toured India with the Commonwealth team in 1949–50. His hobbies are Golf, Gardening, Motor Racing and Swimming. His favourite sportsman is the Rev. David Sheppard.

©

PRINTED IN ENGLAND

WILLIAM GILBERT A. PARKHOUSE
ENGLAND & GLAMORGAN

Height: 5 ft. 10 in. **34** Weight: 11 st.

Matches	Innings	Not out	Runs	Highest score	Average
27	48	2	1,126	96	24.47

Was born in Swansea. He has played for Glamorgan since 1947 and was awarded his county cap in his first season. He has been chosen for five Test matches and has also toured with the M.C.C. in Australia and New Zealand. Eleven times he has scored more than 1,000 runs in a season, and to date has made more than 20 hundreds in county cricket. His highest score was 201 v. Kent in 1956. His hobbies are Golf and Fishing.

©

DONALD (Matey) KENYON
ENGLAND & WORCESTERSHIRE

Height: 5 ft. 9 in. **35** Weight: 13 st.

Matches	Innings	Not out	Runs	Highest score	Average
22	42	1	1,295	107	31.58

Born in Wordesley, Staffs, he has been connected with Worcester, his only county, since 1946, and was awarded his county cap in 1947. A stylish right-hand opening bat, he has scored 53 centuries, 1,000 runs in a season 11 times and 2,000 runs in a season seven times. His highest score is 259 v. Yorks in 1956. He has played in eight Test matches and toured India, Pakistan and Ceylon with the M.C.C. in 1951–52. His hobbies are Gardening and Motoring and his favourite sportsman is Len Hutton. Don's ambition is to score 3,000 runs in one season.

©

NORMAN FREDERICK HORNER
WARWICKSHIRE

Height: 5 ft. 7½ in. **36** Weight: 10 st. 6 lb.

Matches	Innings	Not out	Runs	Highest score	Average
30	50	1	1,476	155	30.12

Born in Bradford, he joined Warwickshire in 1951 after six years with Yorkshire and was awarded his county cap in 1953. A stylish right-hand opening bat, his highest score is 155 v. Middlesex at Lords last season. He has topped 1,000 runs or more in a season six times, and has scored eight centuries. A good field he held 14 catches last season. His hobby is Gardening and his favourite sportsman is the West Indian cricketer, E.A. Martindale. His ambition is to score more than 2,000 runs in one season.

©

FREDERICK SEWARDS (Fiery) TRUEMAN
ENGLAND & YORKSHIRE

 Height: 5 ft. 9½ in. **37** Weight: 13 st. 9 lb.

Overs	Maidens	Runs	Wickets	Average
446	125	958	84	11.40

Born, Stainton, Yorks. Joined the county 1948 and awarded county cap 1951. One of the best fast bowlers in present-day cricket. A great character on and off the field, best performance is 8 for 28 v. Kent. Has taken 100 wickets in a season four times: most wickets in a season 160. A lusty hitter with the bat, his highest score is 74 v. Leicester 1955. Has played in 21 Test matches. Against India in 1952, his analysis of 8 for 31 at Manchester is the best performance by a fast bowler ever in International cricket. Toured West Indies 1953–54 and Australia 1958–59 with the M.C.C. Hobbies are Reading and Snooker, and favourite sportsman, Ray Lindwall. His aim to help others.

©

DOUGLAS JOHN INSOLE
ENGLAND & ESSEX

 Height: 5 ft. 10 in. **38** Weight: 13 st.

Matches	Innings	Not out	Runs	Highest score	Average
27	41	5	1,161	108	32.25

Born in Clacton. Has been connected with Essex since 1946 and was awarded his county cap in 1949. He has played in nine Test matches and was chosen for the M.C.C. tour of South Africa in 1956–57. Ten times he has scored more than 1,000 runs in the season and twice topped the 2,000 mark. Has scored 48 hundreds, one of them in a Test match, and his highest score ever is 219 not out v. Yorks, 1949. As a medium pace bowler, can boast of a best ever performance of 5 for 22 v. the champion county Surrey in 1955. His hobby is Soccer, where he has been a stalwart of the Corinthian Casuals XI for some years now. His favourite sportsman is Peter May and his ambition is to retire gracefully.

©

MALCOLM JAMESON HILTON
ENGLAND & LANCASHIRE

 Height: 5 ft. 9 in. **39** Weight: 10 st. 10 lb.

Overs	Maidens	Runs	Wickets	Average
692.4	292	1,518	94	16.14

Was born in Oldham. He was taken on the staff of Lancashire County Cricket Club in 1944 and in 1950 was awarded his county cap. He has played in four Test matches as well as touring India, Pakistan and Ceylon with the M.C.C. party in 1951–52. A slow left-arm bowler, five times he has taken more than 1,000 wickets in a season and his best performance was taking 8 for 19 for Lancashire v. New Zealand in 1958. In his best season he took 158 wickets. He can claim one distinction as a batsman and that is one century to his credit when he scored 100 not out.

©

ALBERT JOHN ALLAN WATKINS
ENGLAND & GLAMORGAN

Height: 5 ft. 6 in. **40** Weight: 13 st. 6 lb.

Matches	Innings	Not out	Runs	Highest score	Average
27	46	5	1,242	143 n.o.	30.29

Born in Usk, Mon. Has been connected with Glamorgan since 1937 and received his county cap in 1947. Has played in 15 full Tests and four unofficial Tests for England. Was chosen for the M.C.C. tour of South Africa, 1948–49, India, Pakistan and Ceylon, 1951–52. A talented all-rounder, has twice taken more than 100 wickets in a season, bowling medium pace left-hand swingers. Best bowling performance was 7 for 28 v. Derbyshire in 1954. With the bat he has 11 times scored more than 1,000 runs in a season. He has also scored 25 centuries, two of them in Test cricket. His highest score was 170 not out v Leicester, 1954. His hobbies are Golf, Badminton and Driving.

JOHN VICTOR (Big Vic) WILSON
GLAMORGAN

Height: 6 ft. 1 in. **41** Weight: 15 st.

Matches	Innings	Not out	Runs	Highest score	Average
31	45	4	894	80 n.o.	21.80

Born in Scampton, Yorkshire, he has been with Yorks since 1946 and was awarded his county cap in 1948. A hard hitting left-hand bat, he has scored 27 centuries, 1,000 runs in a season 10 times, and 2,000 runs in a season once. His highest score is 230 v. Derbyshire in 1952. He is also a very fine close field and in 1955 held 61 catches. He was selected for the 1954–55 M.C.C. tour of Australia and New Zealand, and has been twelfth man in seven Tests. When not playing cricket he spends most of his time farming. His ambition is to score 20,000 runs for Yorkshire.

JOHN DAVID (Jack) ROBERTSON
ENGLAND & MIDDLESEX

Height: 5 ft. 11½ in. **42** Weight: 12 st.

Matches	Innings	Not out	Runs	Highest score	Average
29	48	4	1,525	99	34.65

Born in Chiswick, London, he made his début for Middlesex in 1937 and received his county cap in 1938. Although now in the veteran stage, he is still a fine opening bat, as he showed last season by topping his county's averages. His highest score is 331 not out v. Worcester in 1949, all scored on the first day. He has scored 1,000 runs in a season 14 times, 2,000 runs in a season seven times, and 67 centuries, two in Test cricket. He has played in 11 Test matches and toured the West Indies in 1948 and India 1951–52 with the M.C.C. His hobby is Photography, and his ambition is to play cricket as long as possible.

ALEC VICTOR BEDSER
ENGLAND & SURREY

Height: 6 ft. 3 in. **43** Weight: 15½ st.

Overs	Maidens	Runs	Wickets	Average
457	169	816	48	17.00

Born in Reading, has played for Surrey since 1938 and was awarded his county cap in 1946. Has played in 51 Test matches and three times has been on M.C.C. tours to Australia and once to South Africa. A lion-hearted fast medium bowler with the ability to swing the ball both ways, his best bowling performance ever was against the Australians when he took 14 wickets for 99 runs. The most wickets he has taken in a season is 162 but 11 times he has taken more than 100. Two other notable performances were 8 for 18 v. Warwick and 6 for 18 v. Notts. Not renowned as a batsman, one landmark in his career that will stand out was when he scored 126, his only century, v. Somerset, 1947.

PRINTED IN ENGLAND

DONALD VICTOR (Slasher) SMITH
ENGLAND & SUSSEX

Height: 6 ft. **44** Weight: 12 st.

Matches	Innings	Not out	Runs	Highest score	Average
27	45	3	1,135	142	27.50

Born in Broadwater, Sussex. Has been connected with his present county since 1946 and received his county cap in 1950. Has played in three Test matches for England. Has scored 14 hundreds in his career, five times he has scored 1,000 runs in a season and one topped the 2,000 mark. His highest individual score was 206 not out in 1950. A more-than-useful slow-medium left-hand bowler, he has taken as many as 73 wickets in one season and his best bowling performance was 7 for 40 against Oxford University in 1956. His hobbies are Youth Work, Gardening and Golf accounting for the fact that his favourite sportsman is Peter Thompson and his ambition to achieve a hole in one.

PRINTED IN ENGLAND

A. C. D. INGLEBY-MACKENZIE
HAMPSHIRE

Height: 5 ft. 10 in. **45** Weight: 11 st. 2 lb.

Matches	Innings	Not out	Runs	Highest score	Average
29	44	4	1,059	113	26.47

Born in Dartmouth, Devon, he first played for Hampshire in 1951 and was awarded his county cap in 1957. Renowned for his adventurous tactics, he is always more than ready to "have a dip". A left-hand bat, his highest score is 130 not out v. Worcester, 1956. He has scored five centuries and twice topped 1,000 runs in a season. In 1958 he scored 100 in 61 minutes, the fastest century of the season. He toured Kenya with the M.C.C. in 1957–58. He is interested in all forms of sport, especially Ski-ing, and Philately. His ambition, he says with a grin, is to be a millionaire.

PRINTED IN ENGLAND

ROY EDWIN MARSHALL
WEST INDIES & HAMPSHIRE

Height: 6 ft. **46** Weight: 12 st. 10 lb.

Matches	Innings	Not out	Runs	Highest score	Average
30	51	2	1,876	193	38.28

Born in Barbados, he made his début for Hampshire in 1953 and was awarded his county cap in 1955. An aggressive right-hand bat, he has scored 1,000 runs in a season five time; 2,000 runs in a season twice and 22 centuries. His highest score is 193 v. Oxford in 1958. A useful off-spinner, his best performance is 6 for 38 v. Surrey in 1956. He began his career with Barbados in 1946 and has played in four Test matches for West Indies; he also toured England in 1950 and Australia and New Zealand in 1951–52. His hobbies are Golf, Fishing, Squash and Swimming. His favourite sportsman is Sir Donald Bradman, and his ambition is to see Hampshire win the County championship.

©

PRINTED IN ENGLAND

DENNIS BRIAN CLOSE
ENGLAND & YORKSHIRE

Height: 6 ft. 2½ in. **47** Weight: 13 st. 10lb.

Matches	Innings	Not out	Runs	Highest score	Average
32	49	4	1,335	120	29.66

Born in Rawdon near Leeds, he has been connected with Yorkshire since 1949, and was awarded his county cap in the same year. He has played in six Test matches and was chosen for M.C.C. tours of Australia and Pakistan. An all-rounder, he has scored 11 centuries, 1,000 runs in a seaon six times and his highest score is 164 v. Combined Services in 1954. An off-spin bowler, his best performance is 6 for 38 v. Northants, and he has taken 100 wickets in a season twice. His hobbies are Golf, Fishing and Shooting, and his ambition is to score a hundred hundreds.

©

PRINTED IN ENGLAND

RAMAN SUBBA ROW
ENGLAND & NORTHAMPTONSHIRE

Height: 6 ft. ½ in. **48** Weight: 14 st. 5 lb.

Matches	Innings	Not out	Runs	Highest score	Average
27	40	6	1,498	300	44.05

Born in Streatham, London, he joined Northants in 1955 after two years with Surrey and received his county cap the same year. A strong left-hand bat, he set up a new county record last season by scoring 300 v. Surrey. He has scored 1,000 runs in a season three times, and 14 centuries. A useful leg break bowler, his best performance is 5 for 21 for Cambridge v. Oxford in 1951. He played in the Manchester Test match v. New Zealand last season. His hobby is Motoring and his favourite sportsman Frank Worrell. His ambition is to lead Northants to a Championship victory.

©

PRINTED IN ENGLAND